PREHISTORIC RELIGION

A Study in Prehistoric Archaeology

by

E. O. JAMES

D.Litt., Ph.D., F.S.A.

Professor Emeritus of the History of Religion in the University of London. Fellow of University College and Fellow of King's College

ISBN: 978-1-63923-672-5

All Rights reserved. No part of this book maybe reproduced without written permission from the publishers, except by a reviewer who may quote brief passages in a review to be printed in a newspaper or magazine.

Printed: February 2023

Published and Distributed By:
Lushena Books
607 Country Club Drive, Unit E
Bensenville, IL 60106
www.lushenabks.com

ISBN: 978-1-63923-672-5

By the same Author

HISTORY OF RELIGIONS
THE NATURE AND FUNCTION OF PRIESTHOOD
THE CONCEPT OF DEITY
MARRIAGE AND SOCIETY
THE BEGINNINGS OF RELIGION
THE SOCIAL FUNCTION OF RELIGION
COMPARATIVE RELIGION
THE ORIGINS OF SACRIFICE
THE STONE AGE
THE BEGINNINGS OF MAN
INTRODUCTION TO ANTHROPOLOGY
PRIMITIVE RITUAL AND BELIEF
AN ANTHROPOLOGICAL STUDY OF THE OLD TESTAMENT, ETC.

CONTENTS

PREFACE   *Page* 13

I. PALAEOLITHIC BURIAL RITUAL   17

   The Cult of Skulls   17
      Choukoutien   17
      Monte Circeo   19
      Ofnet   20

   Ceremonial Interment in the Middle Palaeolithic   21
      Le Moustier   21
      La Chapelle-aux-Saints   21
      La Ferrassie   22

   The Upper Palaeolithic   23
      The Grimaldi Burials   23
      Paviland and other Upper Palaeolithic Sepultures   25
      The Palaeolithic Cult of the Dead   28

   The Mesolithic Transition   30
      Azilian-Tardenoisian Interments   30
      Maglemosean   31
      Ertebølle   32
      Danish Dyssers   33

II. NEOLITHIC BURIALS IN THE ANCIENT EAST   34

   Egyptian Neolithic Cemeteries   34
      Badarian   35
      Amratian   36
      Merimdian   37
      Gerzean   37

Contents

The Earliest Dynastic Tombs	39
The Mastaba Tomb and the Pyramid	40
Neolithic Tombs in Mesopotamia	43
Hassuna	44
Tell Halaf	44
Al 'Ubaid	46
The Royal Tombs of Ur	47
Burials in Elam and Baluchistan	50
Susa	50
Baluchistan	51
The Nal Cemetery	53
The Indus Valley	54
Mohenjo-daro	54
Harappa	55
Cemetery R 37	55
Cemetery H	56

III. MEGALITHIC BURIAL IN EUROPE — 58

Eastern Mediterranean	58
Tholoi in Cyprus	58
Vaulted Tombs in Crete	61
The Cycladic Tombs	63
The Siculan Rock-cut Tombs	65
Western Mediterranean	65
Sardinian Gallery-tombs	65
Rock-cut Tombs and Navetas in the Balearic Isles	66
Maltese Megaliths	68
Iberian Peninsula	72
The Almerian Megaliths	72
South-west Iberian Tombs	76
Pyrenaean Megaliths	78
Atlantic Europe	79
Megalithic Tombs in Brittany	79
The S.O.M. Culture	83

Contents

The British Isles — 83
- British Long Barrows — 84
- The Severn-Cotswold Barrows — 86
- The Boyne Passage-graves — 88
- The Clyde-Carlingford Gallery-graves — 90
- The Medway Megaliths — 92

The Northern Megalithic Tombs — 94
- The Danish Passage-graves — 94
- Battle-axes and Single Graves — 95

CREMATION, INHUMATION AND MUMMIFICATION — 97

Cremation in Europe in the Bronze Age — 97
- Partial Cremation under Long Barrows — 98
- Round Barrows — 99
- Urn Burial — 101
- The Terramara Cemeteries — 102
- The Villanovan Cemeteries — 103
- The Lausitz Urnfields — 104
- The Alpine Urnfields — 105
- The Hallstatt Cemetery — 107

Cremation and Inhumation — 108

Mummification in Ancient Egypt — 109
- Natural Desiccation — 109
- Preservation and Embalmment — 109
- "Substitute Heads" — 110
- Portrait Statues — 111
- The "Opening of the Mouth" Ceremony — 112
- Making a Mummy — 113
- The Burial Rites — 115

THE CULT OF THE DEAD — 117

The Disposal of the Body — 117
- Cave-burial — 118
- The Skull-cult — 118
- Secondary Burial — 119

Preservation and Cremation	122
Desiccation and Mummification	123
Images of the Dead	127
The After-life	130
The Relation of Body and Soul	130
Burial and the After-life	132
Orientation	133
Status	136
Duration	139
Grave-goods	139
Human Sacrifice	142
The Cult of the Dead	143

VI. THE MYSTERY OF BIRTH — 145

The Mystery of Birth in Palaeolithic Times	145
Sculptured "Venuses"	145
Cowrie Shells	148
Fertility Dances	148
Neolithic and Chalcolithic Female Figurines	153
Arpachiyah	153
Tepe Gawra	154
Tell Hassuna and Al 'Ubaid	155
Warka	155
Susa	156
Anau	156
Baluchistan	157
The Indus Valley	157
Phallic Emblems	159
Anatolia, Cyprus and the Cyclades	161
Crete	162
The Mother-goddess	162
The Great Minoan Goddess	162
The Maltese Goddess Cult	165
The Iberian Goddess Cult	167
Statue-menhirs	168
The Goddess Cult in Britain and Northern France	171

Contents

I. FERTILITY AND THE FOOD SUPPLY 172

   Palaeolithic Hunting Ritual 172
     Increase Rites 173
     The Control of the Chase 174
     Hunting Art and Ritual 179

   The Vegetation Cultus in the Ancient Near East 181
     The Divine Kingship in Egypt 183
     The Cult of Osiris 183
     The Solar Theology 184
     The Annual Festival 187
     The Sacred Marriage of the King and the Goddess in Mesopotamia 188
     The Dying and Reviving Year-god in Western Asia 189

   The Cultus in the Aegean 195
     The Minoan-Mycenaean Goddess of Vegetation and the Young Male God 196
     Zeus and Demeter 197

   The Vegetation Cult in North-west Europe 201
     Aegean Influences in Wessex 202

I. THE SKY-RELIGION 204

   The Idea of God 204
     Animism and Polytheism 204
     Supreme Beings 206
     The Universality and Antiquity of the Sky-god 208

   The Sky-god in the Near East 209
     The Sky-religion in Egypt 209
     The Babylonian Triads 213

   The Indo-European Sky-gods 216
     The Indo-Iranian Sky-gods 216
     Zeus and the Olympian Divine Family 221
     The Sky-father and the Earth-mother 224
     The Scandinavian Heavenly Deities 225
     Sky-worship in Wessex 227

IX. PREHISTORIC RELIGION — 229

The Ritual Control of Natural Processes — 229
The Nature and Function of Symbols — 232
Totemism and the Sacred Dance — 234

Fertility and the Mystery of Birth and Generation — 235
Cow-symbolism — 235
Generation and Maternity — 238

The Goddess Cult — 239

The Cult of the Dead — 241
Palaeolithic — 241
Ancient Egypt — 243
Mesopotamia — 246
The Indus Valley — 247
The Mediterranean — 248
Western Europe — 251

The Sky-religion — 254
The Celestial After-life — 254
The Concept of the Universal Sky-god — 256

NOTES — 264

BIBLIOGRAPHY — 285

INDEX — 295

ILLUSTRATIONS

Figure		Page
1	Collar on a skeleton from Barma Grande, Mentone	25
2	The development of the mastaba tomb	41
3	Entrance to passage-grave at Los Millares, Spain	74
4	Reconstruction of entrance to passage-grave at Los Millares	75
5	Passage-grave at Kercado, near Carnac, Brittany	81
6	The Bryn Celli Ddu chambered cairn, Anglesey	87
7	New Grange chambered tomb, Co. Meath, Ireland	89
8	Dancing scene in the rock-shelter at Cogul, near Lérida, Spain	149
9	The "dancing chieftain" scene, a detail from a painting in the rock-shelter at Alpéra, Albacete, Spain	151
10	Cult scene on the Hagia Triada sarcophagus in Crete	165
11	Owl-eyed female figurines, Almeria, Spain	169
12	"The Sorcerer" in Les Trois Frères, Ariège, France	175
13	Dying bison and claviform designs in Niaux, Ariège, France	177
14	Minoan Goddess scene on a signet ring, Ashmolean Museum, Oxford	197

MAPS

The principal groups of painted caves and other Palaeolithic sites in France and northern Spain	261
The ancient Near East	262
Prehistoric cultures in Europe	263

CHARTS

Pleistocene and Palaeolithic Periods	291
Mesolithic Period	291
Sequence of Cultures in Western Europe	292
Sequence of Cultures in the Eastern Mediterranean	293
Sequence of Cultures in the Near East	294

SOURCES FOR ILLUSTRATIONS

G. H. Luquet: *The Art and Religion of Fossil Man*, 1930 (1, 8, 9, 12); T. E. Peer: *Harmsworth's Universal History*, vol. v (2); Daryll Forde: *American Anthropologist*, N. S. vol. 32, No. 1, 1930 (3, 4, 5); W. J. Hemp: *Archaeologia*, vol. xxx, 1930 (6); T. G. E. Powell: *Proceedings of the Prehistoric Society*, N. S. vol. IV, Pt. 2 (7); G. R. Levy: *The Gate of Horn*, 1948 (10); V. Gordon Childe: *The Dawn of European Civilization*, 5th ed., 1950 (11); Max Raphael: *Prehistoric Cave Paintings*, 1945 (13); Ashmolean Museum, Oxford (14).

PREFACE

In the considerable literature on prehistoric archaeology that has accumulated in recent years, covering almost every aspect of the subject, so far as I am aware there has been no attempt in this country to bring together and interpret in a single volume the available material relating specifically to religious phenomena. There have been and are, of course, many excellent and quite invaluable regional studies which describe and discuss much of the data in particular areas and cultures—indeed but for them the present volume could not have been produced. There are also a number of works on various aspects of prehistory in general, directly or indirectly bearing on evidence analysed and reviewed in this book to which reference frequently has been made in its compilation, as will be seen from the footnotes and bibliographies. Nevertheless, for some time, and especially when the subject was discussed at a conference of the Prehistoric Society at the London University Institute of Archaeology in 1953, and at the meeting of the British Association at Bristol in 1955, it has seemed that an investigation of the field as an organized whole should be undertaken in the light of the evidence now at hand.

In opening such an inquiry an initial problem was to decide how the term "prehistoric" should be interpreted, and what should be the *terminus ad quem*. To have drawn the line at the invention of the art of writing would have excluded all consideration of the texts, documents, and inscriptions written or carved on prehistoric or protohistoric tombs, temples, stelae or tablets which, particularly for this investigation, constitute an all-important source of information, not only for contemporary belief and practice but also for their more remote background. The main purpose, however, of a study of Prehistoric Religion must be an examination of the discipline in its earliest manifestations prior to the recording of events in written documents in sufficient quantity to make possible a precise determination of their occurrence, chronology and significance through the ordinary channels of historical research. Therefore, it has been upon the Palaeolithic and Neolithic periods that attention has been primarily concentrated, where no written records obtain.

The term "Neolithic" however, is now exceedingly difficult to define and determine as the transition from food-gathering to food-production certainly was not a uniform and orderly sequence of events, as was formerly supposed, even though it may not have been quite so revolutionary as is now sometimes asserted. Thus, as the use of metals was firmly established in the Near East at least 2,000 years before it was introduced into Britain and other outlying regions far removed from the centre of prehistoric civilization, it is impossible to draw a hard and fast line in any chronological sense between the Neolithic and the Bronze Age in the study of a specific aspect of prehistory which covers the whole field. Therefore, I have not hesitated to include the developments in the second millennium B.C. in the background of the higher religious systems of the Fertile Crescent and Western Asia, of India and of pre-Homeric Greece, calculated to throw light on their prehistoric antecedents, though in some instances the faiths may have passed into the realms of recorded history.

At the other end of the scale a quantity of material exists concerning the observable beliefs and practices still, or until very recently, current in primitive societies on the fringes of civilization, or in its background, all over the world, many of which appear to have persisted little changed throughout the ages. Some of them, in fact, go back apparently to a very remote period in the prehistory of mankind. In employing these sources of information to throw light on ancient institutions, customs and traditions extreme caution is needed, forewarned by the uncritical theoretical reconstructions of "origins" and "developments" of an earlier generation of social anthropologists. Then general conclusions were drawn from disparate phenomena, often haphazardly assembled and brought together on the principle of superficial resemblance, regardless of their diversities, comparability and provenance.

But notwithstanding these fruitless attempts to produce an

orderly stratified sequence of cultural and "spiritual" ascent from savagery to civilization, successive in time and progressive in development, reasonably reliable first-hand accounts, and especially intensive studies of existing primitive societies by properly trained observers for the purpose of ascertaining the part played by beliefs and institutions in a given social structure which happily now are becoming increasingly available), constitute valuable data for the interpretation of the archaeological data. Such studies are able to throw light on analogous activities and organizations, beliefs and practices, and their significance within living religious systems under conditions not very different from those which prevailed in prehistoric times. This is most apparent in the case of the anthropological evidence derived from existing peoples, like, for example, the Nilotic tribes in East Africa representing the remnants of the substratum out of which the higher civilization of the Nile valley arose, and who have retained in their material and spiritual culture and linguistic affinities definite links with the prehistoric Egyptians.

It cannot be denied, then, that the past is contained in the present, even though the earlier theory of "survivals" has had to be abandoned in the form in which it was formerly held. Moreover, while it may be impossible to determine what lies behind the existing culture in some primitive societies devoid of any ascertainable history, this certainly does not apply in the case of the ancient civilizations out of which the higher religions emerged with their roots deeply laid in a prehistoric past now in process of recovery by the spade of the archaeologist. Herein lies the justification for a study along the lines adopted in this volume, prehistoric religion having been one of my principal preoccupations since, after completing my anthropological training at Oxford, I first became acquainted with ancient Near Eastern religions forty years ago as a post-graduate student working under the supervision of Sir Flinders Petrie. In the intervening period much of the data here reviewed and discussed have been collected or examined at first hand in decorated caves and rock-shelters, tumuli and other prehistoric sites and excavations (as well as in many museums), especially in the Dordogne, Ariège and the Pyrenees; in Brittany, Ireland, Wessex and the adjacent region; in Spain, the Aegean and the Eastern Mediterranean. As the book has been written mainly in the excellent library of the Ashmolean Museum, it has been possible to consult the original sources with comparative ease, aided by its efficient staff, who have been always so willing and anxious to be helpful. While in preparing the text a general knowledge of prehistoric archaeology has been assumed, I have endeavoured to make the inquiry intelligible to as wide a range of readers as possible, without, I hope, diminishing whatever value it may have for professional archaeologists.

Oxford   E. O. JAMES

CHAPTER I

Palaeolithic Burial Ritual

SINCE of all the mysterious, disintegrating and critical situations with which man has been confronted throughout the ages death appears to have been the most disturbing and devastating, it is hardly surprising that the earliest traces of religious belief and practice should centre in the cult of the dead. Therefore, an examination of mortuary ritual constitutes a convenient and appropriate starting-point for an investigation of the archaeological evidence relating to prehistoric religion, and takes us back at once to a remote period long before the arrival of *Homo sapiens* on the human scene, or even of his predecessor, *Homo neanderthalensis*.

THE CULT OF SKULLS

Choukoutien

In the caves at Dragon-bone Hill near the village of Choukoutien in China, about 37 miles south-west of Peking, fossil hominid teeth were found in Middle or Lower Pleistocene strata in 1922, but it was not until 1927, on the strength of a very youthful molar unearthed by a Swedish excavator, Dr Bohlin, that Professor Davidson Black announced the discovery of a new genus of very Early Man, *Sinanthropus pekinensis*. This event, in addition to the light it has thrown on human origins, for the time being at any rate may be regarded as affording the earliest evidence of the ritual treatment of the dead, since the remains of Peking Man in the Choukoutien deposits are believed to be the debris of cannibal feasts. Unfortunately, the exact age of the strata is as difficult to determine as is the precise correlation of the phases of the Pleistocene in China with the European glaciations and interglacials. The layers being 50 feet in depth, they extend over a very long period, but the fauna was the same throughout, and as the bison, mammoth and woolly rhinoceros have not been detected it would seem to be older than the Upper Pleistocene (Loess) and younger than the Late Pliocene.[1] On Zeuner's calculation *Sinanthropus* is dated "in the neighbourhood of 500,000 years".[2] The crude pebble and flake implements that were scattered through the caves had affinities with their Clactonian counterparts in Europe and the Soan artifacts of North-west India. If the industry that takes its name from the East-Anglian-type station was an offshoot of the Choukoutien-Soan prototype, as has been suggested, it may have flourished in its original form in China in the Middle Pleistocene contemporary with the Javanese deposits.

So far as the skeletal remains are concerned, with which we are here primarily concerned, since the discovery of the molar in 1927, fragments of human skulls of at least fourteen individuals of varying ages have come to light with teeth and pieces of jaws belonging to more than forty persons, together with a few long bones. These in their general features conform to those of the pithecanthropoid type of hominid, familiar in the notorious *Pithecanthropus erectus*, the so-called ape-man of Java, and the subsequent Javanese examples of the species.[3] They are, therefore, proto-Neanderthaloid just as the implements foreshadow the Mousterian flint tradition. The bodies had been decapitated after death, buried until they had decomposed, and the heads were then carefully preserved for ritual purposes, doubtless, as in Borneo today, because in them it was supposed that soul-substance resided having the properties of a vitalizing agent.[4] As the skulls show signs of injuries they may have been those of victims who had been killed and their crania broken open in order to extract the brain for sacramental consumption. If this were so, probably they represent the remains of cannibal feasts, organized cannibalism in that case having been an established feature of the cult of the dead in the Mid-Pleistocene in North China in which the cutting off and preservation of the head, skull or scalp was a prominent feature during or after the sacred meal, either to extract its soul-substance or as a trophy.

Monte Circeo

That this practice was widely and persistently adopted in prehistoric times, doubtless for a variety of reasons, is clear from the numerous skulls and headless bodies that have been found in Palaeolithic, Mesolithic and Neolithic sites.[5] An interesting and significant example is that of a Neanderthal skull discovered in 1939 in the grotto at Monte Circeo on the Tyrrhenian coast of the Pomptine Fields within a circle of stones in a small inner chamber. Bones of deer, horse, hyena, elephant and lion were on the floor and heaped up round the walls in piles, and on the floor beneath the cranium were two fractured metacarpals of an ox and of a deer. The skull showed signs of having received a fatal blow on the right side of the temple, and at its base the foramen magnum connecting the brain with the spinal cord had been cut away after death, probably to extract the brain.

It would seem, therefore, that here we have the trophy of a Neanderthal man who in the last glaciation, after having been murdered or killed by a serious accident perhaps 70,000 to 100,000 years ago, was deposited ceremonially in a cave used for ritual purposes as a sacred ossuary. It would appear further that the brain had been extracted and eaten to imbibe its magico-religious qualities very much as in the Ngandoeng terraces of the Solo river in Eastern Java (which may correspond in time to the Riss-Würm Interglacial in Europe) skulls appear to have been hacked open, possibly at a cannibal feast, and subsequently used as bowls.[6] Thus, in an Upper Palaeolithic cave at Placard, Charente, drinking cups made from the upper part of the vault of human skulls occurred in the Magdalenian and Solutrean layers.[7] At Krapina near Zagreb in Croatia in a Mousterian deposit on a terrace which also belongs to the Riss-Würm Interglacial, a quantity of human and animal bones occurred in a fragmentary condition, some having been split open to obtain their marrow and charred, suggesting the remains of a cannibal feast. One of the skulls contained artificial cuts, the result doubtless of a deed of violence.[8]

Ofnet

The most convincing evidence, however, comes from two deposits near Nördlingen in Bavaria, where in a spur of the Jura known as Ofnet, and assigned to the Mesolithic period after the last glaciation, a nest of twenty-seven human skulls was found in a group embedded in red ochre, the skulls looking westwards. A few yards away was a second identical group of six skulls. In some of them the cervical vertebrae were still attached, and from their condition the heads must have been severed from the body after death with flint knives, and ceremonially preserved when they had been dried. As those in the centre were more tightly packed together and crushed, it seems that they had been added one by one from time to time. Since some of them were brachycephalic and others dolichocephalic they must have belonged to two distinct races, the one broad-headed and the other long-headed, probably survivors of the so-called "Brünn race" from the Upper Palaeolithic. Twenty were those of children ornamented with snail shells, nine were of women with necklaces of deer teeth, and four only were of adult males.[9] To explain this high proportion of women and children it has been suggested that they were the victims of an attack in which most of the men escaped, leaving the women behind to be decapitated. This hardly accounts for the ornamentation of the skulls with shells, the burial in red ochre, and the provision of all but one of the men with their implements, and signs that fires had been lighted near them. From the equipment it would seem more likely that some particular significance was attached to the skulls, whether the victims had been killed *en bloc* or singly, and so they were treated as trophies comparable to those collected in head-hunting expeditions in Borneo and elsewhere in modern times.

In the grotte de Trou-Violet at Montardit a fragment of a skull from which the flesh had been peeled off, together with a few small bones and a number of pebbles arranged in the form of a human body, may have been in the nature of a cenotaph commemorating some notable person, the head being the object of veneration.[10] In the pre-pottery levels at Jericho seven skulls in varying states of preservation have been recently discovered with features moulded in plaster and shells, including in one case cowries and in the others flat shells in two leaves, separated by vertical slits to represent the pupils of the eyes.[11] Here, again, some form of trophy, or object of worship possessed of great potency, is suggested. For the same reason animal heads were interred, it would seem, as, for example, those of bears in two Mousterian caves at Drachenloch in Switzerland, collected into groups and orientated in stone cists covered with a rock slab. At Petershöhle near Nuremberg bear skulls were erected in niches along the walls of a cave of the same period, and on a stone platform, while in Austria at Drachenhöhle in Styria fifty-four bear femurs were orientated in another Mousterian site.[12] Doubtless it was the great strength of the bear that caused it to become a cult object at a very early period, and as this was likely to be concentrated in the head it would be the skull that would be preserved and venerated.

CEREMONIAL INTERMENT IN THE MIDDLE PALAEO-LITHIC

Le Moustier

It was not, however, only the cranium that was ceremonially treated after death in Palaeolithic times. Thus, at Le Moustier, the site that has given its name to the characteristic industry of the last group of flake tool-makers in the middle of the Palaeolithic, situated near Peyzac on the right bank of the Vézère in the Dordogne, the skeleton of a Neanderthal youth was discovered in 1908 under fragments of animal bones. It had been placed with the back upwards, the forearm under the head, which rested on a pillow of flint flakes. Near the left arm were a fine Acheulean hand-axe and a scraper. In the grave were the bones of the wild ox, charred and split, suggesting the remains of a funeral feast.[13]

La Chapelle-aux-Saints

The similar interment in a small low-roofed cave near the village of La Chapelle-aux-Saints in the department of

Corrèze lay in a pit dug in the floor surrounded with flints which included excellent scrapers and quartzite and crystal flakes of various colours. Near the hand was the foot of an ox, and behind it part of the vertebral column of a reindeer. Above the body, which had been buried in the contracted position, the earth contained broken bones of the woolly rhinoceros, bison, horse and ibex, together with Mousterian implements. Near the skeleton was the leg of a bison buried apparently while the flesh was still on it.[14] Some of the flints were broken near the point, probably in the process of splitting the long bones of the animals to extract the marrow[15] consumed at the funerary feasts held in the cave. Judging from the quantity and variety of the bones, these must have been considerable and could hardly have been confined to the time of the interment.

La Ferrassie

In a cave at La Ferrassie near Les Eyzies in the Dordogne the remains of a man and a woman occurred, the head and shoulders, the right leg and the left forearm of the man having been protected with slabs of stone and covered with bone flakes. In the trenches near by lay the remains of two children, while those of a baby were found under a tiny mound. A fourth child was buried in a grave in the floor and covered by a stone with artificial cup-markings on it. All the skeletons, which may represent members of one family, were orientated east to west, and associated with Mousterian implements. In front of the graves of the children a ditch containing bones and ashes (perhaps those of an ox) may have been a funerary deposit.[16]

The care bestowed on the disposal of these bodies leaves little room for doubt that a cult of the dead was definitely established in the Middle Palaeolithic, though, of course, it was only in districts like the Dordogne where caves and rock-shelters were readily available that intentional interments have survived the ravages of time, weather and wild beasts. At this stage it may not have gone further than a belief in human survival under conditions in which food and implements would be required beyond the grave in a life like that lived before death, for none other could be conceived. The attitude towards the dead which found expression in the funerary ritual may have been a combination of respect, fear, veneration and concern for their well-being. All of these, however, presuppose a prolongation of existence after the dissolution of the body.

THE UPPER PALAEOLITHIC

This becomes clearer in the Upper Palaeolithic with the arrival in Western Europe of a variety of forms of *Homo sapiens* of which the Crô-Magnon type, named after the rock-shelter near Les Eyzies in the Dordogne where it was first detected in 1868, is the most characteristic in the later stages of the last glaciation. Nevertheless, as the burials reveal, in addition to the tall, dolichocephalic, muscular, well-proportioned Crô-Magnons there was a shorter rather less advanced type with a somewhat higher head and broader nose, exemplified in a skeleton at Combe Capelle, Dordogne, and in Moravia at Brno (Brünn) and Předmost, where in a collective burial in a common grave containing fourteen complete skeletons and six fragments, a third variant occurred with heavy brow-ridges, high-vaulted skull and more prognathous jaws. Finally, in the lowest level of the first of the series of caves at Grimaldi on the Italian side of the frontier between Mentone and Ventimiglia —that known as the *Grottes des Enfants*—an old woman and a youth were found in 1901 who differed considerably in their physical features from the rest of Upper Palaeolithic Man.

The Grimaldi Burials

The boy was about sixteen years of age and lay on his right side with the legs doubled back under the thighs so that the heels almost touched the pelvis. The woman was tightly flexed with her knees as high as her shoulders, and her feet touching her pelvis. She was laid to the left of the youth. Round his head were four rows of pierced shells, and his skeleton was stained red with peroxide of iron. On the arms of the woman were shell bracelets. Between the heads lay two pebbles of serpentine, another pebble against the jaw of the woman. The trench had been dug in a Mousterian stratum immediately below the first Upper Palaeolithic level to which the grave belonged. The heads were protected by a flat stone supported by two others, and the space between them was filled with peroxide of iron.[17] The skulls are high and very dolichocephalic; the nose is flatter and broader than in the Crô-Magnons, the jaws are prognathous, and the proportions of the limb bones and the dentition have suggested negroid affinities. About this, however, expert opinion is divided, and the Grimaldi remains may be merely a variant of the Combe Capelle and Předmost types, or possibly of the Crô-Magnon variety of Upper Palaeolithic Man. Thus, a somewhat similar skeleton was found in 1927 at La Genière in Ain, and Keith maintained that the relatively greater length of the forearm and shin as compared with the upper arm and thigh respectively was a recurrent feature in Crô-Magnon skeletons.[18]

In the stratum above this burial were the remains of a very tall man of normal Crô-Magnon type in the extended position with his forearms drawn up, bringing the hands to the level of the neck. The head had a similar crown of shells to that on the youth below, and about its thorax was a quantity of shells which apparently had been fixed to a sort of apron made perhaps of hides. Over the body stones had been placed and the head rested on a block of sandstone reddened with ochre. On the hearth on which it was laid were rough limestone and quartzite tools. Above this came the two young children clad in a shroud composed of nearly a thousand Nassa perforated shells. From this interment the cave has been named. Nearer to the surface were the mutilated remains of a woman which appear to have been re-buried and surrounded with trochus shells.[19]

The adjoining Grotte du Cavillon, the fourth in the series, contained 7,868 marine shells (*Nassa neritea*) of which 875 were pierced. Of these over 200 were about the head of a Crô-Magnon man in the contracted position. The skeleton was covered with powdered haematite so that it was coloured

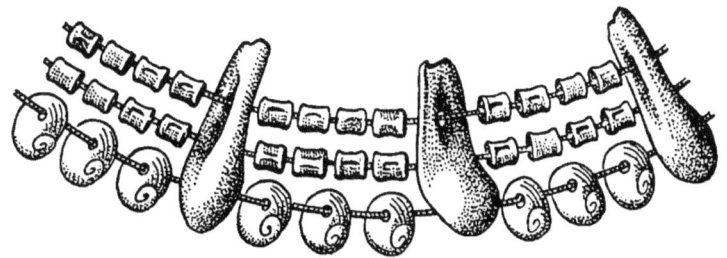

Fig. 1. Collar on a skeleton from Barma Grande, Mentone

scarlet. On the cranium was a fillet of seashells, and twenty-two perforated canine teeth of deer were near the frontal bones. A bone-point made from the radius of a deer lay across the forehead, and two flink flakes against the occiput.[20]

At Barma Grande, the fifth cave, the bodies of a tall man, a young woman and a boy occurred in a grave lined with red ochre. The male skeleton, which lay on its back with the head resting on the thighs, was adorned with Nassa shells, the canine teeth of deer and a fish's vertebrae, all perforated, together with ivory pendants, a necklace and two large perforated cowries (*Cypraea millepunctata*), originally apparently a garter.[21] The female was similarly ornamented and in her left hand she held a flint knife, 26 centimetres in length. Beside her, also lying on his left side, was the boy, whose head was covered with fish vertebrae and Nassas divided into groups by deer teeth (Fig. 1). Above these remains, towards the back of the cave, were two skeletons in the same extended position with an array of Nassa shells, deer teeth and pendants of ivory disposed about the bodies in similar fashion. All these lay in a trench filled with red ochre and were covered with it. Finally, in the sixth cave, Baousso da Torre, a shell collar, a fillet and a girdle with shell pendants recutred in a disturbed burial. Two other skeletons were found in this cave, one of which had been sprinkled with ochre.

Paviland and other Upper Palaeolithic Sepultures
The custom of burying the dead in a deposit of ochreous earths was widespread in the Upper Palaeolithic. Thus, as far from the Italian riviera as the Gower coast of South Wales a skeleton

of this period, long known as the "Red Lady of Paviland", was discovered by Dean Buckland in 1822 buried in red iron ore which had coloured the associated objects. These included a number of Pleistocene animals such as mammoth, woolly rhinoceros, reindeer, bison, hyena, horse and cave bear, together with a quantity of Aurignacian implements and other objects in bone and ivory, and pendants in the form of beans. By the side of the body were small shells (*Neritea littoralis*) and the head and tusks of a mammoth. Only the limb bones of the left side of the skeleton have survived and these, now preserved in the University Museum, Oxford, are thought to be those of a tall Crô-Magnon male.[22]

Between Mentone and Paviland a number of similar burials have been found in Upper Palaeolithic deposits. Thus, at Crô-Magnon among the bones of the skeleton which had been stained red by pieces of haematite were nearly 300 shells, mainly of *Littorina littorea*, and perforated pendants. At Brno (Brünn) immediately above the skeleton were a mammoth tusk and shoulder-blade, and around it were more than 600 conical tubes of a fossil shell (*Dentalium badense*), used apparently as a breastplate, an ivory male figurine without legs, perforated disks in bone, quartzite and stone, and three cut from a mammoth tooth.[23] The skeleton was coated with an iron oxide ochreous powder, and the traces of this red colouring matter occurred on the statuette.

The remains of the tightly flexed body at Raymonden, Chancelade, near Périgueux in the Dordogne, was covered with a layer of peroxide of iron and associated with Magdalenian implements. Although attempts have been made to interpret the anatomical features of the skull as Eskimoid, the skeleton is probably that of a dwarf variety of Crô-Magnon Man considerably later than the Grimaldi type.[24] Thus, three skeletons excavated in the valley of the Roc in Charente in 1923 bear some resemblance to the Chancelade remains. It is clear from other Magdalenian interments, such as those at Obercassel near Bonn and at Laugerie-Basse near Les Eyzies, at Grotte des Hoteaux near Rousillan, Ain, and at Sordes in the Landes, that the Magdalenians were not homogeneous. As an ethnological group they emerged as the consummation of the Upper Palaeolithic with no less than six phases in their industry, establishing themselves mainly in France (with the cave of La Madeleine, Dordogne, as the type station), Spain, Italy, Moravia and Poland, with local variations in England detected at Cresswell Crags in Derbyshire, Cheddar in the Mendips and Kent's Cavern in Devon; while in the Rhine valley in Holland, the vicinity of Hamburg in Germany, and in Eastern Europe, independent groups persisted. That they continued the Gravettian (i.e. the former Upper Aurignacian) tradition in sepulture as well as in art and blade-culture is shown by the recurrence of ochreous burial often in association with an elaborate shell, bone and ivory equipment, as at Grimaldi, Paviland, Brno, Hoteaux, Obercassel and Chancelade.

If the Gravettian culture took the firmest root in the Upper Palaeolithic in Europe, in the second phase of the Würm glaciation the Solutreans from their cradleland, either in the mountainous country of Northern Hungary or in North-west Africa, established themselves sporadically over Western and Central Europe. While their composite culture flourished with its fine pressure-flaking of leaf-shaped points and bas-reliefs in shallow rock-shelters, before it was succeeded by the Magdalenian, the mortuary tradition continued little changed. At the type station of Solutré near Mâcon in Saône-et-Loire were hearth-burials varying in size and associated with perforated shells, pierced phalanges of reindeer, engraved figures of animals in limestone and bone, and the remains of funerary feasts.[25] Unfortunately we know practically nothing about the circumstances and conditions in which a skeleton was found in the important Solutrean site at Laugerie-Haute near Les Eyzies, but at Předmost near Brno there was an intentional burial in a common grave of fourteen bodies with mammoth bones, ivory and reindeer-horn artifacts and a flint industry in a transitional stage from Gravettian to Solutrean. The physical type has affinities with that revealed at Brno and Combe Capelle, and though it may not have been responsible for the

Gravettian industry, or the introduction of the Solutrean in Central Europe, it would seem to have been one of the contributory elements in a composite culture. But from whatever sources the Solutreans and their techniques came, from the few traces left of their graves they appear to have buried their dead in the established manner, which included, as we have seen, a cult of skulls with drinking-cups at the Grotte du Placard, Charente.

The Palaeolithic Cult of the Dead
Thus, from the available evidence concerning the disposal of the body under Palaeolithic conditions it seems that from the beginning of the Pleistocene period a cult of the dead was practised which found expression in the preservation of the skull and the extraction of the brain, ceremonial interment in either the extended or contracted positions with flint implements, and sometimes animal bones suggestive of a funeral feast. In the Upper Palaeolithic the body often was deposited in a grave containing ochreous powder with an abundance of shells and other ornaments in bone and ivory, sometimes apparently after the flesh had been removed from the bones, thereby colouring them red. This widespread custom of coating the corpse with red ochre clearly had a ritual significance. Red is the colour of living health. Therefore, as Professor Macalister has pointed out, if the dead man was to live again in his own body, of which the bones were the framework, to paint them with the ruddy colouring of life was "the nearest thing to mummification that the Palaeolithic people knew; it was an attempt to make the body again serviceable for its owner's use".[26]

Moreover, as blood has been a vitalizing agent from time immemorial, so certain shells, such as the cowrie shaped in the form of the portal through which a child enters the world, seem to have been connected with the female principle and to have been widely employed as fertility charms.[27] It is not improbable, therefore, that this recurrent feature in Upper Palaeolithic interments was in the nature of a life-giving rite which later found expression in female figurines and other aspects and symbols of the Great Mother with which the cult of the dead became associated. Thus, at Laugerie-Basse, Dordogne, cowries were arranged in pairs upon the body: two pairs on the forehead, one near the humerus, four in the region of the knees and thighs, and two upon each foot.[28] Such a distribution can hardly have been other than for the purpose of giving life to the deceased rather than for ornamentation.

On the other hand, the suggestion repeatedly made that the flexing of the body symbolized the foetal position of the embryo and was inspired by the idea of rebirth beyond the grave is most unlikely, at any rate in Palaeolithic times. That the prenatal attitude was then understood or that Early Man would have reasoned along those sort of lines, even supposing that he had any such embryological knowledge, is highly improbable. In some cases the binding was done undoubtedly before rigor mortis had set in, and where this practice has been adopted by modern primitive people normally its purpose has been to prevent the return of the deceased to molest the living. This motive hardly can be eliminated from the Palaeolithic mortuary cult and may very likely explain rigid flexing and burying beneath heavy stones, especially when economy of space is not involved.

Nevertheless, the care taken in the disposal, ornamentation and protection of the body, and sometimes its re-burial, together with its equipment with amulets, fires and the means of sustenance, seem to indicate a respect and regard for the departed that goes beyond fear. The grave was not so much a prison in which the dead were incarcerated within stone walls and made secure from escape by being tightly bound, as a portal to an after-life on the other side of the grave. Even Neanderthal Man, degenerate though he may have become and doomed to extinction as a type in the maximum glaciation, had begun to look forward to survival after death; to a life like that which he had lived on earth, where he would still need food, tools and warmth, as he had always required. The Crô-Magnons appear to have gone a stage further in the development of a cult of the dead by resorting to magico-religious devices, such as surrogates for blood and life-bestowing amulets, in order to re-animate the mortal remains.

Side by side with these attempts to secure a renewal of life in the hereafter there may have been a very real, and perhaps increasing, fear of the return of the dead to exercise vengeance and pay off old scores, or avenge any neglect in the due performance of the mortuary ritual. It is possible that firm trussing of the corpse immediately after the dissolution may have been employed as a precaution against "walking", though the widespread adoption of the contracted position (as distinct from complete and tight flexion in an unnatural posture) may have been merely an imitation of that of sleep and rest or sometimes an economy of space. Among the examples that have been described, however, those of the "negroid" woman at *Les Grottes des Enfants* and the flexed body at Chancelade are very difficult if not impossible to explain on any supposition other than that of fear as the underlying motive of this mode of disposal. On the other hand, the preservation of trophies, as in the cult of skulls, seems to have been inspired by a desire to retain a potent relic of the dead, while brain-extraction was a means of communion with them, or of imbibing their virtue and strength.

THE MESOLITHIC TRANSITION

Azilian-Tardenoisian Interments

That this practice continued into Mesolithic times is established by the nests of skulls at Ofnet, to which reference has been made (cf. pp. 20f). This remarkable ceremonial interment with its thirty-three heads embedded in ochre and ornamented with shells, successively buried in a grotto revealing a sequence of cultures from the Aurignacian and Earlier Solutrean to the Late Magdalenian and Azilian-Tardenoisian, shows that the Palaeolithic funerary cult survived unchanged from the beginning of the Upper Palaeolithic well into the Transitional period at the end of the Pleistocene. Moreover, in addition to this great ossuary, ten burials, including the remains of twenty-three individuals, were discovered in 1928 in another Mesolithic settlement, that at Téviec off the Quiberon peninsula in Brittany. The bodies were crouched in shallow trench graves near the hearths, accompanied by Late Tardenoisian implements, perforated shell necklaces and bracelets, and covered with red ochre and stone slabs, over which small cairns were erected. From the cloak-fasteners it would appear that the bodies were clothed when they were interred, or re-buried, and in one case red deer antlers had been stacked over a skull. On the neighbouring island of Hoëdic male skeletons were similarly crowned with deer antlers.[29] An infant was buried beneath a hearth at Téviec, and at Mugem in Portugal a number of burials have been found under the great middens on the Tagus estuary. In an oval tumulus called Cabeço d'Arruda on these marshes were human skeletons in association with marine shells, a perforated pebble, Tardenoisian flakes and a trapeze.[30]

In Spain near Tres Puntes, Alava, in the neighbourhood of Vittoria, under a tumulus at a mill called Axpea, a number of human bones, including the mandibles of five children, were discovered in 1918, together with pierced shell beads, ochre and Late Tardenoisian geometric flints.[31] At Furfooz on the river Lesse in Belgium, one of the seven caves was an ossuary in which the bones of about fourteen skeletons had been deposited after the flesh had decayed,[32] just as at Mas d'Azil in Ariège portions of two skeletons had been treated in the same way, and painted red after interment.[33]

Maglemosean

Therefore, ritual burial was well established in the Azilian-Tardenoisian culture soon after 12000 B.C., but no clear evidence has so far been produced of intentional disposal of the dead, either in the Maglemosean culture, which flourished in Denmark and along the Baltic coasts about 7000 B.C., or in that of the somewhat later Kitchen middens near the coasts of South Scandinavia and the southern shores of the Baltic about 4000 B.C. Thus, no definite burials have been discovered under the great bog of Mullerup on the west of the island of Zealand, or in any of the other Maglemosean sites, such as Svaerdborg or Holmegaard in the same vicinity, though a few human bones have been found in the peat at Maglemose.

Ertebølle

When salt water poured into the Baltic depression to form the Litorina Sea, near its oyster-beds the people called Ertebølle, after the name of one of their middens, settled down to a sedentary life with shell-fish as their staple diet. In the debris of their refuse they buried their dead in the extended position, and sometimes surrounded them with a few large stones.[34] But there is no indication of their having practised any mortuary ritual, or of their having provided their dead with grave goods. Their outstanding achievement was the production of coarse and roughly made pots for the storage of food, but although some of the later vessels at Havnelev near Strandegaard in South Zealand bore impressions of grain (wheat and barley) no such imprints, or any querns, occurred in the rectangular log-houses inhabited by late Ertebølle folk at Strandegaard.[35]

The earliest signs of agriculture in Denmark came from the Solager midden in North Zealand, and from Brabrand in Jutland in the form of impressions of wheat on potsherds, while simultaneously the bones of the domestic ox, pig, sheep and goat appear in the Ertebølle middens. When the middens were abandoned is uncertain, but it seems that the Mesolithic inhabitants of the region must have been in contact with Neolithic settlers for some time before the arrival of the megalithic migration (c. 2300 B.C.), or encamped on sites which had been occupied previously by food-producers who may have come along the Danube and spread between the Oder and the Vistula beyond the loess lands until they reached the Baltic coasts.[36] In Denmark they continued their tradition of extended burial in earth graves defined by a ring of small stones round the body and covered with a large earth mound. The only stones available being boulders which could not be split into slabs, the Neolithic farmers were the first group in this region to erect small rectangular chambers with single capstones, known as "dolmens" or *dyssers*, like those in the cemetery of Jordansmühl in Silesia in which Danubian and northern grave goods were combined.

Danish Dyssers

The origin of these Danish *dyssers*, however, is far from clear. That they represent the starting-point of the long and complicated process of megalithic burial in slab-built tombs and the associated cult can be dismissed at once. The notion of a unilineal development from the small rectangular chambers consisting of about four large stones set on edge with one larger slab forming the roof, commonly called "dolmens", through passage-graves with round or polygonal chambers leading out of a passage of large slabs and roofed with huge capstones, and the long galleries with forecourts and side-chambers, to the great corbelled vaults of Spain and the Aegean, along the lines suggested by Montelius, has now been abandoned in favour of a series of movements from the Mediterranean and Atlantic littoral during the third millennium B.C. making their way northwards to the British Isles and Denmark, as will be considered in greater detail later (Chap. III). Thus, the "simple dolmen" often has turned out to be nothing more than a late fragment or degeneration of an earlier complex tumulus, and, as Professor Daryll Forde concluded, the traditional classical typology had begun at the wrong end.[37]

In the light of the existing evidence it seems certain that by whatever route the megalithic culture was introduced into Denmark and Sweden, the dolmen tomb-form was the first to arrive. Although it is true that in the Baltic the cult developed along its own lines, with its own Mesolithic tradition in the background, nevertheless its significance can be understood only when it is viewed in relation to all that lies behind the megalithic movement as an integral element in the rise and diffusion of Neolithic civilization in Europe. To this inquiry, therefore, we must now turn, beginning in the Ancient Middle East.

CHAPTER II

Neolithic Burials in the Ancient East

ALTHOUGH the transition from food-gathering to food-production was a very gradual process localized in certain regions, notably in the Fertile Crescent in the Ancient Middle East, where it became an accomplished fact it had a marked effect upon the disposal of the dead in more elaborate tombs and with a more complex mortuary ritual. Graves, however, were still dug in the ground, sometimes covered with a mound of earth or a stone erection, and caves were also used for burial purposes. With the rise of the megalithic tradition massive sepulchral structures developed, while in Egypt a funerary cultus assumed such gigantic proportions that it became the characteristic feature and focal-point of the remarkable civilization of the Nile valley. Indeed the monuments it created have remained throughout the ages the chief sources of information about the culture of which they constitute a permanent record. Upon the decoration and furnishing of their royal tombs the Egyptians lavished their art in mural paintings, sculpture and architecture, and gave expression to their beliefs, hopes and achievements, here and hereafter.

EGYPTIAN NEOLITHIC CEMETERIES

Since Sir Flinders Petrie first discovered the Predynastic cemeteries at Naqada in 1895 hundreds of prehistoric graves have now been excavated which take back the cult of the dead in the Nile valley to well before 4000 B.C. While in Lower Egypt a very early settlement with Mesolithic affinities has been found at Merimde Benisalame near the western edge of the Delta, the three main Neolithic cultures, termed respectively Badarian, Amratian (Naqadaean) and Gerzean

(Semainian), are differentiated in Middle and Upper Egypt. Behind the earliest of these Dr Brunton claims to have detected at the village of Deir Tasa a less developed semi-nomadic cultural phase which he has named Tasian, contemporary with the Merimdian, and which he thinks preceded in the fifth millennium B.C. the more settled agricultural Badarian community.[1] About this, however, there is now some doubt since the graves at Deir Tasa were found in the same cemeteries as the Badarian tombs, and some of them cut into each other.[2] But in any case ritual burial was firmly established in Neolithic Egypt.

Badarian

Thus, at Badari graves occurred in small and scattered groups dug in soft, sandy gravel or limestone detritus on the spur of the desert near to but independent of the dwellings. The bodies were clothed and adorned with their ornaments. One man had a girdle of over five thousand blue glazed steatite beads, and in the hair of a baby were ostrich-tips, while near another infant were a bowl and an ivory spoon. Among the graves were cooking-pots and food bowls, either empty or containing grain and meat, suggesting that funeral meals probably were a feature of the mortuary ritual. Near the hands were slate palettes and pebbles for grinding malachite as eye-paint. The corpse was laid on a reed mat, often on its left side with the head facing west or south, and surrounded with beads, perforated shells, ostrich-shell disks, ivory hair-combs and female figurines, as well as with pottery. Over it was a roofing of matting and sticks, and occasionally hides. The contracted position was adopted with the thighs forming an angle of about 60° with the spine, or at right angles, but tight flexing was rare. The head rested sometimes on a pillow in an attitude which Dr Brunton describes as that for "comfortable sleep".[3] No traces have been discovered of coffins of wood or clay, or any indications of attempts at the preservation of the body, though the skin sometimes was visible as a result of natural desiccation. In some cases the head was wrapped in cloth, but skins were the normal clothing of the dead below the neck. No traces occurred of multiple burial, and females were buried alongside of males in separate graves, though sometimes men were grouped together in a particular part of the cemetery.[4]

Amratian

In the First Predynastic or Amratian culture of Upper Egypt, soon after 4000 B.C., the same general procedure was maintained in spite of infusion of Getulan or Libyan strains from the margins of the desert. The graves continued to be oval with a tendency to become straight-sided with rounded corners, and finally rectangular. Occasionally they were plastered with mud or lined with brick. The bodies were wrapped in matting, though this custom tended to be abandoned in due course, since in the later graves it did not appear. A few traces of wooden coffins were discovered. The contracted position and orientation towards the west, the Land of the Dead, continued, but burials became more communal. Sometimes the body appears to have been dismembered, and in certain instances the head was removed and preserved, and for it either a pot or an ostrich egg was substituted. Pots and animal bones occurred on the grave floors together with fragments of ivory, slate palettes, mace-heads, beads, shells, flint flakes and malachite.

In an undisturbed grave of a female the beads were placed at the neck, mostly carnelian with four turquoise, three calcite and several lapis lazuli. On the right wrist was an ivory bracelet, and on the left two cowries. A slate palette, an ivory pin and resin were at the hands, and close to the head and hands were two pots. On each wrist was a bone bangle, and the leg of a very small animal in front of the face. In another undisturbed female interment, behind the head of the woman was the body of an infant, and both lay on their right sides. At her elbows was a string of carnelians with four blue glazed steatite beads, a white pebble pendant and a short string of columbella shells. A slate palette, a brown jasper pebble, a basket containing malachite, two flint flakes and three limestone "stoppers" were in front of the arms.[5]

Merimdian

In the western marshes of the Delta at Merimde, west of the Rosetta branch of the Nile, where the black soil brought down the river from Abyssinia, a prosperous agricultural community more or less contemporary with the Badarian settlements in Middle Egypt flourished on the fertile soil among the network of small streams until the encroachment of the desert caused it to be abandoned. Like the Badarians and Amratians, in life they wore linen clothes and decked themselves with necklaces of shells, bone rings and ivory bangles. Women had slate palettes on which they ground malachite for painting their eyes to counteract the glare of the sun. As the communities were small no extensive cemeteries have been found, the dead having been buried in trench or pit graves in the flexed position among or within the huts of the settlement near the fire-place, but without any furniture. There is the same lack of evidence in the Fayum lake-side settlements which may be rather later, though closely related to the Merimdians, if rather less advanced.[6]

Gerzean

As Asiatic influences began to make their way in Lower Egypt in the fourth millennium B.C. (c. 3500) they gave rise to a more advanced culture in which copper, painted pottery and cult objects were features, together with marked changes in dress, weapons and religion. In the mortuary tradition no very significant break occurred. Burial in the contracted position in oblong trench graves, dug rather deeper than formerly, was continued. But either a ledge was added for the rapidly increasing offerings, or, if they were placed in the grave, the corpse was laid on a bier of twigs, or in a niche cut in the rock, unless it was enclosed in a coffin. In the Gerzean cemetery at Hierakonpolis, the predynastic centre of the Horus cult of Upper Egypt, a late prehistoric brick-lined tomb decorated with coloured drawings consisted of a chamber 15 by 6½ by 5 feet, divided into two equal parts by a low transverse wall of small crude bricks, like those with which the floor was paved. The whole was plastered over with mud mortar which on the walls was then covered with a coating of yellow ochre. On it hunting scenes, combats and ships had been painted in red, black and white, the designs resembling those on the pottery of the period found in the tomb, together with a flint lance and a small limestone or chert vase. But there was no trace of the body, which can hardly have been other than that of a chief in view of the proportions and decorations of the sepulchre. Near by were two more brick-lined decorated tombs with divided compartments, but as they had been plundered no furniture remained except a few jars. The rest of the graves were rectangular trenches often roofed with wood, mostly disturbed and containing little except coarse pottery and spheroidal spindle-whorls.[7]

Thus, throughout the Neolithic period in Egypt the disposal of the dead followed the same general pattern. Interment invariably was in the contracted position in graves dug in the ground in cemeteries near but, except at Merimde, not within the settlements. The bodies frequently were clothed in skins and provided with ornaments, amulets and the means of sustenance, and at Merimde they were buried near the fire within the family circle. At Badari the burial grounds were near the village and so in close touch with the relatives of the deceased. But later they were placed at a distance from the habitation, suggesting that the next life was becoming less closely connected with that in this world.

Orientation towards the west may indicate that already an occidental land of the dead, which became so prominent later, was in process of development. This ancient doctrine of the "West" as the permanent realm of the dead was submerged, however, in the Dynastic Pyramid Texts in favour of the East as the region in which the dead pharaoh had his abode.[8] Moreover, at the end of the prehistoric period at El Amrah, Gerzeh and Turah the head faced eastwards, while at Merimde the graves were so arranged that the body looked towards the north or the north-east. There was, therefore, no hard and fast rule about orientation, or the side on which the body lay. The normal position for the corpse in the grave was on the left side from the Badarian period to the Middle Kingdom in the second millennium B.C. Where this was not adopted it is possible that if the land of the dead was thought to be where the sun sets, the renewal of life after death was more appropriately associated with the east, since it was there that the sun rose in the morning.

Another home of the dead in some of the Pyramid Texts was among the circumpolar stars in the Elysian Fields in the northern sky. But to what extent, if at all, these beliefs about the realms of the dead in the historical period have their antecedents in the Neolithic mortuary ritual can be only conjectures in the absence of precise information other than the evidence concerning modes of disposal of the body and the position of the tombs and their contents. All that can safely be affirmed is that a life after death was an established belief, and from all appearances it was not very different from that which had obtained elsewhere from Palaeolithic times, since it found expression in almost identical funerary practices.

THE EARLIEST DYNASTIC TOMBS

When the unification of Upper Egypt was effected, it would seem by a king of Hierakonpolis soon after 3000 B.C., with the establishment of the First Dynasty of the pharaohs, significant changes in tomb construction became apparent. The simple predynastic pit graves continued to be the normal method of sepulture for the mass of the people but the elevation of a local chieftain to the exalted position of the single ruler of the "Two Lands" of Upper and Lower Egypt, with all the divine prerogatives the office acquired, found expression in a rapid elaboration of the royal tombs and their contents and cultus. Already, as we have seen, the sides of predynastic graves had been lined with bricks made of Nile mud dried in the sun, and equipped with a plentiful supply of offerings. They were also covered with sand or stones over a wood roof, the brick lining often being carried up to contain this covering and make it secure from hyenas and jackals. The pit was undercut on one side to allow more space at the bottom for the grave-furniture.

As the digging proceeded deeper and deeper into the sand, rock steps were required to gain access to the chamber below, which was also expanded by the addition of smaller rooms to contain offerings. The royal tombs at Abydos illustrate several varieties of this phase in the development in attempts to construct subterranean reproductions of the houses (or palaces) of the living.[9]

The Mastaba Tomb and the Pyramid

Thus, in the centre was a large chamber under the superstructure with the smaller tombs grouped around it containing the bodies of courtiers and servants who in all probability had been sacrificed during the royal obsequies. The floor of the tomb of King Den at the end of the First Dynasty was composed of slabs of granite, while in that of Khasekhemui of the Third Dynasty a room was lined with limestone. In the Second Dynasty the wooden roof was replaced by a corbelled vault of mud brick with a small rectangular brick structure resembling the shape of a house (or palace), with a slight slope to its side, and a niche in one face in front of which offerings were laid. The outside walls became ornamented with a series of vertical recesses and projections. In this way the mastaba tomb as a vast rectangular brick creation arose over a series of chambers and a shaft leading to the grave (Fig. 2). The niche or chapel of offerings was sometimes represented by a "false door" on one side, but in royal tombs its place was taken by a temple. In the Third Dynasty stone was substituted for brick to make the tomb an "everlasting habitation" for the occupant. Thus, Zoser had a vast stone oblong constructed of five other mastabas superimposed on each other in steps of decreasing height and size in the form of a pyramid. In the next dynasty the steps were filled in with stones, the ground-plan was made square, the sides were straightened and brought to a point at the top. Surrounding these vast royal pyramids, which about 2900 B.C. reached their climax in those erected at Gizeh for the kings Khufu (Cheops), Khafra and Menkaura, are smaller stepped pyramids constituting the mastabas of royal relatives, courtiers and officials, arranged in rows at a respectful distance.[10]

The Earliest Dynastic Tombs

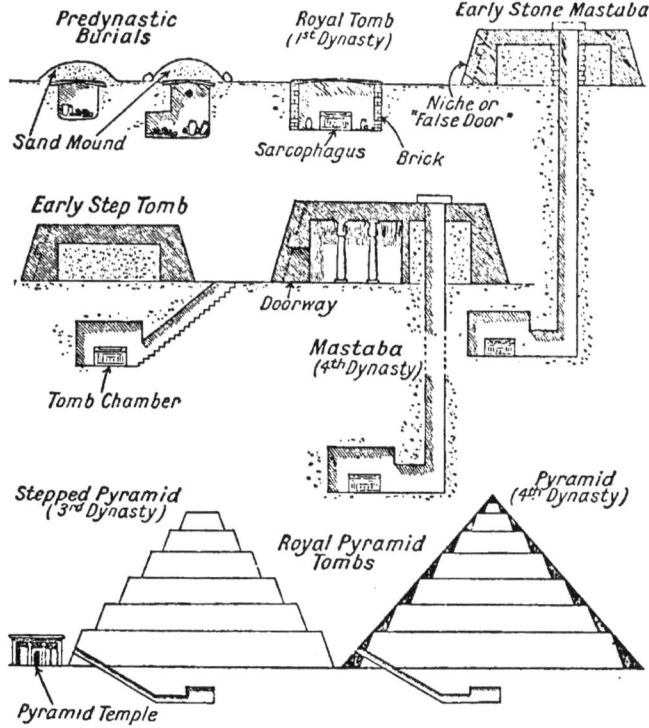

Fig. 2. The development of the mastaba tomb

The burial in the pyramid was in a rock-cut chamber below the surface, and, as in the mastaba, the gigantic superstructure formed the memorial pile above the tomb. Whereas access to the burial chamber under the mastaba was through the vertical shaft which was filled in after the burial, in the pyramid the entrance was in its northern side, near ground-level, along a passage leading to the chamber in the pyramid or in the rock under it. The temple of offerings was in the front of the pyramid on its east side and consisted of several rooms devoted to the royal cultus, corresponding to the chapel and storeroom on the east side of the mastaba, containing provisions for the deceased in the west wall of the chapel and a portrait statue of him sitting at a meal before a table of offerings.

At first the offerings were made at the tomb, and this continued to be the normal practice for all ordinary Egyptians.

Thus, in the mastabas when a niche replaced the tablet of the table of offerings and a "false door" was added, it was through it the *ka*, or guardian *alter ego* guiding the fortunes of the individual in the hereafter, was thought to emerge to partake of the offerings and behold the rites performed in the chapel. But at the end of the Third Dynasty, when the place of offerings in the royal tombs was in a separate court attached to the side of the tomb, it developed into a stately and elaborate independent temple which by the Twelfth Dynasty had become entirely separated from the tomb in the desert.

Originally, however, as the pyramids and their temples stood on the desert plateau 100 feet above the plain, they were approached by a sloping covered passage or corridor of stone at the lower end of which stood a small introductory chapel. Khafra appears to have introduced the custom of placing statues of himself in front of, or between, the pillars of his temple, and the so-called Sphinx temple at Gizeh is the entrance to the corridor of the second pyramid, surmounted by the portrait statue of the pharaoh (Khafra) himself attached to the body of a lion, guarding the great cemetery of Gizeh, the most imposing city of the dead ever conceived. Thus, in the course of a few centuries, between about 3200 and 2900 B.C., the simple grave with its sand heap surrounded by a circle of stones assumed the gigantic proportions of these mighty pyramids, the greatest of which covers thirteen acres and contains over two million blocks of limestone, each weighing on an average two and a half tons, and stands nearly 500 feet high. It may well have been, as an ancient tradition recorded by Herodotus maintained, that 100,000 men were involved in its construction.

Thus, the prehistoric belief that the dead lived in or at the tomb, which must be adequately equipped, therefore, as an "everlasting habitation", persisted until at length it acquired the vast dimensions of these monumental structures which have remained throughout the ages as the most impressive expression of this conception of the hereafter in the ancient world. Even after the Fifteenth Dynasty, when the mortuary ritual and the cult of the dead became crystallized in their final form, the sojourn in the tomb subsisted side by side with the belief in remote realms of the dead in distant regions. When the pharaoh of the Old Kingdom became a god in the celestial realms, the nobility in the Pyramid Age began to seek their own eternity, and so they moved away their tombs from the royal cemeteries to their own domains in sure and certain hope of being able "to join their *kas*" in a future life in their own right. So eventually ordinary mortals, including commoners, returned to the Neolithic and earlier conviction of continued existence beyond the grave as an "effective personality" (*akh*); for every Egyptian at death now was destined to become an Osiris, and so to attain eternal blessedness.

NEOLITHIC TOMBS IN MESOPOTAMIA

In Mesopotamia, on the other hand, the sustained Egyptian preoccupation with the hereafter was conspicuously absent. The contrast between the regularity of the rise and fall of the Nile and the unpredictability of the Tigris and Euphrates, always liable to cause disastrous floods, seems to have been reflected in the cult of the dead. Thus, in Babylonia the hereafter was regarded as a sombre place of darkness and dust beneath the earth, to which all men, both good and bad alike, descended. Therefore, great cemeteries, enduring pyramids and elaborate tomb equipment, which reveal so much about the civilization of Ancient Egypt, are not to be found in Mesopotamia to anything like the same extent. In Sumer, apart from the royal tombs at Ur, the normal procedure was for the body to be clad in its ordinary clothes and wrapped in a mat, or in a linen winding-sheet, in the flexed position with the head resting on a fringed and tasselled cushion. It was then enclosed with a bowl of water and a few personal belongings (a dagger or razor, or a necklace and bracelets) in a wicker or pottery coffin (*larnake*), or in two large pottery jars with their open ends together (*pithoi*), and placed in a simple earth grave, or in a small brick-built vault. In towns the grave often was dug beneath the house in which the deceased had lived, under the pavement of one of the rooms. When the funeral rites had been performed the flooring was relaid and the occupation of the house continued in the customary manner. In the case of family vaults, after each interment the door was bricked up and the food vessels were placed outside before the earth was filled in.[11] Relatively few cemeteries have been discovered as yet in Mesopotamia, but at Ur among the royal tombs in some of the early graves of the commoners (c. 3500 B.C.) there were signs of burning in the upper part of the body. Cremation, however, was not practised in the historic period, and this incineration may have been accidental. Near or over the grave sometimes a model boat of bitumen with a cargo of clay vessels containing food was placed.[12]

Hassuna

West of the Tigris at Hassuna near Mosul in Assyria burials were found at almost all levels in the mound situated in the earliest known Neolithic settlement in Mesopotamia. In the lowest stratum (Level IA) an adult skeleton occurred in a loosely contracted position between two hearths in association with a Neolithic storage jar and a stone hoe, though it is not certain that this was a deliberate interment. From Level IB upwards infant burials in coarse incised and painted-and-incised jars occurred and beneath the floor of a room in Level IC was an undisturbed burial in the fully flexed position with the head to the north. Three sides of the grave were formed by the foundations of the walls of the room, and the fourth side consisted of a row of large stones. No traces of funerary furniture were seen. There seems to have been no uniformity of burial practice in this period, and two skeletons had been flung apparently unceremoniously into a grain bin of Level III, while in a rubbish pit in Level IV there was a skull. In the corner of a room in this level a collection of human bones were found.[13]

Tell Halaf

At Samarra, north of Baghdad on the Tigris, beneath the pavements of Islamic houses are a number of badly preserved graves in a cemetery in a layer showing no stratification. While

Neolithic Tombs in Mesopotamia

most of them were simple inhumations, a few were surrounded by a row of mud bricks. The bodies were flexed but gave no indication of having been orientated. There was the body of a new-born infant inside a pot of Samarran ware.[14] Both these sites, Hassuna and Samarra, were earlier than that of Tell Halaf on the Upper Khabur on the Anatolian border, which has given its name to the painted pottery it has yielded, and marks a definite advance in culture. Not only did the new technique in well-fired pottery replace the earlier styles, but it was accompanied by beads of metallic copper, emmer wheat and barley, and the remains of domesticated cattle.

At Tepe Gawra near Nineveh peculiar circular stone structures (*tholoi*) with a domed roof and in some cases a rectangular chamber attached to them, as in the Mycenaean beehive tombs, were used for ritual purposes, and many of the graves were associated with them. Moreover, that they were dedicated to chthonic deities is supported by the concentration of graves within and around them.[15] Throughout the greater portion of its long history the mound of Gawra was used as a burial ground though doubtless other cemeteries await discovery, since less than 500 tombs and graves have come to light during the excavations. This must represent a small proportion of the population during the many centuries of occupation from perhaps 5000 B.C. to the Bronze Age.[16] A pit was found below layer f. sunk into virgin soil, filled with earth and containing skeletons and artifacts at four levels. In the lowest was an adult in a contorted position; above this were the bones of nine skeletons all intermingled as though thrown into the pit. Higher up were the scattered remains of twelve more bodies, together with a pot, two stone pendants and a basalt pestle. Just below the mouth of the well were two more adults, one of which seems to have been a case of burial in the flexed position; the other was thrown on top of it. It may be, as Dr Perkins suggests, that originally it was used as a cistern or well, and later, after it had been filled with soil, it became a place for burial, as twenty-four skeletons were found at different levels.[17]

Al 'Ubaid

At Gawra flexing was the normal mode of inhumation, and only a few skeletons were laid in the extended position, whereas in the Tell Al 'Ubaid deposits, which represent the earliest phase in Sumer, named after a mound near Ur excavated in 1922, the bodies invariably lay on their backs, rigidly extended with the hands crossed below the chest. This, as we have seen, was an unusual practice which seems to indicate a break in the mortuary ritual in Mesopotamia to be explained in all probability by foreign intrusion.[18]

At Tell Arpachiyah near Nineveh, out of the fifty Ubaid graves discovered forty-five were found in the cemetery from which most of the painted ware of this period came. With many of the burials were votive-painted vessels, and the bodies generally were orientated east by west, though the heads lay sometimes at the east and sometimes at the west end of the grave in spite of the orientation of the body. The grave goods were placed at the head or the feet of the deceased. Fractional burial was widely practised, but even so what remained of the body was laid in an east-west direction. This mode of interment has never been recorded in the Halaf period as the pottery suggests, and it may have been introduced from Iranian sources.[19]

Halaf pottery was associated with two or possibly three of the five graves in the Middle phase, but the catalogue of the tombs in the report is not very explicit about the contents of the interments, and Sumerian tradition placed the foundation of their civilization in Dilmun, perhaps the modern Bahrein, on the Persian Gulf. Therefore, Professor Childe thinks that the starting-point may have been farther south, the distinctive features of the Ubaid culture representing merely adaptations of an imported "Eridu culture" to the peculiar conditions of the Delta.[20]

Be this as it may, while the peasant culture of North Iraq gradually changed character the first Al 'Ubaid settlements appeared in the drying Delta in the south. Further immigrations from Anatolia or Trans-Caucasia are associated with the

Neolithic Tombs in Mesopotamia

Uruk (Warka) civilization, and those from Iran with that of Jemdet Nasr, both of which lay behind the First Dynasty of Ur. In these proto-Sumerian cultures sepulture followed a fairly consistent tradition. In the Ubaid period the extended position was maintained, except, as we have seen, at Gawra, where flexing as the normal mode of Neolithic interment was commonly adopted.

In the Ubaid cemetery outside the retaining wall of the acropolis at Eridu extended collective burial occurred orientated to the north-west, consisting apparently of family graves with a flat shallow dish and an inverted bell-shaped cup, and one or more jars or stone vessels placed near the head.[21] Adults generally were interred in cemeteries outside the settlements of the living while infants frequently were laid among the dwellings. In the cemetery at Ur, which goes back to the Jemdet Nasr and Uruk periods, the bodies were definitely contracted and with them were stone vessels, lead cups and painted pots with sharp angular outlines, lug handles and spouts, and an inverted lead tumbler over the mouth of one of the pots.[22]

In the next stage the stone vessels were more numerous and varied with slip decorated ware. In the uppermost level pottery was scarce and its place was taken by cups, bowls and vases in limestone, diorite, steatite and alabaster. The abrupt ending of the Jemdet Nasr period suggests that the infiltration of an alien people with their own funerary tradition was summarily brought to a close when the old inhabitants reasserted their rule and established a new régime marking the beginning of the Dynastic period of Ur.

The Royal Tombs of Ur

In the great cemetery outside the walls of the old town two types of burials have been discovered, the one being the graves of commoners, the other, at a deeper and apparently an earlier level, those of the kings. These royal tombs are dated by Sir Leonard Woolley soon after 3000 B.C. (i.e. between 2900 and 2700),[23] and differ from the graves of their subjects by being stone and brick-vaulted, chambered structures rather than simple rectangular pits. They do not, however, follow any uniform plan. Usually they consist of one or more long outer chambers which are vaulted, and one or two smaller chambers roofed with domes in stone or brick, together with a pit for offerings and additional burials.[24]

The outstanding features are the amazing wealth of funerary furniture and a ritual involving human sacrifice on a grand scale. The grave goods included a fine head of a bull in gold with eyes of lapis lazuli, exquisitely fashioned stags, gazelles, bulls and goats also in gold with clusters of pomegranates and branches of trees with stems and fruits of gold and carnelian, silver and gold bowls and stone vessels, clay jars, silver tables for offerings, harps or lyres, an inlaid gaming-board, the statue of a ram on its hind legs with its front legs bound to the branches of a tree with silver chains, a wooden chariot decorated with mosaic and golden heads of cows and bulls, and cockle-shells containing green paint. With such a galaxy of priceless objects it is not surprising that many of the tombs had been rifled so that it is impossible to estimate the total wealth of the contents of the cemeteries. But it must have been immense.

Moreover, the bodies on their biers were richly clad and ornamented, and accompanied by a retinue of courtiers, attendants and guards also dressed in their finery. The soldiers were in two ranks with copper spears by their sides and were distributed elsewhere in the chamber carrying daggers and spears with heads of silver or gold. The women wore a gala head-dress of lapis and carnelian beads with golden pendants of beech leaves, ear-rings, necklaces of gold and lapis lazuli, and on top of their bodies were two wooden harps with the head of a bull in gold and copper respectively. These remains were those of victims who were sacrificed during the obsequies of a ruler who, according to an inscription on a cylinder seal found in the tomb, was named A-bar-gi, and his supposed queen was called Shub-ad. The stone chamber of the king had been plundered, but traces of a retinue survived, together with two model boats. Behind it a second vaulted chamber with a

Neolithic Tombs in Mesopotamia

cylinder seal of lapis lazuli above the roof bearing the name of the occupant, Shub-ad, was undisturbed.

Here by her body on a wooden bier was a golden cup near her hand and a large quantity of beads from the cloak in which she must have been clad. Three fish amulets and three gold pins were against her arm. Over the skull was a head-dress of greater elaboration than those of the court-ladies, fortified with amulets in lapis shaped as a bull and a calf. Near it was a second head-dress composed of thousands of lapis beads and some gold animal figures, with the bodies of two female attendants, one at the head and the other at the foot of the bier. Inside the entrance stood the wooden chariot used as a hearse. The chamber was strewn with offerings and around the interment were the remains of fires and of a funeral feast.

In another similar grave lay the bodies of six men and sixty-eight attendants arranged in an orderly manner in the rectangular pit in the slightly flexed position, suggesting the absence of a struggle of any kind or a violent death. The women wore head-dresses and were arranged with all their ornaments over crimson garments, adorned in their full glory to accompany their sovereign to the next life. The supposition is that they walked to their appointed places in the chamber and then took a drug such as hashish or opium, and after their sleep of death the gaily dressed voluntary victims were put into position before the grave was filled in.[25] Therefore, it is suggested that the kings of Ur were regarded as divine rulers who "did not die as men die, but were translated". Under these circumstances it would be a privilege for his courtiers to continue their service beyond the grave.[26]

Nevertheless, though kingship in Sumer is said to have "descended from heaven" after the flood in the third millennium B.C., presumably as a gift of the gods, it never occupied the position attained by the pharaohs in Egypt; Mesopotamia being divided up into a series of city-states loosely bound together rather than a single nation with the throne as its dynamic centre, as in the Nile valley. No Sumerian king, therefore, was a cohesive force in the entire realm. This, however, apparently did not prevent the prehistoric rulers of Ur from acquiring a divine status by virtue of their office and its insignia in which divinity was inherent,[27] and so of gathering around them at death a select company of the devoted members of their court and of their bodyguard to accompany them to their final abode, there to carry on their customary service. If this interpretation of the mortuary ritual is correct it follows that the conception of "the Land of No-Return" where rulers and commoners alike dwelt in darkness and dust was a later development as in Israel, where the notion of Sheol arose largely under prophetic and Babylonian influence in the eighth century B.C. In the royal tomb ritual in the Early Dynastic period in Mesopotamia there was some approximation to the Egyptian cult of the dead, and in prehistoric times the two contemporary civilizations seem to have developed along more or less parallel lines in respect of funerary practice and belief, until in the third millennium B.C. they diverged as the structure and functions of the State in the valleys of the Nile and the Euphrates underwent a fundamental change.

BURIALS IN ELAM AND BALUCHISTAN

Susa

In Elam, where at Susa in the lowest level of the site (Susa A) a culture flourished contemporary with that in Sumer, the grave goods in the cemetery were in advance of those in the Ubaid burials.[28] In the succeeding higher levels, corresponding to Uruk (B), Jemdet Nasr (C) and Early Dynastic (D),[29] the cultural development was maintained. Interment was in the extended position coupled with some flexed bodies which de Mecquenem thinks had been inserted in the graves after decomposition.[30] The funerary pottery was of a very high quality in form and design, based mainly on basketry models and ornamented with magico-religious patterns and symbols. Stamp seals were engraved with animal figures and female figurines moulded in clay. Children's graves contained toys, as in Warka IV in the Uruk culture in Southern Mesopotamia, but inscribed tablets do not occur in these earlier levels (A, B).

Burials in Elam and Baluchistan

It is not until C level is reached at Susa that proto-Elamite tablets appear together with food vessels and seals of the Jemdet Nasr period.[31] The tombs become richer but similar to those below, though they contain little pottery. At the D level the designs reveal affinities with the Early Dynastic scarlet ware in Mesopotamia[32] and the seals, pins and metal vases resemble those found in the Ur royal cemeteries and the "A" cemetery at Kish.[33] The polychrome vases, however, suggest relations with Baluchistan rather than with the Euphrates valley.

From Early Dynastic times in Sumer a fairly uniform culture seems to have existed in the Zagros mountains from Susa to Tepe Giyan, near Nihavend in Va, the divergences being most marked in the north and south. That Dynastic influences predominated in the cult of the dead can scarcely be doubted in the light of the evidence from the cemeteries concerning mortuary procedure. In the Musyan area on the Mesopotamian border the tombs and their contents conform to Sumerian types in relation to the royal cultus, and in both regions the sacred kingship seems to have been an established institution. But in which of the two areas the "dynasty" arose is a matter of conjecture.

The Iranian highlands geographically represent the natural position for a common cradleland of the whole range of cultural achievements in the Ancient East in the fourth millennium B.C. If it was the source of the first civilization of Elam, it may well have been the centre from which similar movements and influences radiated across the Zagros mountains into Mesopotamia through Baluchistan and the Himalayas to India. In Western Turkestan at Anau near Askabad the settlements unearthed by Pumpelly in 1904 have revealed further evidence of another outpost of the same civilization on the alluvial land of Transcaspia, while in Baluchistan Indian pottery has been found in association with wares having Persian affinities (Hissar I).[34]

Baluchistan

Although the course of events in Baluchistan before 3000 B.C. is still obscure, it would seem to have been in the small settled farming communities there that the sources of Indian civilization are to be found. These villages had behind them the earlier Iranian settlements such as Sialk and Giyan, but in addition to these centres on the edge of the Persian desert, the ancient cities of the Tigris-Euphrates valley made their contribution to the urban culture of Mohenjo-daro and Chanhu-daro on the Indus, and Harappa on the Ravi, which flourished in the third millennium B.C. Thus, Baluchistan appears to have been the connecting link between the Indus valley civilization and that of the Fertile Crescent and Western Iran, though neither in Baluchistan nor in Sind was there apparently a genuinely Neolithic stage, such as occurred in some parts of Europe, in which cultivation, herding and pottery-making were practised without any knowledge of metal. This indeed applies throughout the greater part of the Ancient East.

In the secluded mountain valleys of Baluchistan the self-contained peasant communities at Quetta, Nal, Kolwa and Zhob developed a prehistoric culture with a considerable measure of uniformity but with certain local distinguishing features. Thus, in the pottery techniques, while, as in Persia, buff ware was characteristic of the south and red ware of the north, black on red predominated in the Zhob valley in the north and black on buff in the south at Nal, Quetta and Kulli, and at Amri in Sind, where typologically the earliest pottery occurred.[35] The latest came from a mound near Nal in Southern Baluchistan, first described by Sir John Marshall in 1904.[36] This proved to be a necropolis which had been excavated in a very unscientific manner at the beginning of the century by an antiquarian in search of pottery before Mr Hargreaves of the Archaeological Survey began operations there in 1925. These "pioneers" had dug down on the western slope of the mound and further excavation revealed stone structures which may have been used for funerary purposes, as they were part of the necropolis in which some forty groups of burials were discovered associated with 270 mortuary potsherds.

The Nal Cemetery

everal methods of inhumation appear to have been practised t the same time, but fractional burial predominated. Only one omplete adult skeleton and those of three infants were dis/ overed intact, the rest consisting of a few bones scattered among he pots. Some of the vessels contained bones or fragments 'xed with earth. Two phalanges were in one vessel, parts of wo small ribs in a second, and three metatarsals in a third, and o on, whether they were placed there deliberately or had erely drifted in by accident. Bones of animals were also ecovered from the groups. In one grave a broken bowl con/ ained earth and five other smaller vases, with pieces of a rib, part of a pelvic bone and many small bones in the earth and between the vases. These would seem to have been placed there, and may have belonged to a single individual, probably a woman. Besides these fractional burials, the three complete inhumations—the adult and two infants—were enclosed in rectangular sun/dried brick graves. With the infants were six/ teen beads and a pear/shaped crystal pendant. The adult lay on its left side with the head to the east, face to the south, and the left and right arms bent in a slightly contracted position of about 50°, suggestive of sleep. In this grave there was no furniture. Near the grave of the infant a skull and some bones were found, and around the neck the remains of a necklace of eighty/nine white disk beads.[37]

Making due allowance for disturbance by the earlier excava/ tors, there can be little doubt that at least some of the bones of the fractional burials had been interred as fragments and not as complete bodies. As in the Damb Buthi cemetery in Makran in Sind,[38] they had been collected after the body had been exposed for some time and then either put in a pot or laid on the floor of the necropolis without any protection. The grave goods were chiefly pottery vessels, apart from the bead necklaces and pendant and the discoid beads found with the second infant's skull. There were also a grinding stone, a stone weight, a stone chisel, copper tools, and a marble ringstone. The presence of a piece of red ochre in one of the funerary vessels, and of a carefully moulded cake of red ferruginous earth in a broken vessel with a colour grinder, hardly can have been fortuitous, especially as red pigment recurs at Damb Buthi, and, as we have seen, it has a long history in ceremonial interment going back to Palaeolithic times.

THE INDUS VALLEY

Mohenjo-daro

In Sind and the Punjab the remarkable homogeneous urban civilization which flourished from 2500 to 1500 B.C., revealed by the excavations in and around the Indus valley at Mohenjo-daro, Chanhu-daro and Harappa since 1922, has produced singularly little evidence of the disposal of the dead and of funeral ritual. At Mohenjo-daro no trace of a cemetery has been discovered, and the few bones in the vicinity of the houses and in pits seem to have been those of people killed when the city was raided in its last period and their bodies summarily thrown away.[39] As some of the bones show signs of charring it has been suggested that cremation was practised, generally on the banks of a river, and the incinerated remains collected for the performance of funerary rites before they were deposited in the "ossuary". But the skeletons in the pit on the southern side of the city in what is called North Lane give every indication of having been disposed of in haste and disorder, and at least one had been decapitated. If cremation was in vogue some attempt at incineration may have been made by the relatives when the raid was over, but the general conditions, as Mackay has suggested, point to a massacre by raiders among a group trying to escape, whose bodies were hurled into a pit near an exit of the city.[40]

Much the same explanation applies probably to the other fractional burials which have been noted. Thus, the twenty-one skeletons recorded by Sir John Marshall do not represent intentional burial and their attitudes point to simultaneous death. None was deposited in an orderly manner or provided with grave goods.[41] Moreover, they belong to a late period. In one case a tragedy seems to have occurred in the last phase

The Indus Valley 55

of the city, in an attempt to escape from a well-room, during which four persons were killed. Two lay on or below the stairs where they died, trying to climb to the street; one of these seems to have fallen backwards. The other two came to an untimely end in the lane outside or near by, where some of their bones were found.[42] At Chanhu-daro near Sakrand in the Nuwabkah district of Sind, the only graves came from the Muhammadan cemetery.[43]

Harappa

On the south-eastern outskirts of the ancient city of Harappa in the Montgomery district of the Punjab, a lightly packed mass of twenty complete skulls and other fragments intermingled with long bones, animal remains and pottery were found in what seems to have been an ossuary.[44] In the deserted corner of a house fragments of two skulls were recovered and said to have been a fractional burial,[45] but it seems more likely that it was a modern interment. Some of the bones had been buried with the ligaments upon them, and Sir Mortimer Wheeler suggests that they may have been interred ceremonially after a plague or battle when vultures and jackals had done their grim work on the bodies.[46]

Cemetery R 37. To the south of the citadel mound in what is known as cemetery R 37, fifty-seven graves have been identified as belonging to the main Harappan period. The bodies in them were extended from north to south with the head towards the north. Large quantities of pottery were placed at the head, some at the feet and along the sides, and occasionally below the body, ranging from as many as forty pots to from fifteen to twenty as a fair average. Personal ornaments and toilet objects were sometimes worn. These included a copper ring found on one skeleton, and on others a necklace of steatite beads, two anklets of paste beads, a copper ear-ring and shell bangles, together with a copper mirror, a stock of antimony, a large shell spoon, and mother-of-pearl. In one grave was a small pottery lamp and bones of a fowl on the floor near the feet of the deceased. One of the graves was lined with mud-brick as at Nal in Southern Baluchistan,[47] and in another the body, probably that of a girl, had been buried in the extended position in a wooden coffin and wrapped in a shroud of reeds, of which traces remained. With it were thirty-seven pots, the majority near but outside the head of the coffin. On the right middle finger was a copper ring, to the left of the skull a shell ring (perhaps an ear-ring) and two others above the left shoulder.[48]

Cemetery H. Between this cemetery and the citadel on the south side a second cemetery in Area H was excavated by Vats in 1929 and the succeeding seasons, in the lower and older stratum of which were extended burials, sometimes with the knees slightly bent, orientated towards the east or north-east. Some of them may have been fractional, unless they were normal interments disturbed by later burials or other causes. The red ware was not Harappan, and among the food offerings was a dismembered goat. Apart from a gold bangle on the wrist of a woman and three teeth on a gold wire on the skull of another, no ornamentation occurred. On the stratum above this lower level about 140 true fractional burials were found, together with babies enclosed in urns in the contracted position. The jars, again, are not Harappan, and on them are depicted scenes which it has been suggested have Vedic affinities.[49] Although the friezes on the urns display the same decorative characters in both the upper and lower strata, the symbolism, with its bulls, goats, waisted animals, crested peacocks between groups of stellar or solar motifs with the figure of a centaur with horns, has no really convincing parallel in any of the cultures of the Ancient East. But as cemetery H is subsequent to the true Harappa civilization, its contents do not come within our present inquiry.

What is significant is that in the earlier Harappa cemetery R 37 inhumation in the extended position was the normal mode of disposal, and that it conformed to the usual mortuary procedure in respect of food offerings, grave goods and personal ornaments, though fractional burial also may have been adopted. If cremation, which subsequently became predominant in Vedic India, was practised it has left no very convincing races of its occurrence prior to the destruction of the cities in the middle of the second millennium B.C.

Throughout the Ancient East, from the Fertile Crescent to the Indus valley, the funeral ritual underwent singularly little change from the beginning of the Neolithic to the break-up of the urban cultures. This uniformity is an indication of the solidarity of the area as a cultural unit in which, despite marked differences in climatic and economic conditions and in respect of the social and religious structures, there was a uniformity of procedure in the burial of the dead, and in the funeral ritual and equipment. In the Indus valley the evidence is surprisingly meagre, and although it appears to have had a theocratic state with a sacred kingship,[50] no royal tombs, comparable to those in Egypt or at Ur, have come to light. Whether or not the practice of cremation played any part in the absence of extensive cemeteries has yet to be determined by further excavation.

CHAPTER *III*

Megalithic Burial in Europe

WHEN the Neolithic culture passed from the Ancient East westwards into Europe in the second half of the fourth millennium B.C. (i.e. from about 3500 to 3000 B.C.), following either an overland route from the south-east to and along the Danube or by way of the Mediterranean littoral to Spain and France and the north-west, with in addition a continental route from South Russia, Poland, Central Europe and Germany, the cult of the dead underwent considerable development. If in the Middle East the use of copper and later of bronze played an important part in the beginnings of the more highly organized urban communities, in Europe the knowledge of metal spread relatively slowly in a northerly direction and was still unknown long after it was well established in the Fertile Crescent, Iraq, Persia, Turkestan and Anatolia. But this did not prevent a general advance in culture over the greater part of Europe in the third millennium.

EASTERN MEDITERRANEAN

Tholoi in Cyprus

So far as the disposal of the dead is concerned, in Cyprus with its close links with the neighbouring Chalcolithic cities of southern Anatolia, at Khirokitia, between 4000 and 3500 B.C., the remains of tholoi have been found similar to those of the Tell Halaf period at Arpachiyah in Iraq near Nineveh.[1] These lie on either side of a long wall resting on the older structure of the small tholoi, 4 to 6 metres in diameter, made of *pisé*, or sun-dried bricks, forming a kind of corbelled roof, or with mud-plastered reeds or brushwood. The larger ones, 10 metres wide with walls 2 metres thick, are fewer in number and were built on either the left or the right of the wall. In many cases they are surrounded by open spaces enclosed by walls. In the area were round tables built of stone slabs and burnt bones. The foundations are deeper and more substantial than are those of the smaller tholoi, and on them the earliest attempt at corbelling in the whole of the Mediterranean was constructed in the form of a vault built of river stones and resting on the walls.

The floors were usually made of beaten earth or mud, sometimes plastered with a layer of fine mud, and in them the graves were dug. Whether large or small, nearly every tholos contained one or more skeletons, mostly in the contracted position. Over the head or chest a large stone quern was placed, necklaces of beads and shells sometimes were worn, and bowls, intentionally broken, surrounded the body. In one of the larger tholoi a woman had been buried under a square platform in the foreground, with the hands, it seems, bound behind the back, as in the Neolithic strata at Jericho. Near the summit of the hill two skeletons were found below a rectangular platform of mud plastered over with clay on the floor of a fine tholos. One had a necklace of carnelian beads and dentalia, and was surrounded by broken vases. The other, that of a young person, had the hands behind the back and a bowl under the middle part of the body.

One of the most important of the upper group of tholoi contained twenty-five infants in successive floors, in some cases buried on top of adults, elsewhere in small holes surrounded with stones or covered with slabs. On the lower floor were a "throne", or seat, made of river-stones, and three small round hearths, on one of which lay the skeleton of an adult. Higher up was a clay head of a figure, probably representing a male god, ornamented at the back with what appears to be a snake design. This may suggest a connexion with the cult of the Great Mother whose emblem in Crete was the snake. Or the head may represent a chthonian deity with the snake as his attribute; a belief that recurred in the Bronze Age in Cyprus.[2] The infants may have been sacrificed as part of the funeral ritual, and the whole tholos and its equipment indicate that it was a place of peculiar sanctity. In fact, all the larger structures and many of the smaller ones seem to have been connected with the cult of the dead as their contents show that they were reserved for burials and the prescribed mortuary ritual, which may have included sacrifices in honour of the chthonian deities. Some of the smaller tholoi, on the other hand, appear to have been habitations, or used for grinding grain, without any connexion with burials.[3]

In the succeeding culture localized at Erimi (3500–3000), which marks the transition from the Chalcolithic to the Bronze Age in Cyprus, the tholoi have a stone substructure with a central support. On or along the inner face of the foundation post-holes occur, suggesting that there had been a superstructure of brushwood or reeds supported by posts and covered with mud. On the floor of rammed earth there were traces of occupation, but burials have been found along the outer ridge of the stone foundation or under the floor. Towards the end of the period, in addition to the mortuary ritual practised at Khirokitia, the presence of female figurines in graves suggests that the cult of the Mother-goddess had been introduced, probably as a result of foreign influence.[4]

In a later necropolis at Vounous Bellapais (c. 2800–2000 B.C.) a vase from Palestine shows that contacts with the Fertile Crescent continued into the Bronze Age (i.e. 2800–2600 B.C.). The cult of the dead became more developed and tombs cut in the rock were either short with roughly parallel sides and rounded back, or long and narrowing towards the end, which was either straight or rounded. The long sides sometimes sloped inwards. Each *dromos* gave access to a main chamber through a rectangular or rounded doorway. On either side of the tomb were from one to three smaller side-chambers blocked by rectangular, rounded or irregular slabs of rough blocks of limestone. In some the bodies were placed in niches with grave goods on the floor. In the earliest period the burials generally were in the right and left parts of the chamber with large vessels on top of them, though in one case they covered the greater part of the floor. The bodies were clad in their usual clothes with bronze daggers, pins, necklaces and small bottles on or near them. Large bowls containing animals' bones and smaller vessels were used in the sacrificial ritual in honour of the dead, the animal victims having been deposited on the floor of the chamber with vases placed over their remains. As new burials were introduced in the family or clan tomb the previous ones and their furniture were grouped along the back wall of the chamber.[5]

Vaulted Tombs in Crete

In Crete a succession of vaulted beehive tombs have been investigated along the borders of the plain of Mesara since 1904, containing hundreds of interments. Those grouped round Koumasa, south-east of Gortyna on the upper slopes of the Kophina mountains, consisted of four tholoi, three circular and one square, varying in internal diameter from 4·10 to 13 metres. They were enclosed within dry-stone walling composed of undressed stones bonded by a quantity of clay and projections inwards. The whole had been roofed with a corbelled vault, or with wood and thatch. It was entered through a doorway to the east, formed by two large stone uprights supporting a massive lintel. In one case (tholos B) the doorway was divided into two by a large upright stone deeply fixed into the ground. The natural rock was left as a floor, as was also the case at Hagia Triada and Platanos. On the outside of the northern wall five slabs in a row projected from 0·15 to 0·20 metre at a height of about 1 metre from the ground, possibly to serve as scaffolding during the building of the upper part of the tomb, or if it was covered with earth it may have been a key binding it with the earth to make it more compact. A square pit lined with stones often stood before the doorway, and a court paved with slabs recurred in front of several tholoi.

Inside was a hearth at which numerous fires must have been lighted in the middle of the circle immediately under a smoke-hole. But it would seem to have been for ritual purposes other than cremation, as no genuine evidence exists for this mode of disposal having been practised in these tombs. The thickness of the burial stratum and the mass of bones indicate hundreds of interments, which at Hagia Triada were estimated by Professor Halbherr at 250, and at tholos B at Koumasa the number was far larger.[6] The bones, however, were so dislocated and often heaped together in various parts of the chamber to afford space for subsequent burials, that the manner of disposal could not be ascertained. Throughout the Mediterranean communal sepulture was the common custom, a community burying in the same ossuary for hundreds of years, generation after generation in this way being "gathered to their fathers". Thus a chronological sequence of objects occurred in the tombs though the more valuable articles, especially those of metal, frequently were extracted from the preceding interment when a tholos was reopened. To judge by such things as remained, the equipment included stone vases and palettes not unlike those in the royal tombs in Egypt at the beginning of the Dynastic period,[7] cylinder seals and clay figurines, amulets, scorpions on ivory seals, and pins, awls and daggers in copper, suggesting intercourse with Egypt and the Aegean, while geometric vases, the spiral motif on seals and vases, and obsidian, show Cycladic influences. Fires were burnt on the floors of the tombs but no traces of cremation occurred, and although no evidence was obtainable from the Mesara tholoi concerning posture, elsewhere in Crete contracted burial in coffins or clay pithoi was the usual procedure.[8]

In Eastern Crete single graves or cists were grouped in small cemeteries, and at Mochlos large ossuaries or chamber-tombs were entered through doorways closed by huge upright slabs of stone, or cists were constructed with walls of similar slabs. Sometimes the walls were built of small stones like those used in house construction, or with a combination of large and small stones. Occasionally bodies were interred in holes in the rocks with no attempt at a fashioned grave and very little in the way of mortuary objects. These all belonged to the Early Minoan period, but in the Middle Minoan large terra-cotta jars, or pithoi, came into use. These were found standing upside down over the earlier tombs or in cemeteries, as at Pachyammos and Sphoungaras, in a state of confusion as a result of subsequent interments. The body had been placed in the jar with the head downwards, and the jar had been then put in the ground bottom up, the corpse occupying a sitting or crouched position; the knees often trussed up under the chin and the arms doubled back against the body.[9]

The Cycladic Tombs

Notwithstanding the influence of Egypt on the Mesara tholoi, which may indeed have been erected by Libyan settlers soon after 3000 B.C., in Early Minoan II and III in Crete and the Aegean, collective burial in stone-built or rock-cut tombs, or in natural caves, prevailed in successive interments numbering many hundreds, as against the separate sepulture in Egypt and Mesopotamia. In the Cyclades, connecting Crete with the mainland, the early graves included cave-burial, rock-cut tombs and small slab-cists. In these barren islands, however, colonized from Anatolia about 3000 B.C., as in Eastern Crete individual burial in the contracted position was prevalent in the later tombs (i.e. Early Cycladic III, about 2400 B.C.) containing human figures called "idols", marble vases and weapons. In the oldest prehistoric cemeteries at Pelos in Melos the graves were cists constructed of four erect slabs from the neighbouring hill-side with the bottom paved with thin plates of schist and covered with a huge capstone, roughly flattened on the underside. Burial apparently had been in the contracted position, and several of the graves had held at least half a dozen bodies, as at the cemetery of Antiparos, where most of the tombs contained more than one skeleton. The head in most cases was laid against the west wall, but no attempt was made at orientation. The vases were at one end but not more than two were found in a single grave.[10]

In the majority of the island tombs the contents were much the same and included earthen or stone pots, varying in shape and colour from light red to black, marble idols, sometimes shaped like a "fiddle", obsidian blades, copper daggers and axes and silver ornaments, but in later cemeteries (e.g.

Antiparos II, Amorgos, Siphnos, Syros) the metal ornaments were prevalent, the idols better shaped and the grave more elaborate. For example, at Antiparos I on the western side, bones were heaped together in confusion, and most graves contained the remains of several bodies which would seem to have been cut up and tightly wedged together between the side slabs. In the later sites on the south-east of the island the tombs were longer and better built, and contained only one body in each, the head resting on a slab or pillow. In both, the nature of the goods was the same, but the large marble bowls and plates, obsidian implements, pottery designs and representations of the human form in marble, showed an advance in technical skill.[11]

In the southern group of tombs at Phylakopi in Melos irregular pits, sometimes semicircular, were sunk beneath a shelf of rock, or subterranean rectangular chambers were cut out of the soft rock, entered through a rectangular doorway and approached by a short uncovered dromos about 1 metre in length and 1·60 metres in width. Unfortunately these chamber-tombs were not reopened or thoroughly examined when they were found. They and the shaft-graves of uncertain date are by no means rare in the Phylakopi district, trapezoid cists being the earlier mode of burial. On the west side of the Bathing Creek, the graves are quite small, sometimes round with a dromos and a low beehive roof. On the east side is a two-chambered tomb with a gable roof, well-squared walls, and a ledge for the head of the corpse to rest on. The pottery was mainly of local geometric ware, with obsidian chips lying about. Fragments from the chambers included Mycenaean imports, showing that later influences were felt in the Early Cycladic settlements.[12] In Guboea, only single interments occurred in the pit-grave excavated in the ground, and the same applies in the rectangular or oval corbelled tombs in the hill-side of Syros. On the island of Pantelleria between Sicily and Africa are a series of elliptical structures, locally called "sesi", containing one or more burial chambers approached by a passage to which a low door gives access and having a

orbelled roof. They are solid masonry with an outer casing
f large blocks of stone, and are believed to be Neolithic in
rigin.[13]

The Siculan Rock-cut Tombs

Farther to the west, Sicily became a cultural centre in the third
millennium B.C. As early as 2500 agricultural settlements of
Eastern-Mediterranean type situated on hill-tops began to replace
Neolithic villages. The cemeteries were composed of rock-cut
tombs, usually entered through a *domos* leading to oval or
circular chambers which contained a number of burials. The
narrow portal or window cut out of the slabs at the top,
probably a survival of the doorway of the chamber-tomb, was
sealed with a slab which in one case at Castelluccio near
Syracuse was decorated with spirals in relief. In the same
cemetery another tomb was closed with two carved slabs which
together represented a breasted female figure.[14] At Monteracello
the vault was later reproduced above ground as a rectangular
cist built of squared slabs of limestone set on edge with a
window-entry at one end to represent the door. The chambers,
however, were generally more or less circular in plan, though
natural cave-tombs and old flint mines were in use as family
graves, and followed the Aegean funerary technique and ritual
in its main characteristics.[15]

WESTERN MEDITERRANEAN

Sardinian Gallery-tombs

The elaborately constructed Siculan port-hole slabs ornamented
with raised bosses and engraved spirals recur in the Sardinian
gallery-tombs, in the Maltese tholoi, and in the Spanish
passage-graves, while a similar entrance is found in British
barrows and in cists in Brittany, in the valley of the Seine and
in Sweden. In Sardinia, where collective burial in caves and
rock-cut tombs was common, gallery-graves, known locally as
tombe di giganti, or giants' tombs, were constructed of rude blocks
roofed with flat capstones or corbelling and covered by a cairn
enclosed by masonry walls rounded at the closed end. At the

front the entrance was effected through a huge slab carved and bordered in relief with a small hole at the base and gabled above.[16] The narrow corridor of dressed slabs opened into a rectangular chamber enclosed by large slabs of stone set on edge and roofed with similar slabs, the intervening space being filled with earth. The chamber was a family tomb, and from the entrance two wings branched off, prolonging the double walls of the corridor, which were sometimes covered with clay mortar, not unlike in plan the horned cairns of Northern Ireland except that the stones were dressed with metal tools. Some of the Giants' Tombs were contemporary with the rock-cut graves known as *domus di giganti*, or "Witches' Houses", with an upright slab forming the entrance to both of them from a semicircular space flanked by masonry.

The rock-cut tombs consist of a circular or elliptical chamber with a beehive ceiling and approached by a short corridor rectangular in form, though sometimes the chamber is rectangular with a flat roof. It is not easy to date these graves in the absence of very much in the way of well-attested furnishings. Mackenzie attempted to establish a typological sequence from the "dolmen" to the Giants' Tomb,[17] following that of Montelius for the evolution of megalithic monuments in general. But the process can as easily be reversed unless it is supported by datable contents. The connexion would seem to be rather with the Mediterranean tholos type of tomb, though there may be some relation between them and the truncated conical drystone towers of clay mortar and blocks of stone called *nuraghi*, which in their more complicated forms continued in their final development until the Late Bronze Age in the first millennium B.C. as fortified refuges, sometimes containing traces of a third upper chamber approached by a stairway, and revealing signs of habitation.[18]

Rock-cut Tombs and Navetas in the Balearic Isles

In the Balearic Isles a similar mystery surrounds the *talayots*, commonly found in Menorca, which while sometimes used for burial purposes generally had neither entrance nor interior chambers. In construction they resembled the *navetas*, or stone-built tombs shaped like a ship, built of cyclopean masonry in which a slab-roofed passage leading to a rectangular burial chamber had a very small door.[19] Closely associated with them in Mallorca were a number of rock-cut tombs, dating from the Bronze Age, consisting of a long narrow gallery with one or more smaller side-chambers opening out of it. Those on the level ground are approached by a descending stair contained in a chamber cut in the rock and open to the sky. Others are entered through a low opening cut in the rock and giving access to an uncovered courtyard in the hill-side. Both types may have courtyards and a single or double vestibule which may or may not contain a stair. In one instance a mound was erected over a cave covering the entrance. The main chamber was filled with earth in which the bodies were buried in the extended position with pottery, copper or bronze daggers and awls, perforated shells, and buttons. In the side-chambers they were laid in the contracted posture, and in some of the vessels human bones and ornaments were found.[20]

In the *navetas* of Menorca the structure of the rock-cut tombs is reproduced above the surface of the ground in the form of megalithic chambers along boat-like lines. That known as Es Tudons ("the wood-pigeons") stands on slightly rising ground in a sloping valley, measuring in length about 45 feet with a height of rather under 15 feet. The entrance at its western end is nearly square with three courses of upright masonry inclining towards an angle of 67°. The eastern end is rounded and gathered in at an angle of about 55°, the sides perhaps meeting originally in a ridge before the upper part collapsed. The appearance was that of an overturned ship (*naveta*) with a square stern and rounded prow. The monument stands on a platform above the level of the rock, and forms the forecourt bounded by rough stones. In front of the entrance are two slabs which formed a second semicircular area concentric with the forecourt. The door of the entrance may have been a slab of stone, suggested by a groove shown in the floor, and through this opening a passage led to an antechamber some 10 feet high.

A second narrow passage led into the main chamber constructed like that in the rock-cut tombs, except that the roof made of great slabs is flat instead of being rounded. At the far end is a terminal ledge, 2 feet above the floor-level, as in the caves, but no side-chambers have been discovered. Since in all probability the *navetas* were used as tombs for chieftains in the manner of the Giants' Graves in Sardinia, while commoners were buried in the rock-cut tombs, they doubtless were carefully sealed after interment. This is indicated by the rebate for a door-slab at the two Rafal Rubi *navetas*. At Es Tudons fragments of prehistoric pottery and two pieces of a bronze armlet in the soil by the entrance suggest that it was a tomb which remained unopened until fairly recently.[21] But until more is known of their contents the Balearic graves will remain obscure notwithstanding their structural importance in the megalithic tradition of the long cairn type of grave.

Maltese Megaliths

Of all the islands in the Western Mediterranean, however, the one of greatest sacred significance from the third millennium B.C. was Malta. Although it was uninhabited apparently until the megalithic civilization reached its barren shores about 3000 B.C., it was there that the elaborate labyrinthine burial vaults or apsidal "temples" of Mnaidra, Hagia Kim and Hal Tarxien were created, with the Gigantea on the neighbouring island of Gozo and the Hal Saftieni Hypogeum to the northwest of the village of Tarxien, prior to the arrival of the Bronze Age immigration about the middle of the second millennium when cremation was introduced at Tarxien. It is true that Ugolini has endeavoured to make the island the centre from which Mediterranean civilization originated,[22] but this claim can hardly be seriously maintained. Nevertheless, it certainly does seem to have been the meeting-place of a number of streams of culture over a considerable period from western Asia and the Eastern Mediterranean, including Thessaly and the Balkans, as well as from Egypt, and nearer at hand from Italy, beginning perhaps, as Zammit contended, about 3000 B.C.[23]

It may, however, have been rather later that the tholos-architecture of Near-Eastern (Sumerian) origin, in its western diffusion, reached the island.[24]

The three successive Neolithic temples at Hal Tarxien reveal a chronological series extending from the Neolithic in the third millennium B.C. to the Bronze Age in the middle of the second millennium. Within these broader periods, which in Malta in the Phoenician colonization continued into the first millennium B.C., contemporary with the final phases of the nuraghic culture in Sardinia, there were subdivisions each displaying its own insular characteristics as well as its contacts with the outside world, ranging from the Near East and Anatolia to the Cyclades, Italy and Sicily. It was, in fact, not until the Bronze Age that this seclusion was interrupted by the arrival of a cremating immigration at Hal Tarxien from the Eastern Mediterranean, and only there has a cremation cemetery been found containing copper and bronze implements and a type of pottery with its duck-shaped vessels, quite distinct from the preceding Neolithic ware.[25] It may be that it was only one of several similar groups which happened to have been isolated before it was influenced by the native Neolithic culture, but in any case it shows how vigorous was the indigenous prehistoric civilization known to us very largely from its megalithic monuments.

Notwithstanding the complexity of their structure, the general plan is that of the megaliths of the Siculan and Sardinian type with corbelled vaulting, a curved forecourt and a passage leading to several chambers. Thus, at Mnaidra two elliptical chambers are placed one behind the other, the southern half consisting of a paved passage of upright stones leading to an enclosure composed of a wall of vertical and horizontal masonry. To the left of the entrance stands a trilithon table with a horizontal block above it. A window 16 by 12 inches has been cut in the vertical slab of the wall of the enclosure beyond the aperture, and similar port-holes occur in the south-west wall communicating with two other rectangular spaces, while the whole of the southern half of the structure is surrounded by a series of rough stones set alternately with the broad faces and their narrow edges outwards. The roofing of the apses was by corbelling, of which a few traces are still visible.[26] The northern half of the temple was added later, and at Hagia Kim and Hal Tarxien a complicated sanctuary was produced, apsidal elliptical chambers with cup-marks and spiral cuts on many of the slabs being suggestive of Minoan influences.

The Hal Tarxien group of temples, to which a fourth has now been added, are all prior to the Bronze Age influx with a common approach from a large semicircular forecourt leading to a corridor terminating in an apse. The succession of developments was spread over centuries within the Neolithic period, with a fourth smaller temple to the east dating from the Bronze Age more or less contemporary with the cemetery overlying the other temples. The whole structure may have been surrounded by a mound of earth up to the level of the capstones, while the apses were domed with corbelled cupolas and the corridors sheltered by long horizontal slabs, with the spaces between the apses only open to the sky. The walls were decorated with geometric designs, spirals and friezes of animals.[27]

The temple called Gigantea in Gozo, which originally consisted of a single shrine, contained stones with spirals and animal designs in relief, and ornamental pittings. Like Mnaidra, when a second temple was added it became two separate buildings, each having two sets of parallel elliptical areas with the remains of niches and altars in the second elliptical enclosure.[28] The great rock-cut Hypogeum at Hal Saflioni with its domed vaults decorated with spirals is an underground series of caves, passages and chambers with trilithons built in front of them, reproducing below ground in three storeys the main features of the temples. The middle room is the largest and has a number of small chambers and two decorated rooms, with the lowest storey reached by a flight of steps partly cut in the rock. Before it became a vast ossuary extensively used for burial purposes, containing, it is estimated, 7,000 interments with shell necklaces, polished stone amulets and funerary pottery, it may have been used as a anctuary for oracular and initiatory rites, as Zammit has uggested,[29] in which, as will be considered later,[30] the siatic Mother-goddess probably played an important part. But whatever may have been the precise nature of the cultus performed in these sacred edifices, Malta unquestionably was an important religious centre in the third millennium B.C., and while its megalithic cult may not have been essentially a mortuary ritual, despite the absence of burials except at Hal Saflieni, the plan of construction adopted with the semicircular court with apses, port-holes and slabs used as doorways and approached through a passage, conforms to that of the collective tombs of the Eastern Mediterranean. The oldest examples were elliptical apsidal shrines with a door on one long wall and a niche facing it on the other, branching into lateral and terminal apses. This is merely an extension of the rock-cut tomb, familiar as we have seen elsewhere in the Western Mediterranean in the tholos tradition, with the addition of a semicircular paved forecourt.

The numerous graves cut in the rock at Malta are assigned to the Phoenician occupation in the first millennium, prior to the Roman domination in 218 B.C. The earliest of these are circular tombs with a domed ceiling and shallow circular shaft and a square entrance sealed on the outside by a rectangular stone slab. Cinerary urns of an amphora type, globular in form and covered with a circular plate, occur in them, with ashes in one or more urns. These oldest graves were followed by an almost identical structure except that the shaft became deeper and rectangular, until in the third stage the funeral chamber was rectangular with a flat ceiling and the floor ran at right angles to the entrance dividing the tomb into two parts with a flat ledge on each side of the trench on which two bodies were laid. Occasionally, rectangular chambers were added to the single shaft. The furniture became progressively more and more abundant and varied in the later graves, inhumation being the rule in the second stage, though cinerary urns in the shape of a simple Maltese olla persisted throughout the sepulture. Copper jewellery occurred in the third type of rectangular tomb as well as glass, beads, stone and ivory objects, and a bilychnis lamp with Carthaginian affinities. Roman influences were very evident in the later graves, but although they were used by the Phoenicians and their successors down to the Christian era, some of the rock-cut tombs may have been built in the pre-Phoenician period. Indeed Zammit maintained that some of those of the first stage cannot be much later than about 3000 B.C.[31] If this can be substantiated by further discoveries and examination of the furniture, the sepulchral origin of the temple architecture will become more apparent.

Isolated from commercial relations with the Aegean the culture contacts of Malta in Neolithic times seem to have been mainly with Anatolia and Western Asia, notwithstanding the presence of querns of lava from Sicily, and Siculan bossed bone-plaques, and the spiral designs and other Minoan influences which reached it by the second phase of Hal Tarxien. The pottery shows resemblances to that of Southern Italy and Sicily, while the rotund female figurines and ancient figures in bas-relief are Thessalian and Asiatic in appearance, and the polished grey ware is reminiscent of Syria and Palestine. Besides Danubian, Macedonian and other Eastern European connexions, the closest affinities appear to have been with Sardinia. Notwithstanding the traces of Minoan contacts the sacred isle stood apart from the rest of the Aegean world, and having practically nothing to export it remained relatively in isolation from the commercial activities of the region. This doubtless explains the survival of the Neolithic culture long after the use of copper and bronze had become established elsewhere. But as the centre of the megalithic cult it occupied a unique position in the Western Mediterranean in the third millennium and exercised a far-reaching and powerful influence in the diffusion of this essentially religious prehistoric civilization.

IBERIAN PENINSULA

The Almerian Megaliths

It was, however, on the southern and eastern shores of the Iberian peninsula that the commercial and cultural enterprises were most apparent from about 2600 B.C. onwards, and nowhere is the megalithic tradition more strongly represented than in Almeria and the surrounding district. Communal graves, ossuaries, cists, simple and chambered or galleried "dolmens", corridor-tombs, corbelled vaults with or without entrance passages; in short, practically every known type of great stone monument is to be found on the land bridge in the sea route from the Ancient Middle East to the Atlantic littoral and the North-west. Its wealth in metals made it a centre of commercial enterprise for traders and voyagers, and the Chalcolithic invasion of Spain, which introduced the megalithic cult, may have been preceded by metal-using navigators who settled at Valez Blanco, Palaces, Campo and Puerto Blanco, where they buried their dead in stone-walled trenches containing from eight to ten bodies, or in stone cists, each under a round cairn, rather like the North African pit-graves or the Early Minoan rock-cut cists. But collective burial in natural caves and circular cists was also coming into vogue with collective necklaces, stone beads, bracelets, *Pectunculus* shells, stone figurines, and copper pins, among their funerary furniture.[32]

The Neolithic folk settled on hill-tops like El Garcel near the Mediterranean coast in South-east Spain, and brought with them a culture having affinities with that of the Badarians and Merimdian peoples of prehistoric Egypt and the Fayum. But they also had adopted collective burial and the use of calläis beads which might connect them with Brittany rather than the Fertile Crescent. It was apparently upon this first genuine Neolithic civilization in Western Europe that the megalithic voyagers made their impact when they established themselves in Almeria among the hills at Los Millares. There within very easy reach of the coast in a region rich in copper, gold, silver and lead, they erected a settlement on the spur of a plateau overlooking the fertile valley of the Anderax river with a cemetery of collective tombs behind the town containing copper daggers and axes, flint arrow-heads, ornaments of ivory and calläis, amulets, bone figurines, stone jars, beakers, bowls and vessels decorated with conventionalized animals.

Rectangular houses were built with dry-stone walling and supplied with water by an aqueduct from a spring in the hillside. Whether or not it was contemporary with or subsequent to the Garcel Neolithic culture is a matter of debate, but in any case it represents an influx of a group of megalithic builders in Almeria who became sufficiently powerful and established to fashion and erect imposing stone tombs with corbelled roofs.

Over a hundred of them were constructed in small groups, either with entrance passages, circular corbelled chambers and dry-stone walling, like those at Khirokitia in Cyprus or at Mesara in Crete, or as quadrangular megalithic gallery tombs. The chambers in the tholoi generally are from 3 to 6 metres in diameter, and the walls are lined with stone slabs plastered and painted, while pillars of stone or wood support the roof. A single or double ring of upright stones constitutes the retaining wall of the earth mound, and on the side where it descends, generally on that facing the sea (i.e. the east), the

Fig. 3. Entrance to passage-grave at Los Millares, Spain

Fig. 4. Reconstruction of entrance to passage-grave at Los Millares

wall of the chamber and the slab at the entrance are pierced by a doorway or port-hole, frequently divided into a series of antechambers by other doors. This passage is constructed with upright slabs or dry-stone, the roof is of flat slabs or corbelled, and the portals are formed of several slabs or of a single holed-stone (Figs. 3, 4). Access to the circular mound is gained by two or three steps leading down to the passage. The semicircular forecourt where the rites were performed, often is outlined by stone slabs.[33]

In one tomb up to a hundred burials were found, and everywhere there are indications of collective interment on a considerable scale over long periods, the earlier bones having been put on one side to make room for later additions to the necropolis. The skeletons often overflow into the passage, and it has been suggested that a family likeness occurs in some of the skulls. Be this as it may, there is little room for doubt that these great tombs belonged to a family or clan, as elsewhere in the megalithic region. In this neighbourhood in South-eastern Spain similar cemeteries existed at Almizaraque and Las Canteras, and farther to the west at Belmonte, Purcherra, Tabernas and Velez Blancho.[34] There were also in the area slab-built graves, some rectangular or in the form of trapezoid cists with short entrance passages.

Although there were traces of partially burnt bones, inhumation was the normal method of sepulture, the fires probably having been for ritual purposes as purifying agents. The furniture everywhere was rich, and while this included an abundance of copper daggers, awls and pins, there were also superbly flaked flint arrow-heads, halbert blades and knives together with ivory, turquoise, calläis, *pectunculus* shell, amber and jet objects. The pottery was mainly Almerian with decorated incised geometric and ritualistic designs, but a few beakers occurred in some of the tombs as an intrusive element. Highly stylized female figurines made by painting or incising knucklebones were among the cult objects in the graves, which included flat-stone croziers, a few undecorated schist plaques, and stone or bone models of sandals used apparently as amulets as were the stone-axes.

South-west Iberian Tombs

Granada on the plateau also contains several large cemeteries of collective burials in the neighbourhood of Guardix, Gor and Gorafe. A few were corbelled tholoi, but most of them were smaller cists, often entered through port-holed slabs, and containing Almerian funerary furniture, but of a rather inferior and less varied character. In fertile Andalusia, rich in minerals, vast tombs were erected, as, for example, at Antiquera at the base of the Sierra de los Toreales, between Malaga and Granada. There the Cueva de Menga consists of a short lofty passage leading to a rectangular chamber, 25 metres in length and 6 metres in width, rising to 3 metres in height at its inner end, which is cut out of a ridge of a cliff and covered with four large slabs and a low mound of earth supported by three large central pillars. The chamber is walled with carefully dressed upright stones inclined inwards, and the gallery is covered with a single slab. The entrance is composed of four stones rather lower in height than the rest of the uprights but showing no indication of an inward incline. On the last of the vertical blocks on the left wall of the passage elongated cruciform figures are incised comparable to the designs of

Neolithic shelters in the provinces of Malaga and Granada, and similar in patina to that of the surrounding rocks. These may have been a later addition, but they reveal the antiquity of the monument.[35]

On the same hill overlooking the plain, about 80 yards from the Cueva de Menga, there is a second chambered tomb, the Cueva de Viera, following the same method of construction but on a smaller scale and entered through a long gallery divided from the chamber by a stone doorway at one end and by a similar portal from an outer passage of rough stones at the other end. The cover-stones of the inner gallery and chamber are less regular than those of the Cueva de Menga, and on the stones of the outer passage are cup-markings. Two kilometres away a double-chambered tomb of cupola-type, the Cueva de Romeral, stands on an isolated hill, while a simpler form of the same construction recurs at Gor in Granada, and Matarrubilla in Sevilla.[36] In fact, from Almeria to the Portuguese province of Algarve on the South-west Atlantic coast, a long line of megalithic collective tombs mark the sites of ancient settlements in this metalliferous region. Thus, in the cemetery of Alcala in Algarve there are seven corbelled tombs of the Los Millares type with galleries, portals leading to a circular chamber, paved and divided into rectangular compartments, though in some dry-stone walling takes the place of vertical slabs.[37]

At Palmella in Estremadura on the Tagus estuary near Lisbon circular rock-cut tombs approached by passages with antechambers reappear and extend along the Atlantic coast to Alapraia (Cascaes), and Folha de Barradas (Cintra), and inland to Badajoz and Salamanca in Spain. In them the funerary furniture was less elaborate and metal objects were rare. Nevertheless, the essential features of the Almerian characteristics were retained in the cylinder-head pins, clay plaques, marble figures, often with incised eyes and bands, and excellently fashioned and polished halberd blades in flint and arrow-heads. From elsewhere came calläis beads, schist plaques, gold, amber, ivory and croziers decorated with rectilinear designs and a squat type of beaker ware, globular pots and carinated bowls. Copper was only used for small objects in most of the graves, its place being taken by stone and flint axes.[38]

Pyrenaean Megaliths

While Almerian influences were extending westwards to Portugal, along the east coast and the Ebro valley, they were also penetrating northwards until they reached Catalonia and the Pyrenees. The indigenous population continued to bury their dead in caves and trench graves but in North-eastern Catalonia, Navarra and the Basque province megalithic passage-graves under round cairns, gallery and bottle-shaped tombs, dolmens with polygonal chambers and short passages began to make their way from the south, together with an abundance of copper objects, calläis beads, cylinder-pins, *Pectunculus* bracelets, zoned beakers, bone buttons, and knuckle-bone figures. The segmented galleries divided into two compartments by slabs like a series of cists, prevalent in the Pyrenees, may have arisen as a result of a fusion between the Almerian and El Carcel immigrations in this area.[39] Caves were still used, however, for burial, but it was the gallery-graves and their culture that became the dominant influence in the Pyrenaean region, spreading from Catalonia across to the west coast of France, representing a combination of the passage-tomb and the slab-cist of the original Almerian colonists.

On the Atlantic littoral and in the hinterland a similar movement occurred, with the megalithic architecture becoming less complex, with small passage-dolmens of inferior workmanship taking the place of the great tombs of the south, until in Galicia, the Basque provinces and the Spanish Pyrenees free-standing rectangular closed dolmens or cists became prevalent, polygonal in the north-west and square in the north-east. These are mere shadows of the great megalithic tombs of the south with their long ancestry in the Middle and Eastern Mediterranean.[40] The rarity of metal in these more remote megaliths is, however, no indication of their age, since the Neolithic culture persisted in North-west Iberia and Northern Europe long

Atlantic Europe

after copper and bronze were in general use in the Middle East and the Mediterranean littoral. Nevertheless, it suggests that the quest of ore was not the principal motive of the diffusion in this region, however much it may have been one of the articles sought in the south. Indeed there is no single object, or group of objects, which characterizes these graves, notwithstanding the fact that beaker pottery has revealed the spread of a new cultural influence not only in the Iberian peninsula but throughout western and Central Europe from Brittany and the Rhine to Bohemia and Moravia, and sporadically in Sardinia, Sicily and Northern Italy.[41] But this diffusion could not have given rise to the megalithic civilization, in either the Eastern Mediterranean or Atlantic Europe because, as will be considered later, while the Beaker folk buried their dead in megalithic tombs, they merely adopted the practice when they settled in areas in which the cult was already established.

ATLANTIC EUROPE

Megalithic Tombs in Brittany

Undaunted by the hazards of the Bay of Biscay, the megalithic mariners after colonizing Iberia made their way in a north-westerly direction from Portugal and Galicia to the Breton peninsula. Thus, in the Gulf of Morbihan and the neighbouring isles, which with Jersey may have been joined to the mainland, five types of tombs are distinguishable based on the Iberian tradition but adapted to local conditions and materials. While the corbelled passage-graves on the coasts and islands reproduce their Portuguese and Spanish prototypes, they are clearly imitations displaying local variations. In Southern Morbihan the Iberian plan reappears, although corbelling is less frequent than in the south of Spain and is distinct from the small corbelled graves of the Breton Bronze Age. To the north-east of Carnac the great passage family dolmen of Kercado in the form of a circular tumulus, 20 metres in diameter and 3·5 metres in height, is surmounted by a menhir over the burial chamber and surrounded by a stone circle (Fig. 5). Originally it had an ashlar retaining wall which splayed out towards the entrance to form a forecourt with a stone-built portal in the centre and a huge slab on each side of it. Encircling the mound was a causeway at the base of the wall constructed of closely packed stones from 3 to 6 metres wide flanked by the stone circle which seems to have been a development of the ritual enclosure at the entrance to some of the tombs at Los Millares and of forecourts in the Aegean tholoi and rock-cut tombs, but extended to embrace the entire structure.[42] Of the rites which were performed in it the only indications are two hearths and a slab on which offerings may have been cooked before presentation to the dead or to their tutelary spirits.

In some of the Breton passage-graves several chambers occur, as, for example, in the tomb of Mané Rutual, Locmariaquer, where behind a smaller rectangular chamber lies a larger polygonal chamber covered by a huge slab, as in the Spanish megaliths. But in Brittany sometimes transepts were added on either side of the gallery at or near the inner end (e.g. Mané-Bras (Goderon) and Clud-er-Yer). Whether or not these transepted galleries evolved in France out of normal Iberian tholoi with lateral cells as at Los Millares,[43] or, as Dr Daniel now maintains, they represent an independent line of diffusion from the gallery-graves set in wedge-shaped barrows related to the Balearic *navetas* and the Scandinavian *giganti*,[44] the elongated straight covered chamber indistinguishable from the passage-grave became a prominent feature in megalithic construction in Brittany (other than in Southern Morbihan) and in the basins of the Loire and the Seine. It is common also in the south of France and in many islands of the western Mediterranean, often covered with a long barrow in contrast to the Breton passage-graves in round barrows. In Morbihan, however, the unchambered long barrows of the Manio type near Carnac, which are not strictly megalithic in structure, may not have been inspired by the great Iberian megalithic tombs,[45] and, unless Dr Daniel is correct in deriving the *allée couverte* from the gallery series in the islands of the Western Mediterranean,[46] which is by no means improbable, the transepted galleries may have been borrowed from the long cairns.

Atlantic Europe 81

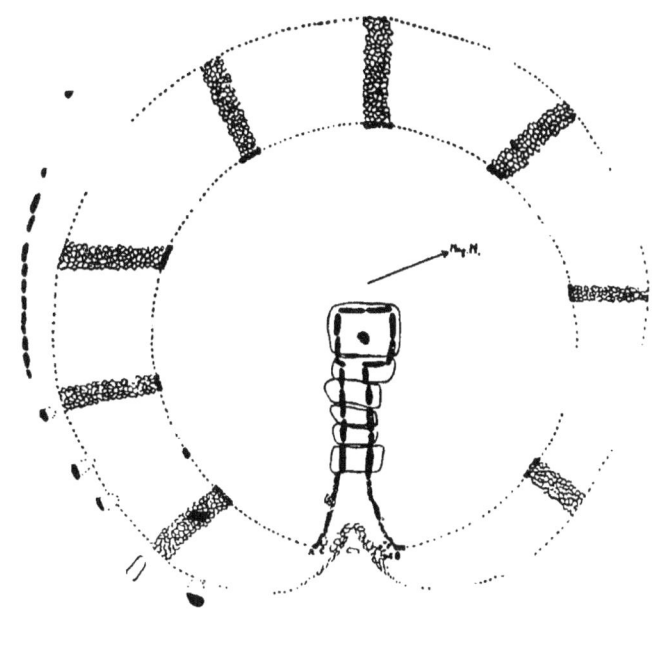

KERCADO
(CARNAC)

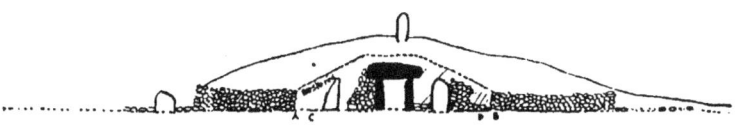

Fig. 5. Passage-grave at Kercado, near Carnac, Brittany

Another type of gallery occurs in Brittany consisting of two sections at right angles, the one leading into the other, with carvings of an exclusive design on the vertical slabs. Since this form is unknown south of the Pyrenees, probably it represents a Breton peculiarity. In Southern Morbihan shortened galleries without entrances, such as the closed chamber in the tumulus of Tumiac, Arzon, are built largely of dry-stone walling under huge barrows. That at Mané-er-Hroeck was 100 metres long and covered a square chamber of very large slabs placed horizontally to form a chamber roofed with capstones. On one side of the chamber an upright was decorated with schematic sacred carvings like those on the Iberian chamber tombs, idols and plaques. Spiral designs recur on the pillars at Gavr'inis and Mané-Lud, similar to those in the Middle Mediterranean megaliths.[47] At Mont S. Michel the central chamber was surrounded by a number of small cists, and although they have been assigned to the Bronze Age,[48] greenstone ceremonial axes and calläis beads, which abound in them, suggest that they belong to the established tradition in Brittany, where practically every example of megalithic monument is to be found from corbelled tholoi to small cists.

Corbelling, in fact, is not a prominent feature in this area, having been introduced in all probability by the mariners from the south. A few rock-cut tombs were dug in the softer rocks, but the common practice was to bury commoners in stone cists, or dolmens, consisting of three or more upright slabs roofed with one or two capstones, either under small tumuli or sunk in the ground, containing jadite axes and bracelets, calläis, amber and rock crystal beads, together with some copper and gold objects, stone double axes, mace-heads and ritual carvings. This assortment of grave goods shows that Brittany became the centre of the megalithic cult in north-western Europe, and so attracted devotees from a very wide area. In addition to those who brought the chambered-tombs with their forecourt and walling and Mediterranean antecedents from Southern Spain and Portugal, there were unmistakable connexions with the valley of the Loire and Southern France; while from the Paris basin came the galleries with port-hole slabs, figurines of the Mother-goddess and "collared flasks" characteristic of the Seine-Oise-Marne (S.O.M.) culture. The occurrence of beakers in most types of graves, except the corbelled tombs of Morbihan and Jersey, indicate that the Beaker folk were also a dominant element in the population, since they adopted the local cult and buried their dead in megaliths with their own drinking-cup.

The S.O.M. Culture

The distribution of the monuments suggests in the first instance a maritime diffusion with concentrations at certain focal-points, such as the Gulf of Morbihan, Southern Finistère and, in a lesser degree, the Lower Loire and Vendée with extensions to the Côte du Nord and Jersey. But they are densest in the Breton coastal districts and the lower reaches of the estuaries, diminishing on the western coasts and dwindling to a few isolated spots in the north-east. From the Paris basin a late form of megalithic cult, characteristic of the S.O.M. cultus, made its way to Brittany with its collective burial in rectangular chambers and its appropriate furniture as indicated above, while commoners were interred in family ossuaries. This tradition had been inherited from the Pyrenaean region in the south of France, Sardinia and the Balearic Isles, as appears in the gallery of Grotte des Fées, 82 feet long, derived from the rock-cut tomb of St Vincent in Mallorca. Passing up the Rhône valley to the Paris basin, it then spread westwards to Brittany and Jersey but not to Guernsey. To the north-east the S.O.M. galleries occurred in Belgium and Westphalia, and finally reached the south of Sweden. In the Marne, chalk cemeteries have been found containing rock-cut graves entered by a descending ramp or dromos, as in the Mycenaean tombs, and in the more elaborate structures equipped with richer furniture but fewer bodies than the smaller collective burials of forty or more corpses. In the valley of the Seine and Oise slabs generally have been used to produce a trench with a chamber at one end divided from the rest by a port-hole at the entrance, often with a conventionalized figure of the Mother-goddess inscribed on the wall.[49] In the Paris basin trepanning holes in the skull was practised as a magical device.

THE BRITISH ISLES

From Brittany the megalithic mariners proceeded northwards across the English Channel soon after 2500 B.C., settling on the chalk downs and uplands in the south of England from Sussex to Eastern Devon in an environment not unlike that to which they had been accustomed in their continental homelands. They organized themselves in small agricultural communities on patches of arable land and pasture with causewayed enclosures on high ground, perhaps for impounding cattle at the end of the summer, in such places as Windmill Hill near Avebury in Wiltshire (the site which has given its name to the earliest or "A" Neolithic culture in Britain), Knap Hill between Marlborough and Devizes, Whitehawk Camp near Brighton racecourse, Goodwood near Chichester, Coombe Hill near Eastbourne, Maiden Castle in Dorset, Hembury near Honiton in Devon, and Carn Brea in Cornwall. Near the Thames at Abingdon a Neolithic promontory has been identified on low-lying ground.[50]

The absence of metal in these sites and in the graves indicates that the first Neolithic colonists arrived before they had become acquainted with the processes of metallurgy, and their pottery was also of the pre-Beaker type, consisting of well-proportioned round-bottomed, baggy or carinated bowls, sometimes copied from leather models, with moulded rims and upright lips. They were well baked and often burnished, either plain or ornamented by drawing the finger or a comb over the wet clay and making imprints with the finger-nail, and pricks by bone-pins under the rims. They engaged in large-scale flint-mining on the open chalk of the downs at Cissbury, Harrow Hill, Blackpatch and Easton Down in Sussex and Wessex, at Peppard on the Chilterns, and Grimes' Graves in Norfolk, where phallic figures carved in chalk or bone have been found.

British Long Barrows

Skeletons having been discovered in the shaft of a flint-mine and in the ditch at Whitehawk Camp, it might appear that commoners were not interred in prepared tombs. Collective burial in communal graves, often in a confused condition, was, however, a feature of the Windmill Hill culture, together with secondary interment in stone vaults or chambered tombs covered with an earth mound. These long barrows are of very frequent occurrence on the downs from Sussex to Dorset, and on the Yorkshire and Lincolnshire Wolds; the primary interments in the chambers beneath a small cairn or sods at the end of the mound usually are associated with Windmill Hill pottery. In districts where stone was not available—e.g. in South Wiltshire, Hampshire, Dorset, Sussex and Berkshire— these elongated mounds were composed of earth, chalk and timber heaped over with subsoil excavated from ditches, as in the very long unchambered Holdenhurst barrow near Bournemouth. In Brittany, as we have seen, long mounds as an alternative to burial in round cairns were in vogue before this mode of sepulture reached Britain, soon after 2400 B.C., and became a characteristic feature of the Neolithic "A" culture. It was also under Breton influences, it would seem, that chambered barrows began to make their appearance rather later on the Cotswolds and in the neighbourhood of the Severn in the form of genuine megalithic gallery-graves, where suitable stone was readily obtainable, as it was in Ireland, Scotland and the Orkneys.[51]

The origin and relation of these two types of barrows, however, is still a matter of debate. The earth mounds on the Sussex Downs are situated near the causewayed camps rather than in association with the flint-mines, but their focus would appear to have been Salisbury Plain, where stone was accessible and megalithic monuments abounded. Indeed the great long barrow at West Kennet, which was virtually an appendage of Avebury, contains stone chambers. But stone was not difficult to obtain on the Yorkshire Wolds where earthen barrows were erected. The distinction between the two techniques, therefore, has the appearance of being an established tradition rather than a matter of the material, though doubtless accessibility of stone facilitated its use in tomb construction. It may be, as Hawkes and Piggott suggest, that earth barrows were introduced by the Neolithic "A" immigration from Brittany before the megalithic builders arrived.[52] But the two groups of tombs seem to have been more or less contemporary in the Windmill Hill and Cotswold-Severn regions, and they may have reached their respective destinations along parallel but distinctive routes, the one landing on the south coast of England, the other making its way along the Bristol Channel and settling on the Gower coast of South Wales, and on the opposite side in the Mendips, spreading thence to the Cotswolds where it continued the megalithic tradition.

The Severn-Cotswold Barrows

Thus, the great mound known as Belas Knap near Charlton in Gloucestershire, 200 feet long and 75 feet wide, has at the end a false portal with uprights, lintel, blocking-stone and dry-stone walling curving inwards, together with the remains of a forecourt in which the funerary rites were held. On the west and east sides are openings leading to a small chamber composed of five great slabs of stone with a second long narrow chamber on the east side, and a passage running north and south at the southern end. It is said to have been surrounded by a circle of stones, but no trace of it has been found. Numerous dolichocephalic skulls occurred in all the chambers, and below the portal were those of five children. The remains of a brachycephalic young man, it has been suggested, may have belonged to a prisoner of war sacrificed during the funeral ceremonies.[53]

At the east end of a very long barrow at Maiden Castle a body apparently had been hacked to pieces and the brain extracted from the skull in the same manner and doubtless for the same reasons as those we have already considered.[54] Near by were pits which could have contained offerings for the dead, and judging from the length of the barrow (1,790 feet) the person interred in it must have been of some significance unless the site was a place of peculiar sanctity. In the communal tumuli the dead apparently had been deposited in the family vault to be gathered to their fathers without very much circumstance or elaboration of furniture.[55] Only at Nympsfield in the Cotswolds have infant bones been recorded in barrows in southern England.[56]

On the other side of the Bristol Channel long cairns of the Cotswold type recur in Wales along the Glamorgan and Gower coast, in the Black Mountains in Brecknockshire, and

The British Isles

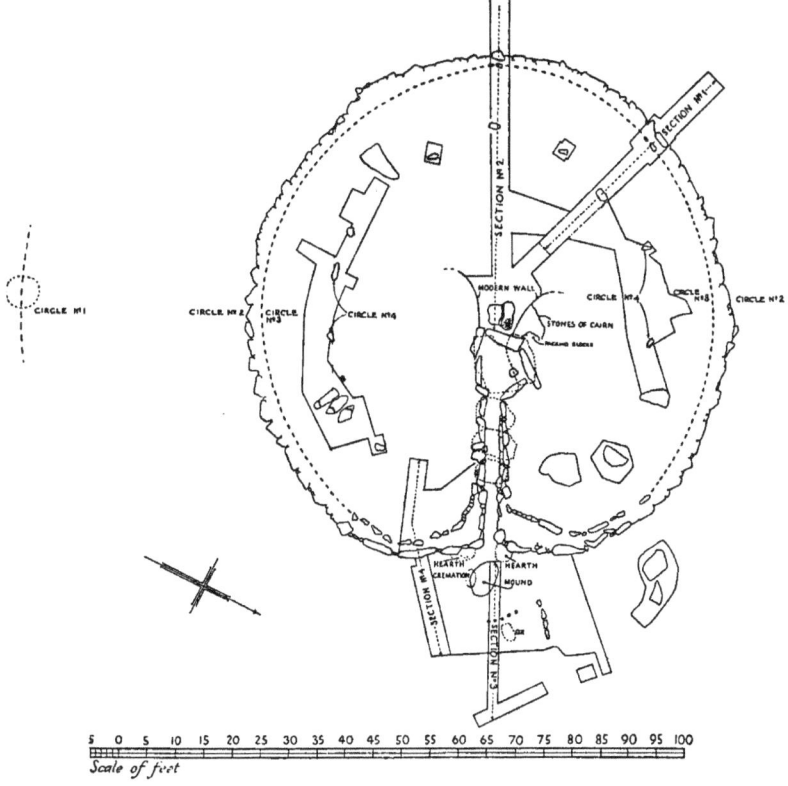

Fig. 6. The Bryn Celli Ddu chambered cairn, Anglesey

in the Conway valley in the north. In the western peninsulas they are more prevalent in the north of the Principality than in the south, and reveal connexions with North Ireland and South-western Scotland. Thus, Bryn Celli Ddu in Anglesey is a chambered cairn consisting of a single polygonal chamber about 8 feet wide covered by two capstones, and approached by a passage 6 feet in length with a roofed portal and an inner passage 20 feet long, and originally placed in a round barrow 90 feet in diameter with a ritual pit behind the chamber and a menhir in the centre of the tomb. Inside the portal are two recesses which may have been an antechamber, and outside the circular wall were the remains of a forecourt, suggesting possible parallels with the Mallorca tombs[57] (Fig. 6). Ten miles to the west at Trecastle Bay is a similar round barrow 80 feet in diameter with a passage leading to a small central chamber with three side-chambers opening out of it, and at Plas Newydd near by a small chamber opens out of a larger one, either as a single chamber with an antechamber at the south,[58] or, as Dr Daniel maintains, a side-chamber with a passage running to the east.[59] In any case both Bryn Celli Ddu and Plas Newydd are passage-graves displaying the customary features.

The Boyne Passage-graves
The centres of this widely dispersed group of tombs with an elongated gallery divided into segments by upright slabs and often opening on to a forecourt with stone-walling recessed at one end to form horns, seems to have been the estuary of the Clyde and Carlingford Lough in Northern Ireland. From these two ports of entry the colonizers spread through the Hebrides, Arran, Bute, Kintyre and Galloway in Scotland, to the Isle of Man, Anglesey and Ulster, with westward extensions as far as Sligo and County Mayo, bringing with them the gallery-grave tradition of Sardinia, Southern France and the Pyrenees. Meanwhile, around Dublin a passage-grave cult had been established with tholoi tombs in the Boyne valley beneath circular cairns on high ground arranged in cemeteries. The best known of these, New Grange, is a circular chambered barrow 280 feet in diameter and 44 feet high (Fig. 7) surrounded by a stone circle originally numbering probably not less than thirty-five free-standing menhirs now reduced to twelve. Around the mound runs a kerb of large flat stones on end, each about 10 feet long, some of which are decorated with sculpture and geometrical patterns in low relief typical of Breton and Iberian tombs. The octagonal chamber with a corbelled vault 20 feet high is approached by a passage 62 feet long roofed with capstones and having three cells opening out of it independently roofed. On the floor of each cell and in the centre of the main chamber are large shallow stone basins.[60] When the mound was first opened in 1699 it is said that a

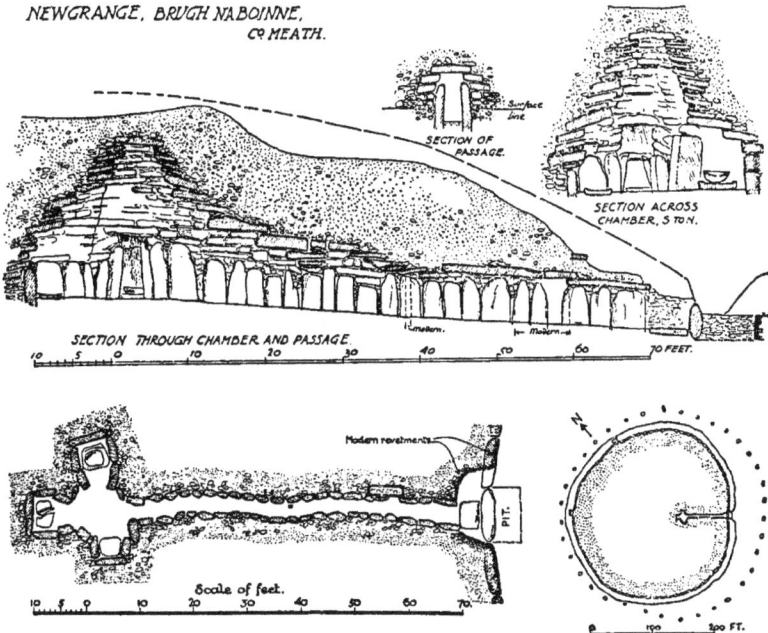

Fig. 7. New Grange chambered tomb, Co. Meath, Ireland

menhir lay on the ground in the burial chamber, and another stood on the summit of the hill.[61] In the neighbouring tumulus of Dowth two sets of chambers occur, one of which is cruciform in plan but with a subsidiary passage opening out of one of the side recesses. The other is circular with an antechamber leading out of it. The stones in both these tombs have sculptured symbols and elaborate incised conventionalized designs on the walls and roofs, including those of the Goddess,[62] suggesting their Breton and Iberian prototypes.

The passage is not divided into segments as in the Clyde-Carlingford graves, and although entrances in the Boyne group often splay to form a forecourt, this feature is not prominent. At Carrowkeel in Sligo a vast corbelled tomb has sills in the passage and at the entrance to the three polygonal chambers, reminiscent of that at Antiquera in Spain;[63] a feature that recurs at the magnificent tomb of Maes Howe in the Orkneys, where it was doubtless reproduced from the Boyne model rather than from the Iberian original structure. Closed round cairns at Carrowkeel resemble those of Mané and Tumaic in Brittany, but by the time the cult had reached Sligo it had passed its zenith apparently, as burial in simple round stone dolmens in walled cairns was the more general procedure.

From Dublin, Boyne, Armagh and North Antrim the passage-grave tradition developed along familiar lines with inland and southern outliers.[64] The chambers with one or two cells are reminiscent of the plan of Los Millares and Almizaraque in Almeria, and at Alcala in Algarve. These features were further developed at New Grange and Dowth into three cells as apse and transepts. In the Dublin group at Tibradden Mount the tholos scheme of a circular chamber with corbelled roof (now mainly destroyed) and dromos built of dry masonry, together with chambers having cells opening out of them, is reproduced.[65] Furthermore, the Iberian tradition of erecting the tombs on mountains or hills in groups was followed, while the symbolic and geometrical stylized designs recall similar patterns on Iberian passage-graves.[66] Another common feature are the large shallow stone bowls. Therefore it is in Spain that the origins of the Boyne Hill megalithic tradition would appear to lie, with Brittany as its area of characterization.

The Clyde-Carlingford Gallery-graves

The Clyde-Carlingford galleries, on the other hand, belonged, it would seem, to the Severn-Cotswold group, derived ultimately from the Pyrenees and Southern France, Sardinia and Sicily, introduced into Ulster and Sligo either direct from its continental cradleland, or as a secondary colonization from Scotland. The resemblance to the Sardinian Giants' Graves is so close that it could be explained as the result of an immigration from the Western Mediterranean, and the decorated pottery conforms to the Pyrenaean technique. But in the absence of a chronological sequence in the Sardinian megaliths all that can be affirmed is that the Clyde-Carlingford "horned cairns" have remarkable affinities with their prototypes in Southern Europe by whatever route they may have reached the North Channel and settled in small agricultural communities in Ayrshire, Galloway and the Hebrides, and on the Irish side in Ulster and Sligo. There they may have found the passage-grave people in possession of the uplands near the coast of Dublin and the Boyne valley, and on the limestone hills in Sligo and the formidable headland of Antrim. Therefore, they concentrated on the light soils above the 400-foot level to the north of the region occupied by the Boyne group. Nevertheless, passage-graves and galleries exist side by side, both at Carlingford Lough and in the Hebrides and Skye, suggesting that the two intruders probably overlapped, and perhaps intermingled in certain districts to some extent while retaining their respective characteristic modes of sepulture, both of them being essentially colonizers and devotees of a megalithic cult rather than aggressive conquerors of territory.

If they were primarily a religious movement led by sacred chiefs, as Childe suggests, whose magic power ensured the fertility of the crops and herds, of game and fish, the two groups may have been sectarian branches of the same cult, not adverse to intermarriage—a union that found expression perhaps in "hybrid" tombs in which a passage-grave might be enclosed in a gallery.[67] Be this as it may, whatever may have been the object of their quest, they wandered freely and fearlessly by perilous maritime routes in the northern seas, and settled often in the bleakest and wildest places—the Hebrides, Caithness and the Orkneys—as well as in more congenial and fertile localities in Ulster, Galloway, the Isle of Man and Anglesey. Thus, an Iberian type of passage-grave, known as Rudh'an Dunain, similar to New Grange or Bryn Celli Ddu, stands in a remote hollow on the western coast of Skye. At Callernish on the stormy coast of Lewis a small circular cairn 21 feet in diameter encloses a rectangular chamber $4\frac{1}{2}$ feet deep and $6\frac{2}{3}$ feet wide, entered by a passage from the east, with a portal formed by two slabs on end. Surrounding the cairn is a circle of thirteen stones having a diameter of $37\frac{1}{2}$ feet with four avenues of menhirs leading to it from the four points of the compass.[68] On the top of it is a single tall menhir nearly at the centre of the circle, doubtless for the same purpose as the cylindrical pillar in the chamber at Bryn Celli Ddu in Anglesey.[69]

Other Hebridaean cairns stand within circles, suggesting that collective burial persisted on these islands, while in Caithness the cairns often occur in cemeteries, as at Camster on Warehouse Hill, comprising in addition to chambered cairns, others covering merely a short cist designed for individual interment. These may have been used by the Beaker folk who settled in Caithness while collective burial was still in vogue. In fact, Childe regards them as the last degeneration of the long cairn under the influence of the individualist tradition, the round-chambered cairns being intermediate forms.[70]

The Medway Megaliths

At the other end of the British Isles a small group of megaliths occur in Kent on the uplands of the Medway valley. These small closed chambers in long mounds enclosed by rectangular palings of large blocks were erected apparently by immigrants from Holland and North Germany. If Stukeley's sketches of it are accurate, Kits Coty House at Aylesford, with what Crawford believes to be a dummy portal like Belas Knap in the Cotswolds, and the rectangular barrows at Addington and Coldrum, have distinctive features of their own,[71] suggesting a separate colonization. But they seem to have been derived originally from the Dutch or Baltic chambered tomb[72] rather than, as Crawford contends, from the Severn-Cotswold group. The skeletons buried in them were on the whole shorter than those found in other British megaliths,[73] and all the circumstances indicate a settlement in the Medway valley from the Low Countries practising collective burial in chambered barrows.

Thus, the British Isles became the meeting-place of a number of streams of megalithic peoples after the foundations of the Neolithic "A" (Windmill Hill) peasant culture had been laid about 2500 B.C. on the uplands. In the river valleys and marshes of East Anglia and the Thames basin, and along the east coast, in Yorkshire, and subsequently in Anglesey, Ulster and Galloway, the Neolithic "B" Peterborough immigrants from the Baltic had established themselves relatively undisturbed by the Neolithic "A" settlements on and beyond the chalk massif of Wessex and Sussex, the wolds of Yorkshire and Lincolnshire and on Lyle's Hill near Belfast in Ulster. Neolithic communities accustomed to burying their dead collectively in long cairns reached the Cotswolds and South Wales via the Bristol Channel from Brittany and the mouth of the Loire. Thence they penetrated to Berkshire, and probably to North Wiltshire, and to the Black Mountains of Brecknockshire up the valley of the Usk. From the south of France and the Western Mediterranean the Clyde-Carlingford gallery-graves were introduced into Northern Ireland, South-west Scotland and the adjacent islands, while from Spain and Brittany came the Boyne group of passage-graves to the south of the Irish gallery territory, with closely related chambered tombs in Tramore near Waterford in the Scilly Isles and in the west of Cornwall. These represent local colonizations from the same sources on both sides of the Irish Sea in the south,[74] corresponding to those in the Hebridaean group at the other extremity.

In Eastern Britain the contacts were with the Low Countries, the Rhineland and Scandinavia. Some of these were of considerable antiquity, going back to Boreal times in the Mesolithic, when land communications with the Continent still existed. It was from this direction apparently that the Medway megaliths came into being as an isolated group, introduced by mariners who reached the Netherlands, North Germany and Scandinavia, either by proceeding straight up the English Channel or by a circuitous route through the Pentland Firth to the Scandinavian littoral. Thence eventually they made their way through Holland to Kent, having in the course of this diffusion developed their own characteristic features, some of which may have been borrowed from other sections of the megalithic culture with which they had come in contact.

THE NORTHERN MEGALITHIC TOMBS
The Danish Passage-graves

As has been considered in an earlier chapter,[75] the cult was firmly established in Denmark on the islands of the Cattegat and the East Danish coast not later than 2200 B.C., but whether or not it came via the British Isles or direct from the south of France is by no means clear. The first Danish farmers appear to have buried their dead in single earth-graves in the extended position within a ring of stones, protected probably by wooden planks and covered by a low elongated mound, from which the *dyssers* may have emerged.[76] Collective interment in passage-graves with round or polygonal chambers approached by short passages covered by capstones, reminiscent of Iberian and Irish forms, except that corbelling was not adopted and dry-stone walling was rare, gives every appearance of having been introduced from the original home of this type of sepulture. In Jutland a smaller side-chamber from 4 to 7 metres in length often was added, with larger dimensions in Sweden,[77] while in Eastern Denmark double passage-graves occur in which one mound encloses two chambers, each with its own entrance. In the latest form the passage opens into a short side flush with the floor of the chamber, and at Alsbjerg a triple-chambered tomb occurs bearing some resemblance to the Caithness graves.[78] Since as many as a hundred skeletons have been found in some of the passage-graves,[79] they must have been used for collective burial for a very considerable time, and this is confirmed by the sequence of indigenous pottery in them.

The angular decorated bowls, however, resemble the Rössen ware of Central Germany and the Rhine valley, a copper dagger could have come from Los Millares, beads from Brittany, and hammer-headed pins from the Kuban tombs. But metal ornaments usually were copied in amber, bone or stone, amber being the chief export and the most widely used material for necklaces and pendants. Denmark, therefore, must have been a cosmopolitan centre to which the megalithic influx

The Northern Megalithic Tombs

brought cultural traditions culled from a variety of sources deeply laid in their ancestry in Iberia, Brittany, and subsequently in Ireland.

Battle-axes and Single Graves

Meanwhile there were also substantial infiltrations from North-west and Central Germany, together with Danubian merchants exchanging metal weapons and tools for amber ornaments and amulets. The most disturbing influence, however, came from the virile Nordic warriors with their battle-axes, who from about 2300 B.C. pursued their aggressive course from the Black Sea and the Urals through Central Europe to the Baltic, passing down the Elbe to Holstein and Jutland. Unlike the megalithic people in the centre and on the east coast of the peninsula, the Battle-axe conquerors buried their dead in the contracted position in single graves dug in the earth and generally covered them with a round mound. In the earliest of the separate graves in Jutland ovoid beakers with an S-profile decorated with horizontal cord-impressions occur, together with polished stone battle-axes, thick-butted flint axes, spherical maces and amber rings and buttons.[80] When subsequently interments were made in the existing barrows the axes had deteriorated and herring-bone designs had taken the place of cord-ornamentation on the beakers, until at the end of the passage-grave period in the adjacent islands (*c.* 1750 B.C.), and in Zealand, where the megalithic tradition survived much longer than in Jutland, the Battle-axe warriors had consolidated the civilization under their rule, and established themselves as the dominant power in Sweden and Finland.

In North-west Germany and Holland they expanded in a southerly direction, swarming over the plains of Schleswig-Holstein, probably driving the peasants in the Elbe-Weser region to seek refuge in Mecklenburg and in the Drenthe-Ems provinces in Holland. There the Elbe-Weser folk continued the megalithic technique, erecting stone cists often with very long galleries entered by a short passage in the middle on the long side, covered by an elongated mound, known as Huns' Beds. In Jutland, passage-graves persist only near the coasts, and there they are exclusively of the earlier variety, while in Zealand later types occur. Only on the islands did the tradition continue without a break. Elsewhere in Denmark the single graves extended northwards until they reached the extreme northerly end of Jutland, and in many of the passage-tombs the megalithic contents in the deepest layers are overlaid by single-grave relics.

On the islands it is estimated that there were nearly 3,500 megalithic graves, and 4,000 in Northern Sweden, mostly in Västergötaland and on the south-west coast, in all probability built by refugees from Jutland. Like the Beaker folk, the Battle-axe warriors sometimes buried their dead in the existing megalithic tombs, but their normal mode of sepulture was their own individual burial with the knees bent in earth graves paved with small stones. The sides were walled with stones and then lined with wood, closed by wooden planks and covered by a low mound. The furniture, though variable, generally, in the case of a man, included a battle-axe or a butted-axe of ground flint, a beaker, a stone mace and two large disks of amber; in that of a woman, a necklace of amber beads. But whereas in the megalithic tombs the contacts were mainly with the Western Pyrenaean and Mediterranean region, in the single graves they were essentially with Central Europe and the Danube, with local characteristics and variations.

Whether the megalithic tradition came to the Baltic by way of the Atlantic route via the British Isles, or directly from Spain through the English Channel, it was an intrusion from the south which became centred in the Danish Isles, especially in Zealand, with concentrations in northern and eastern Jutland and south-western Sweden, and south of Lake Väner, with extensions in the central region and in Norway. Once established in Denmark and Scandinavia, it developed its own peculiar features until in the long cist period it was brought to an end, probably about 1700 B.C., when the warrior culture from Central Europe predominated in the Baltic.

CHAPTER IV

Cremation, Inhumation and Mummification

CREMATION IN EUROPE IN THE BRONZE AGE

In the opening centuries of the second millennium B.C. when the Neolithic civilization in the greater part of Europe had run its course and new cultural influences and traditions everywhere were rampant, the cult of the dead underwent a fundamental change. Before the Bronze Age was firmly established, however, metal had been in general use over a wide area and new modes of sepulture were beginning to appear, so that no sudden or revolutionary transition occurred from one epoch to another, as was formerly imagined. Thus, the elusive but influential people distinguished by the bell-beaker as their characteristic product roved about early in the Chalcolithic period as merchants and traders, opening up new lines of communications diffusing a uniform culture. This included the practice of metallurgy, which had been adopted in their Almerian area of characterization in Southern Spain, but unlike the megalithic mariners they had no hard and fast rule about the disposal of the dead.

As we have seen, they frequently resorted to burial in megaliths, so that beakers have been found in the rock-cut tombs and natural caves in Sardinia, Sicily and Portugal, in the great tholoi of Almeria, in the French galleries, the Catalonian cists, the British round barrows and the Danish passage-graves. But they readily reverted to their original custom of inhumation in single graves in the cemeteries of Moravia, Saxo-Thuringia and the Rhineland, where they mingled with the Battle-axe people, and eventually made their way to the lowlands in South-east Britain, East Anglia, Yorkshire and Scotland, continuing earth burial in isolated graves or grouped together in small cemeteries. Occasionally the dead were placed in stone cists, round barrows or cairns with circular ditches, and sometimes there were indications of cremation.

Partial Cremation under Long Barrows

In Yorkshire, bodies were actually burnt in a trench or flue at the end of some of the long barrows after having been dismembered and placed under chalk-rubble and wood, among which charcoal and other charred matter were found.[1] But on the wolds inhumation was by far the most frequent practice, and out of 379 burials opened by Greenwell only 78 contained cremations.[2] Moreover, in many cases it would seem that bodies were burnt accidentally as a result of purificatory fires having been lighted in graves, or for the purpose of desiccating the corpse. In many of the British barrows burnt and unburnt bones occurred, and only in relatively few was cremation the rule. When a trench was especially constructed with a flue to aid combustion, as in some Yorkshire barrows, there can be little doubt that genuine cremation was intended. The same applies in the case of those in which the bodies were burnt on a platform of gravelly material and sand reddened by fire as at Tilshead and Winterbourne Stoke in Wiltshire, and at West Rudham in Norfolk.[3]

In the Leighterton barrow in Gloucestershire three vaults arched over like ovens are said to have been found with an urn at the entrance to each containing ashes and human bones imperfectly burnt and broken.[4] Similarly, in the Huggard Wold group of barrows in the East Riding the calcined remains appeared to have been placed in a wooden receptacle, traces of which had survived, but they had seldom been reduced to ashes. Generally they consisted of pieces of charred bones mixed with burnt chalk and soil reddened by fire, the pyre extending outside the area containing the actual cremation. The charcoal from the trenches sometimes was several feet long in a horizontal position, the floor of the trench being a continuous stratum of incinerated adult and juvenile bones, broken and splintered by the action of fire.[5]

It seems, therefore, that while in some cases genuine crema‑ ion probably was attempted as a means of disposal of the dead n the Neolithic and Early Bronze Age, partially burnt remains may be merely the result of an accidental conflagration arising from a variety of causes. Sometimes, as Childe suggests, the wooden chambers in the crematorium trenches may have caught fire,[6] if and when it was the custom to burn fires in the graves for purificatory purposes, or to dry the corpse to preserve it from decay; a practice, as will be considered later,[7] which has been widely adopted in primitive societies in modern times. In any case, the use of fires in mortuary ritual preceded the adoption of cremation as an established mode of disposal of the dead towards the end of the Bronze Age. Prior to this it had occurred only sporadically, perhaps in Syria at Byblos, in Palestine at Gezer, in the Peloponnese at Argive Heraeum, and without doubt in Bohemia, Moravia, Hungary and Central Germany, and in megalithic tombs in Brittany, Wessex and Ulster, where in the Clyde‑Carlingford galleries it predominated.

Round Barrows

Inhumation, however, was the normal form of sepulture in unchambered and in chambered graves in Neolithic Britain, although burnt bones are of fairly frequent occurrence in passage‑graves like Bryn Celli Ddu in Anglesey, Nympfield in the Cotswolds, and in two circular cairns in the Scilly Isles. It would seem, therefore, that the two practices existed side by side, though cremation usually was of the partial variety, either outside the tomb before the incinerated remains were deposited in the grave, or in a specially constructed wooden hut or in a flue‑like trench, while a few barrows covered cremations on platforms. At Dorchester‑on‑Thames the bodies were burnt on pyres within the circular sanctuary and the incinerated bones were then interred in bags in cremation cemeteries. In Dorset four out of five of the round barrows contained cremations, while in Cornwall the practice was almost universal.

The "Disk Barrows" around Stonehenge, composed of one or more small mounds on a circular platform with a small ditch inside it but no entrance passage, had cremations with blue faience beads from Egypt (c. 1400 B.C.), together with amber beads from the Baltic and Central Europe, and jet beads from the north-east coast of Yorkshire. Beneath the chalk patches outside the sarsen circle at Stonehenge (i.e. the Aubrey Holes) a number of cremations have been recorded, and also in the bank and in the silt at the bottom of the ditch in the south-east quadrant. One hole was nearly full of wood ash, but the smallest contained only the remains of a partial incineration in the lowest levels. Although most of the holes bore traces of cremations, the furniture accompanying them was confined to a few bone pins, flint implements, and in Hole 29 a lugged "pygmy" cup bearing some resemblance to a Neolithic "B" Groved Ware vessel of Rinyo type from the Woodhenge area,[8] a few miles to the north-east of Stonehenge, where (i.e. at Woodhenge) only one cremation has been found.[9]

While the ditch, bank and Aubrey Holes may belong to the Late Neolithic period (c. 1900–1800 B.C.), the main structure of the sarsen circle and its "bluestones" probably are contemporary with the round barrows, and may be some 400 years later than the earliest features of the site (i.e. 1500–1400 B.C.).[10] It was then, in the Early Bronze Age, soon after the arrival of the Beaker "A" people from the Lower Rhineland, that a small influx of warrior chiefs from Brittany practising cremation established themselves temporarily in Wessex, equipped with a new type of flat dagger having a tough midrib and mounted on wood or amber, spherical stone battle-axes, sceptres, and blue glazed beads from the Eastern Mediterranean.[11] It may have been this invasion which facilitated the transition from the Early Bronze Age to the Middle Bronze Age in Britain, characterized by the change from inhumation to cremation as the established mode of disposal of the dead, associated with round barrows.[12] Many of their graves occur at the two principal cult centres of this period, Avebury and Stonehenge, nd very probably it was these warrior chiefs who were esponsible for the remodelling of Stonehenge. Outside Wessex hey expanded to Exmoor, the Mendips and along the Icknield Way from South Wales to East Anglia, and established colonies around sacred sites marked by clusters of their bell-barrows containing mainly primary cremations.

Urn Burial

Parallel with the Wessex culture a more permanent Middle Bronze Age culture flourished in Britain marked by cremations with the remains buried in cinerary urns, frequently under barrows or in cairns, except in the north, where they were grouped in cemeteries. These urns were made of coarse clay and were similar in design to the food-vessels with flat bottoms which accompanied interments in the contracted position in stone cists and under barrows in the British Isles about 1700 B.C., immediately after the Beaker invasion. With them occurred also stone axes, metal ear-rings, buttons with V-shaped perforations, bracelets and crescentic jet necklaces with gold *lunulae* of Ireland. Therefore, if the antecedents of the Urn culture are to be sought in that of the Food-vessel folk, a fundamental change in the disposal of the dead must have occurred by the Middle Bronze Age, inhumation having given place to cremation in the meantime.

On the Continent, cremation cemeteries in the form of urn-fields became general at this time (i.e. from the Middle Bronze Age to the Early Iron Age, from about 1500 to 800 B.C.), first in Hungary and Northern Italy, and then extending from Western Asia Minor throughout Western, Central and Northern Europe to Ireland. Genuine cremation with the ashes deposited in urns which were buried in large cemeteries now was so widely adopted that it marks a definite transition in the cult of the dead, notwithstanding the fact that partial incineration, as we have seen, was prevalent in the Early Bronze Age and the Late Neolithic from the Early Helladic graves in Greece to the British barrows. Even in Food-vessel graves cremated ashes are not unknown, and as cremation increased, the food-vessels seem to have become cinerary urns, though as a general practice this transition was not effected until the Middle Bronze Age.

The Terramara Cemeteries

Thus, in Northern Italy south of the Po and Lake Garda westwards towards Brescia and Cremona, outside the settlements of pile-dwellings known as Terramara, were cemeteries on small piles and protected by moats containing ashes in urns closely packed together and covered with basins. It is possible that these prosperous agriculturists (*terra-maricoli*) may have arisen as an Urnfield group with Danubian, Asiatic and Iberian affinities, crossed with those of the Corded-ware warrior Nordic and Slavonic intruders in the Middle Danube basin,[13] before they were driven into the Middle and Lower Po valley and Taranto by a general westward movement, and there established themselves as a dominant but localized group. In any case they had come into contact with the practice of cremation and urn burial before they reached Italy about 1500 B.C. in the Middle Bronze Age, probably in Hungary, where in the Pannonian cemeteries, extending from the Austrian border to Central Hungary, and in those of the Banat and North-east Serbia, urn burial was the only mode of disposal of the dead. Elsewhere inhumation was generally adopted.

It was this expansion from Hungary which took cremation in urnfields through North-western Serbia and Slavonia and the intermediate regions along the Save and the Danube to Transylvania, and along the Theiss to Perjamos and Tószeg, where after 1400 B.C. it gradually ousted inhumation.[14] In Saxony and Western Silesia and Brandenburg the Lausitz culture became a powerful influence from about the middle of the second millennium B.C., which eventually was destined to play an important part in the establishment of cremation. When iron was just beginning to come into use in Italy for small objects, the vigorous community of peasant farmers called Villanovans, after the suburb of Bologna where their culture was first identified, had become established in what are now Umbria and Tuscany. Randall-MacIver regards them as an immigration from Hungary,[15] but they may have been merely descendants of the Terramaricoli[16] who continued the cremation and urnfield tradition.

The Villanovan Cemeteries

Around their villages, composed of small huts which were reproduced in the hut-urns that became common in Latium in the south,[17] graves were dug in the adjacent cemeteries, sometimes lined with stone slabs in which the cinerary urn was placed. The ossuary and grave furniture were often enclosed in an immense jar, or *dolio*, marked in several instances by sandstone stelae roughly carved with rosettes, human figures or animals. The *dolio* generally is a two-storeyed structure resembling a bowl with an inverted rim and a horizontal handle surmounted by a conical neck with splayed rim. It might be covered with a slab of stone and within the jar was the pottery ossuary, with its cover and several other pottery vases ornamented with meander patterns in high relief. In the graves were bronze pendants, palette-knives with handles, armlets, fibulae inlaid with amber, and bronze pins headed with disks of bone and spheres of glass, gold and glaze pendants, gold head-bands with four masks of human heads, and a gold fibula covered with figures of lions.[18] While they employed iron, the Villanovans were expert workers in bronze and exported their products as far north as the Balkans and east as Transylvania. They also had contacts with Phoenicia and Assyria, whence from the south the knowledge of iron may have spread through Italy.

Only a very small number of inhumations occur in their cemeteries. Thus, at Villanova only 14 skeletons were found as against 193 cremations, and these are said to have lain "pell-mell among the tombs containing burned bodies, almost at the same level", and with the same grave furniture.[19] These inhumations may have been the interments of members of adjoining communities who died among the Villanovans but continued their normal mode of disposal of the body in the local cemeteries. This would explain the absence of any such intrusions in those of Selciatello at Corneto in Etruria, and in the Etruscan Vetulonia near the village of Colonna.

The Lausitz Urnfields
While Italy and Southern Europe were experimenting with iron at the beginning of the first millennium B.C., the central region north of the Alps was still in the Bronze Age, and in the thirteenth century was in a state of ferment. The Barrow and Tumulus culture of the Middle Bronze Age, which survived in the highlands, was invaded by the Urnfield folk who occupied the valleys and the plains of the Upper Danube basin and practised cremation and the deposition of the ashes in large urns after the manner of the Terramara people, but sometimes under barrows. A smaller vessel for votive offerings, familiar in the Villanovan graves, was associated with these urns, revealing affinities with northern Italy, suggesting that they may have come from south of the Alps. It was, however, in that part of eastern Saxony and western Silesia known as Lausitz that it developed its characteristic features, among which were its ossuaries constructed by placing two truncated cones base to base and covering them with an inverted dish. In the earlier burials a hole was bored in the sides, presumably to enable the soul to leave it at will, and with the ossuaries were buff-coloured pots ornamented with large conical warts (*Buckeln*). In the later graves the warts became flutings or corrugations and the ware was dark-faced. Vases with side spouts called "feeding bowls", and vessels shaped as animals and clay rattles appeared. Since moulds have been found in the graves, the Lausitz folk must have been metallurgists, and they may have invented the socketed celt, developing it out of a flanged celt with a bronze sleeve.[20]

Wherever they may have originated, having established themselves in Eastern and Central Europe they carried on the Early Bronze Age cultural tradition called Aunjetitz, after the cemetery at Unětice near Prague, and extended their sphere of influence across Southern Germany and Upper Italy to the Rhône, although in the Lausitz culture inhumation in stone graves was abandoned in favour of cremation. Like their predecessors, the Lausitz people controlled the trade-routes and valleys on the loess between the Elbe and the Oder. Thence their culture spread to the Vistula, the Austrian Danube and the mountains of Slovakia, its influence being felt farther afield in Spain, the British Isles and Scandinavia, so that it became a predominant unifying force in the Late Bronze Age, and continued to flourish when iron was beginning to make its way northwards from Italy into Bohemia, Moravia and East Prussia. Throughout its diffusion urnfield burial in extensive cemeteries was retained, and the biconical ossuary was of frequent occurrence in the graves.

The Alpine Urnfields

In the North Alpine region a less coherent urnfield culture developed on the Upper Danube and its tributaries, and spread down the Rhine and across Switzerland, establishing itself in the fertile valleys and along the trade-routes as in the case of the Lausitz. Its main centres, however, were the copper mines of the Tyrol and the salt deposits at Hallstatt and Hallein in the Salzkammergut, Reichenhall in Upper Bavaria and Mergentheim in Württemberg, where it absorbed elements from trading contacts with the Tumulus culture, and especially with the Lausitz folk who may have settled within its borders.[21] But while cremation was universally practised, the urnfields were less uniform than those of the Elbe and the Middle Danube. Some of the urns were under barrows in Bavaria, the Rhineland and Eastern Bohemia, while inhumations in cists were not unknown.

In the graves stone axes and winged celts were common, together with socketed chisels, bronze swords with engraved hilts, rapiers, knives, razors, fish-hooks, sickles, bronze-tipped arrows and a great variety of ornaments. The urns were globular or piriform, sometimes fluted or roughened, with a cylindrical neck and wide brim which in the Tyrol was supported by pillar-like handles. Biconical ossuaries of Lausitz type occurred sporadically in the earlier urnfields throughout the region. Even the Tumulus-builders, who survived in the highlands above these valleys inhabited by the Urnfield folk, practised cremation, though, except in Bohemia, they seldom deposited the ashes in urns. Beyond the Main and Saône the culture declined, judging from the impoverished conditions of the cemeteries in this area. This may have been a result of its having become isolated from its Alpine centre as it spread into Central France and the Low Countries, where it mingled with the surviving elements of the earlier Tumulus culture and was overlaid by influences from north-western Bohemia.

It was not until towards the end of the Bronze Age that urn burial and Lausitz ossuaries reached Northern Germany and Scandinavia, notwithstanding the contacts between the Baltic and Central Europe at the beginning of the period. From the Eastern Mediterranean, probably inspired ultimately by Egypt and travelling along the amber route, came the custom of representing the grave in the form of a ship in which the deceased made his voyage to the next life. This practice was common in the Iron Age and reached its climax in Viking times. Boat-burial also appeared in Britain in the middle of the second millennium with other Scandinavian affinities like the amber cup found at Hove. It was not until much later (*c*. 700 B.C.) that groups of Late Bronze Age Alpine urnfield invaders reached the southern shores of England and settled in the Thames valley at Brentford and elsewhere in the lowlands, bringing with them bronze swords with a point shaped like a carp's tongue, together with "winged axes", horse trappings and knives resembling a hog's back. As would be expected, they buried their dead normally in urnfield cemeteries, according to their established custom, or sometimes at the south or south-east end of barrows of the Early or Middle Bronze Age, as, for example, at Deverel and Rimbury in Dorset. In the Deverel barrow the burials were placed at the foot of slabs arranged in the shape of a horseshoe, while in some of the cemeteries they were circular in plan.

The Hallstatt Cemetery

These immigrations from the Continent between 850 and 700 B.C. were the result of widespread movements of peoples at the end of the Bronze Age, characterized by the urnfield cultures based on Central Europe. It was at this time that the classic site in the Austrian Alps above Lake Hallstatt came into great prominence with an increased demand for the salt that was mined there. This is shown by the dimensions of the cemetery excavated in 1846, which dates from about 1000 to 450 B.C. The first phases appear to fall within the Bronze Age because the earlier fusions of peoples in the Alpine region lingered on, and towards the end of the period they sought shelter in the mountain valleys from the warlike invaders on the highlands. Thus, the harp fibula of Late Bronze Age type was a characteristic object at Hallstatt, together with the leaf-shaped bronze sword in which the flanges round the hilt disappeared and the tang terminated in a semi-hexagonal finial; the blade being narrower than in most preceding types and the rivets smaller.[22]

Of the 2,000 or more graves that originally were contained within the cemetery, 455 cremations and 525 inhumations have been identified. The bronze objects, numbering 179, were associated with the cremations and only three with the burials. In the case of the cremations, which are the older of the two modes of disposal in this cemetery, urns were rare and iron was confined to a few small knives. The bronze fibulae suggest contacts with East Central Europe, and it is not improbable that at the end of the Bronze Age pressure from the eastern side of the Lausitz province was responsible for a modification of the culture both at Hallstatt and in the West Alpine region, causing further extensions westwards and possibly to Catalonia in North-east Spain. The similarity between the Hallstatt and Alpine cultures may be explained largely as a result of the intrusion of the Lausitz urnfield folk, and it was under Hallstatt influence that the Lusatian urnfield people of Poland adopted the use of iron. The Tumulus-builders of the Middle Bronze Age (c. 1450 B.C.), on the other hand, continued to practise inhumation in the First Iron Age when elsewhere cremation predominated, and even in the Late Hallstatt period (C.D., 800-400 B.C.) intrusive inhumation graves occurred containing objects derived from the south-eastern sides of the Alps.

Urnfield cremation-burial, however, would seem to have come into Central Europe from the south-east out of Anatolia by way of Thrace.[23] By the thirteenth century, urnfields were established in Northern Syria at Carchemish and Ras Shamra, when cremation replaced inhumation,[24] while at the Sixth City of Troy an urn cemetery goes back to the fourteenth century, and can hardly have been derived from Central Europe or the North Alpine region.[25] From Western Asia it reached Hungary and Austria in the Middle Bronze Age (e.g. Tószeg C), following the tracks of the Neolithic colonists 2,000 years before, and interpenetrated the Tumulus culture as it moved towards the Rhine about 1100 B.C., eventually reaching Britain about 750 B.C.

CREMATION AND INHUMATION

While cremation and burial in urnfields were widely adopted in the Bronze Age and in the Middle and Late phases of the period, becoming the predominant mode of disposal of the dead, especially in Central and Northern Europe from the Alpine region to the British Isles, the practice appears to have been an intrusion from the Near East. Inhumation, however, in its various forms persisted everywhere as the basic rite, and not infrequently the incinerated ashes were buried with interments under barrows or cairns, suggesting that cremation was a new element superseding the earlier sepulture without completely eliminating it, except in a few localities towards the end of the Bronze Age. Moreover, as we have seen, partially burnt bones were of fairly common occurrence in graves from Neolithic times onwards. These were really inhumations which had been subjected to incineration to a limited extent, sometimes apparently for the purpose of desiccation, or as a result of accidental firing during a purificatory rite. Or, again, when secondary burial was practised, the body might be reduced to ashes, wholly or partially, after it had been interred for a period for a variety of reasons, as in primitive states of culture today.[26]

MUMMIFICATION IN ANCIENT EGYPT
Natural Desiccation
Although cremation has been a recurrent feature in the cult of the dead since the Bronze Age, the predominant and persistent tendency has been to give some measure of permanence to the mortal remains either in an "everlasting tomb" or through a process of natural or artificial preservation of the body. This was most conspicuous in prehistoric Egypt, where frequently the dead were buried in the hot dry desert sand, which was often impregnated with natronous compounds, so that decomposition was arrested for an indefinite period, as in the case of the natural mummies in the more recent saltpetre caves in New Mexico.[27] The continual discovery of corpses in this condition probably concentrated attention upon the physical survival of the body after death, which soon found expression in a more ample provision of grave furniture and eventually, as we have seen, in elaboration of tomb construction. But burial in more spacious brick-lined graves removed the corpse from the desiccating sand and, therefore, defeated the effects and the purpose of the interments and their equipment. It may have been, as Elliot Smith suggested, that it was as a result of this that attempts were made at the beginning of the Dynastic period to discover ways and means of artificially preserving the bodies of the dead.[28]

Preservation and Embalmment
Thus, the flexed body of a woman has been found from the Second Dynasty which was wrapped in numerous layers of bandages, each leg having been separately treated. Between the bandages and the bones there was a mass of linen corroded probably by crude natron which had been applied to the body to preserve it.[29] Similar contracted burials have been discovered in the tombs of the Third and Fourth Dynasties near Nuerat, Beni Hasan, with the limbs separately wrapped in linen and

the whole body covered with cloth.³⁰ No traces were found of attempts to embalm the tissues, whereas the body in a mastaba of the Pyramid Age (c. Fifth Dynasty) at Medum was shrunk, wrapped in a linen cloth, then modelled all over with resin into the natural form and plumpness of the living figure, completely restoring all the fullness of the form. The eyes and eyebrows were painted on the outer wrapping with green, and the generative organs were modelled with precision showing signs of circumcision. The viscera had been removed and embalmed in a recess in the south end of the chamber in the form of lumps of resined matter wrapped round in linen, while the body cavity of the mummy had been packed with linen soaked in resin. The head had been broken off by violators of the tomb but carefully replaced with a stone under it to keep it in position.³¹

At Deshasheh on the western edge of the plain about sixty miles south of Cairo, in a long trench grave of the Fifth Dynasty on the top of the hill lay the body of a young man on its back with the head towards the north in a coffin carefully placed in a recess. Upon the breast a stout head-rest was set on end, and the generative organs were modelled in cloth in their correct positions. The body was fully wrapped in linen, and the skin and ligaments were firm and strong. There were no signs, however, of embalming or mummification, but, nevertheless, the body had been preserved intact by desiccation. In the well at the foot of the coffin the head of a calf lay face downwards, and on the floor of the well at the other end was the calf's haunch. On the left side, looking out to the well, were two eyes painted opposite the head, and on the inside in addition to a list of offerings was a list of seven sacred oils which might indicate an acquaintance with embalmment.³²

"Substitute Heads"
In two graves of the Sixth Dynasty, Professor Junker found the corpse covered first with a fine linen cloth to protect the mouth, ear and nose from a layer of stucco-plaster which was then applied and modelled according to the form of the body. The

head was so accurately followed that in one case the fallen-in nose and twisted mouth could be clearly seen. In two other instances only the head was covered with the plaster, and on the linen enveloping the head of Idew II the face was painted.[33] These plaster-covered heads he connects with the "substitute heads" carefully portraying the facial features in limestone found among the grave furniture at the beginning of the Old Kingdom (c. 2900 B.C.). Their function, he suggests, was, therefore, that of a portrait statue of the deceased to take the place of the mummy if and when it should fall to pieces. For this reason they were made of the natural size, and they occur only in tombs in which statues or statue-chambers are absent.

Portrait Statues

That effigies of the dead were regarded as permanent substitutes for the corpse is shown by their being accorded the same ritual treatment by the mortuary priests as the actual mummy. Thus, in the periodical funeral services performed in the tomb-chapel it was important that the smoke of the incense should envelop the statue, and to it the food offerings were made in the prescribed manner.[34] Indeed, it would seem that in early times the reanimation of the dead man took place before the statue and not before the mummy. Thus, the rubric states that the ceremony called the "Opening of the Mouth" be performed on behalf of the statue in the "House of Gold"; that is to say, in the actual workshop where the statue was made. Even as late as the New Kingdom (c. 1546 B.C.) it was still depicted in the wall-paintings sometimes as the recipient of these rites.[35]

It is hardly surprising, therefore, that the sculptor was called "he who makes to live" (*s'nh*), and the making and reanimation of a portrait statue was described as a creative act; a rebirth or renewal of life. Similarly, the mortuary priest whose duty it was to supply the needs of the deceased in the hereafter, was for this reason called "servant of the *ka*", and whatever he provided for the *ka* was shared by him with his protégé.[36]

The corpse lying at the bottom of the tomb-shaft in the mastaba[37] was too inaccessible for ritual purposes to be the actual recipient of the funerary rites performed in the chapel above ground, or in the case of the pharaoh, in the pyramid temple. Therefore, it was to the statue as the substitute for the body that the libations were offered and the food and drink presented, just as in the temples the cultus was held before the statue of the god. But before the portrait statue could be employed as the *simulacrum* of the deceased it had to be fashioned with as close a resemblance to the actual person as possible, and then as it were "brought to life" by an elaborate ritual process of restoring the bodily functions and attributes one by one. This act of "Opening of the Mouth" (*Upt-ro*) is mentioned in the ancient texts in close connexion with the fashioning of the statue by the sculptor.[38] In all probability the rite was held where the statue was actually made; in the first instance perhaps in a chamber in the pyramids, since the Egyptian mortuary ritual was derived ultimately from that performed on behalf of the pharaoh in death and in life (e.g. the Toilet ceremonial). Thus, the lustrations in the "House of the Morning" which the king underwent daily, and especially before officiating as the high priest, were repeated at death in the process of the mummification of the corpse and the creation of the portrait statue, the royal ritual being extended to all and sundry when the hope of becoming Osiris after death became a universal aspiration.

The "Opening of the Mouth" Ceremony
Although "The Book of the Opening of the Mouth" was not compiled until the Nineteenth Dynasty, it and the subsequent copies in the Twentieth and Twenty-sixth Dynasties describe rites which originated among the early inhabitants of the Nile valley, and reproduce ancient formulae recited during their performance to reconstitute the body of the deceased and restore to it its *ba* and *ka*.[39] The earliest mention of the observance is in the sculptured tomb of Methen belonging to the Fourth Dynasty[40] when the cult of Osiris came into increasing prominence, but some of the rites may have been in use in predynastic times.[41] In any case, it seems to have been performed on a statue in the first instance and to have consisted in its purification

with holy water sprinkled from different vessels, censings and the presentation of balls of natron. An ox was then slain and its foreleg cut off and given to the statue. The eyes, nose and ears were touched with a copper chisel and various magical instruments, one of which was a rod ending with the head of a ram and called "Great Magician". With this the priest pronounced the formula, "I open thy mouth with the Great Magician wherewith the mouth of every god is opened". Then finally, after a goat and a goose had been beheaded, the statue was invested with a head-dress, clothes and jewels and royal insignia. So arrayed it was anointed and again censed, the rite terminating with a sacred meal served on an altar. It was the duty of the king to perform the reanimation ceremony of the portrait statue of his father.

With the development of the worship of Osiris the rite became practically a repetition of that which was said and done by the sons of Horus for his father (Osiris). As Osiris had become a living soul by receiving from his son Horus the latter's eye, which had been lost in the conflict with Seth, so the body of a dead man must be similarly reanimated by the restoration of the faculties of the living person. It was this that was accomplished in the Opening of the Mouth ceremony, first on the portrait statue, and finally, as it was stereotyped in the Eighteenth Dynasty, on the actual mummy, so that the deceased might be able to take part in the funerary ritual in the chapel at his tomb.[42] The procedure was, however, practically identical with that adopted in the Opening of the Mouth of the statue. The body was purified with holy water, embalmed and censed; the mouth of the mummy was touched with the foreleg of the ox and other sacred objects; the faculties were restored one by one; the toilet ceremonies were re-enacted; a sacred meal was eaten by the mourners, and the coffin was duly installed in the grave.[43]

Making a Mummy
The process of mummification which found its climax in the Opening of the Mouth was essentially a religious act whereby

the dead man was made into a living soul (*ba*) after the technical skill of the embalmers had rendered the body imperishable and the ritual acts of the priests had reconstituted the mental faculties. First, after washing the corpse in Nile water, the brain was extracted through the nostrils by a metal hook and the internal organs were removed, leaving only the heart (and possibly the kidneys) in position. The heart being the seat of life, it had to remain to resume its functions when the operations were complete. The corpse was next soaked in a salt-bath for a considerable time and the epidermis peeled off, while the viscera was embalmed separately, and until the Twenty-first Dynasty placed in canopic jars with stoppers representing the heads of the four sons of Horus familiar in tombs from the Fourth Dynasty onwards. When the body was taken out of the salt-bath it was washed in a conventionalized manner before it was carefully desiccated to free it from all moisture by either placing it in the sun or over a slow fire. When this had been accomplished—and the permanence of the preservation depended largely upon efficient drying of the corpse—embalmment began.

Resin mixed with natron and animal fat were applied to the surface, or poured over the body in a molten condition, and caused to penetrate into every cavity and crevice, and into the structure of the bones. Linen wads dipped in the mixture were packed into the body-cavity, the cranium and the nostrils, the orifices being sealed sometimes with a lump of resin or wax. The body and limbs were then treated with resinous paste and separately wrapped, appropriate spells from the prescribed liturgy being recited during the anointing and bandaging. In and after the Twenty-first Dynasty the viscera was separately embalmed and wrapped in linen parcels and restored to the body-cavity before it was finally packed with preservative material.

The substances used for embalming, which included in addition to natron and resin, incense, cedar oil, honey, olive oil and wax, were regarded as possessed of life-giving qualities which it was maintained had exuded from the body of Osiris, or some other god, or to have been the tears of the gods when they wept for the murdered divine hero (Osiris). Amulets of great potency were inserted in the bandages, on the body, and round the neck, long utterances being recited by a priest during their placing in position. They included a model of the Eye of Horus and the heart-scarab in hard greenstone, or the *crux ansata*, bestowed for the purpose of restoring life to the heart and preventing it witnessing against the owner at the time of judgment. Upon it was inscribed a legend in which it was addressed as the *ka* of the body, "the Khnum (ram-headed Creator-god) who makes my limbs to prosper".[44]

The Burial Rites

The mummification ritual having been completed in strict accord with that which was done by Anubia, the divine funerary physician, to the dismembered body of Osiris to restore it to life and to render it immortal, the mummy was placed in an elaborately decorated coffin, and together with the canopic jars containing the viscera, returned to the family for the burial rites. From its home it was taken to the place of burial in solemn procession on a sledge drawn by a pair of oxen, or in earlier times it was transported in a boat by canal and along the Nile, accompanied by professional mourners, priests and relatives. At the necropolis, ornamented with pictures and hieroglyphic inscriptions illustrating the cult of the dead, the procession was met by musicians and dancers, and the mourners partook of a meal before the ceremonial entrance into the tomb was made and the Opening of the Mouth ceremony performed, when the rites had been transferred from the statue to the mummy. Finally, to enable the dead man to leave the tomb and enjoy the delights of the next life depicted on the walls of the necropolis, he was equipped with the Book of the Dead.[45]

When the worship of Osiris was first established at Abydos it was believed that those who were buried there would come under his protection in the next life, rising from death to immortality, and share in his offerings on festivals. Therefore, in the first instance the bodies of the kings, and then those who could afford the very heavy costs of elaborate mummification, the purchase of a tomb at Abydos and the transport of the mummy to it, were taken to the cult-centre of Osiris (Abydos), often by way of Busiris in the Delta where the "House of Osiris" was situated, there to appear before the dead god. If it was not possible to buy a tomb at the sacred site the mummy was transported to Abydos to rest there for a time in order to imbibe its life-giving qualities and its holy influences and associations before being buried in its local cemetery. Even commoners depicted on the walls of their tombs representations of the royal obsequies, though the transportations of the deceased was in their case purely a ritual procedure. For the most part they had to rely on natural desiccation or simple methods of embalmment, and on portrait statues, for their survival in and beyond the grave.

That attempts at mummification go back to Neolithic times is suggested by the retention of the hieratic use of a flint knife to make the incision for the extraction of the viscera throughout the history of the ritual. This is supported by the occurrence of canopic jars, and the bandaging of bodies, sometimes with traces of embalmment, at the beginning of the Dynastic period. It was not, however, until the Fifth Dynasty that the more elaborate methods were crystallized in the form in which they became the characteristic feature of the cult of the dead in Ancient Egypt.

CHAPTER V

The Cult of the Dead

HAVING examined in some detail the available material connected with sepulture and mortuary ritual that has survived from prehistoric times, it now remains to attempt an interpretation of the data in the light of an anthropological study of the cult of the dead among living primitive peoples. Although this evidence cannot be expected to yield precise information about the significance of the beliefs and customs of Early Man, nevertheless it affords a glimpse of the meaning and purpose of identical practices in vogue under conditions not very different from those that prevailed at the dawn of human history. As man always has been phenomenally conservative in his attitude towards death and the dead, there can be little doubt that in these respects the cultus in remoter regions on the fringes of civilization has not undergone very fundamental changes throughout the ages.

THE DISPOSAL OF THE BODY

Thus, the treatment of the body before civilization had truly begun was almost identical with that adopted in areas where it has scarcely yet penetrated, at any rate until very recent times. From the Mousterian onwards, in both cases, the dead have been placed in graves dug in the ground, often but not always in the contracted position, and supplied with food and drink and other offerings, such as red ochre, shells, amulets and ornaments, believed to be necessary for sustenance on the journey to the next world and efficacious for the renewal of the life of the body, or its spiritual counterpart, beyond the grave, and for its status in the hereafter. The simplest procedure has been interment either in the contracted or extended position in a trench or in a cist of stone slabs, sometimes impregnated with red ochre as a vitalizing agent, and generally equipped with grave-goods. As in the Dordogne in the Palaeolithic, burials of this nature often have been in caves, which may or may not have been used for habitation.

Cave-burial

Disposal in caves, adopted in the first instance for practical reasons of security and secrecy, may have suggested the widespread belief in a subterranean land of the dead, since caverns appear to lead into the depths of the earth. Kruijt, in fact, maintains that in Indonesia the mortal remains are placed in a cave or hole in the ground because these are regarded as the entrances to the underworld. So fundamental was this belief, he contends, that at one time it was universally held in this region, as is shown, he thinks, by the existence of bone-caves among peoples who now place their hereafter in a mountain or a valley.[1] But although it is prevalent, cave-burial is and has been more widely adopted than the conception of a subterranean hereafter, and the correlation is by no means established. Not infrequently the souls of the dead are thought either to remain on earth or to return to the island which was their original home.[2] Therefore, it would seem more likely that in Indonesia the association of the underworld with cave-burial arose as a later interpretation of the earlier form of disposal.

Elsewhere in the Pacific where the dead are interred in caves, particularly in the case of chiefs, the practice often has been adopted to prevent the bodies being molested. In Easter Island, for instance, the corpses of an uncle and two nephews, after being exposed, were lowered with a rope down the crevasses of the cliff in order to evade the enemy.[3] In Aneityum, New Hebrides, where the underworld belief does not occur, it was the custom to bury a chief with his head above ground. Female mourners watched the grave until the skin on the skull was decomposed, after which it was deposited in a cave.[4] In the Banks Islands the normal method is inhumation, but burial in caves also occurs,[5] though it does not appear to have any particular significance with regards to the hereafter. The same applies elsewhere in southern Melanesia, where, in spite of the predominance of the belief in an underworld, a variety of very diverse ways of disposing of the dead have been adopted. Of these the commonest has been interment coupled with the preservation of the skull and certain other bones of the skeleton after exhumation, which sometimes may be kept in caves or in houses for safety.[6]

The Skull-cult

The special attention paid to the skull is reminiscent of the cult of skulls which, as we have seen, has been a recurrent feature of the mortuary ritual of Early Man since it was first encountered in the caves on Dragon-bone Hill near Choukoutien in China at the beginning of the Pleistocene period.[7] While commoners are interred in the usual place of burial where the bones are collected after the flesh has decayed, and heaped on one side, as in the collective Almerian tombs,[8] the corpse of an important person is hung up in his son's house, either in a canoe or enclosed in the figure of a sword-fish. After the lapse of perhaps a year, the bones are buried in the family ossuary but the skull and jaw-bone are enclosed in the figure of a bonito-fish, and set up in the house or in the public charnel-house (*oba*), where they remain. A man may treat the body of his wife in this way and keep her jaw in a basket in the house as a memorial, offering food to the relics from time to time.[9] In the Malay Archipelago after the funeral feast the skulls are washed and taken to the house in baskets where offerings are placed before them. In due course they are deposited in a cave in the mountains.[10]

Secondary Burial

Among the Trobriand islanders, two months after burial the body is exhumed and the bones collected, taken to the seashore or into the bush, where they are smoked over a slow fire. When this process of desiccation is complete they are put in a basket and given in charge of the widow, who keeps it by her side. Three months later a feast is held, and she is then allowed to go to the gardens, but before doing so she must make sure that the basket is guarded by one of her children until she returns to the house. At the end of two months it is placed in a cleft of the cliff, the widow having first painted a horizontal black mark across the forehead of the skull.[11] In Australia the bones are collected from the tree or platform on which the body has been exposed after death, packed in sheets of paper-bark and hidden in a cave, buried in an anthill, or put in the fork of a dead tree. The Warramunga smash into fragments the cranium and all the bones except the radius, and bury them in an anthill. The radius is carefully wrapped up in paper-bark and fastened with fur-string in the shape of a torpedo about 18 inches long and 3 or 4 inches in diameter. One end is decorated with owl or emu feathers, and secreted in the hollow of a gum-tree. The next day it is taken back to the camp just before sunset, where it is wailed over by the women, who cut their thighs and scalps with yam-sticks. For seventeen days the bone is hidden away in the wurley, or bough shelter, of an old woman in whose charge it is placed until at the final ceremonies it is broken with a tomahawk and interred in a little pit on the ceremonial ground near a drawing of the totem of the deceased and certain sacred trees. The grave is filled in with earth and the opening closed with a large flat stone.[12] Thus, the deceased is gathered to his or her totem.

In the Narrinyeri and some of the tribes on the Adelaide plain the skull has been used as a drinking-vessel. A piece of fur-string was fixed to the occiput through the foramen magnum on one side, and to the frontal portion on the other, through the orbital cavities.[13] Parts of the body must be eaten by the mourners in Queensland and the Northern Kimberleys and elsewhere, either before it is exposed in a tree or during the process of drying over a fire or in the sun after the internal organs have been removed and the bones and dried skin made into a bundle to be carried by the mourners from camp to camp. This cannibalistic feast is said to be a symbol of respect and regret for the dead,[14] but over and above this it was doubtless for the purpose of imbibing their qualities. In the Queensland region it is associated with attempts to preserve the body for the period of mourning by evisceration, until at the end of the rites it is cremated, interred or placed in a cave or in the hollow of a tree. On the south-west of the Gulf of Carpentaria usually it is a preliminary to exposure on platforms, and in the south-east it forms parts of the interment ritual. In the north the bodies of the mourners are smeared with the exudations from the corpse.[15] These more elaborate modes of disposal are reserved, however, for chiefs and members of their family, warriors and other fully initiated men who are in the prime of life and full of vitality. But since the bundle is to be preserved only for the duration of the period of the mourning ceremonies, which coincide with that of revenge to compensate for the death, it is in a very different category from that of the mummy in Ancient Egypt.

Concerning the ultimate fate of the departed in primitive society generally there is little or no interest. As one member of the community after another is dispatched to the unseen world with the prescribed mortuary rites, gradually each in his turn is forgotten by his kinsfolk and descendants, his name is never mentioned, and his mortal remains are concealed in some secret and inaccessible spot, such as a cave or crevice, lest molestation of the body should bring vengeance on the survivors. As a precaution against the return of the dead to their former haunts and relatives, tight flexing, blindfolding or mutilation is not infrequently adopted; or the corpse may be taken by a circuitous route to the grave, the mourners making loud noises, unpleasant odours, and brandishing weapons to scare away the ghost. In Melanesia it is driven forth with bull-roarers and conch-shells in the Banks Islands,[16] and everywhere the final funerary feast is the occasion for speeding the departing guest to a land of no-return through a process of initiation into the next life and the ceremonial disposal of the body. Revenge is liable to occur in the case of those who have died violent deaths, or who may be thought to have a grudge against the living or against life for any reason (e.g. childlessness and the unmarried). Since so much depends on the valid and punctilious performance of the obsequies in keeping the dead at bay and happily installed in their proper realm and status, no pain, must be spared in conforming to the prescribed procedures which very often includes the taking back of the body, or of some vital part of it like the skull, to its home when death has occurred at a distance.

Nevertheless, while fear is and has been a very prominent feature of the cult of the dead, the main purpose of the mortuary ritual is by no means confined to rendering the deceased harmless to the survivors. When this is the motive it is accomplished by making him at peace with himself and in harmony with his new surroundings in the spirit-world; and also by removing from those who have come into intimate contact with the corpse and the mystery of death the dangerous sacred contagions they have contracted. The general attitude displayed in the cult of the dead, therefore, is that usually adopted by primitive people in the presence of any ambivalent sacred object, namely a combination of the fear, respect and reverence shown to a being who is half-god and half-devil, or perhaps god and devil by turns.

Preservation and Cremation

Thus, on the one hand a determined effort is made to dispose of the dead as summarily and surely as possible, and, on the other hand, to keep the physical body, or its surrogate, intact either permanently or for a specified period. How closely these two desires are connected is shown by the intimate relation which exists between what might appear to be diametrically opposed modes of disposal, i.e. preservation and cremation. In Australia, as we have seen, after the flesh had been consumed at a cannibalistic feast the bones and desiccated skin sometimes have been made into a mummy bundle by the legs being flexed tightly against the body and the knees trussed up, and in this form preserved for ritual purposes until it was disposed of, often by cremation. Peruvian mummies are similarly compressed, and in Nicaragua a chief after death was wrapped in clothes and suspended by ropes before a fire till the corpse was baked to dryness. When it had been preserved for a year, it was taken

The Disposal of the Body

to the market-place and burned, the belief being that the smoke went "to the place where the dead man's soul was".[17] In Florida, where the dead are said to have been clothed in rich coverings, dried before a fire, and placed in a niche in a cave, fragments of half-incinerated human bones were found in a mound at Cade's Point near Santa Fé Lake in association with other skulls showing no signs of the action of fire.[18]

Similarly blackened human bones embedded in charcoal have been discovered in native cemeteries in British Honduras[19] and east of the Mississippi.[20] In a Cherokee mound at Chote, in the valley of the Little Tennessee, skulls and other bones have been found resting on coals and ashes, and in one burnt-clay sepulchre in this district a corpse had been placed face upwards and covered with mortar. On this was built a fire so that the body was encased in an entire shield of pottery.[21] Among the Aztecs in Mexico the corpse was washed in aromatic water before it was placed on the pyre. This may have been a survival of mummification, since in the series of pictures depicting the Michoacan funeral rite in the sixteenth-century Spanish MS. *Relacion de los ceremonios y rites de Michoacan* the actual body is shown swathed in rolls of cotton and carried on the heads of bearers to be consumed on a blazing fire. Or, again, in a painting at Chichen Itza in Yucatan the preparation of a corpse for cremation is represented with the body opened to extract the heart and viscera, which, after being charred, are to be preserved in a stone urn with cinnabar.[22]

Desiccation and Mummification

In the Basket-maker caves in Northern Arizona bodies were sometimes wrapped in blankets and woven clothes and strung together in the flexed position in the form of mummy-bundles resembling those depicted in the Mexican MSS.[23] At Kimboko in the Kayenta district they were encased in masses of hardened adobe, indicating that they had been packed into cists at the time of interment.[24] In the Lower Mimbres valley in Southern New Mexico the skeletons were tightly packed in red clay, each one resting separate and alone, with large perforated dishes placed over their faces,[25] as in the Lausitz ossuaries.[26] The saltpetre caves in this region have been used extensively for burial, the bodies found in them having been desiccated intact with the skin on most of them almost unbroken, and adorned with anklets, shell ornaments and bracelets of beautifully plaited straw. Next to the skin was a coarse cotton cloth, between the legs a large wad of cotton (sometimes dyed red or indigo) with the feathers of the turkey, the large woodpecker, and the blue jay. Near the head stood a large earthenware jar and in some cases drinking gourds.[27]

In the Eastern States similar burials occurred in the saltpetre caves in Kentucky. In one instance the mummy was placed in a sitting position between broad stones arranged edgewise with a flat stone covering the whole structure. The corpse was enveloped in coarse clothes and wrapped in deer skins, the hair of which was shaved off. Utensils, beads, feathers and other ornaments were enclosed with it in the stone coffin. In the mammoth cave, Kentucky, the body of a woman was in such a remarkable state of preservation that many of the features were discernible. But in none of these natural mummies was there any sign of a suture or incision in the abdomen indicative of the removal of the viscera.[28] This suggests that the process of mummification had been purely natural by desiccation. Nevertheless, the fact that they were clad and adorned with ornaments, or mudded into cists, shows that the bodies had been deliberately placed in the caves because of the preservative properties they contained.

Along the Alaskan coast, on the other hand, evisceration was practised, evidently through the pelvis. After cleansing the cavity from fatty matter, it was then dried in the sun, wrapped up in the form of a mummy-bundle, unless it was placed in a life-like posture, dressed and armed.[29] The Aleutian islanders embalmed the bodies of the men with dried moss and grass, buried them in their best attire in a sitting position in a strong box with their darts and instruments, and decorated the tomb with varied-coloured mats, embroidery and paintings.[30] In a cave in the island of Kagamale, the body of a chief was covered with the fine skins of the sea-otter, as a mark of great distinction, and enclosed in a basket-like structure over which a fish-net was thrown made of the sinews of the sea-lion, and a bird-net. Among the grave furniture were wooden vessels, green stones used for tanning skins, and locks of hair.[31] It is not improbable that these more elaborate methods of preservation were introduced from Asia where among the Ainu anal evisceration was practised and the body dried in the sun. In Virginia the skin was flayed off the bodies of kings, the flesh was removed from the bones which were dried in the sun before they were put back into the skin and the empty spaces filled with white sand. To prevent the skin from corrupting or shrinking, it was oiled.[32]

In the Pacific, evisceration and artificial embalming, though by no means unknown in the obsequies of chiefs and their families, is of comparatively rare occurrence. In Samoa the operation was performed by women in houses built for the purpose. The viscera was removed and buried, and then the body was anointed daily with a mixture of oil and aromatic juices. To enable the juices of the body to escape it was punctured all over with fine needles, and after a lapse of about two months the process of desiccation was completed. The hair, which had been cut off, was then glued on the scalp by resin, the abdomen was filled with folds of cloth with which also the body was bandaged and laid on a mat with the face and head exposed. From time to time the face was oiled with a mixture of oil and turmeric, and so successful was the mummification that bodies embalmed and exposed for over thirty years were found in a remarkable state of preservation. The practice, however, has now been discontinued because the family of chiefs responsible for it has died out.[33]

Similarly, in addition to their established custom of preserving human heads, the Maoris in the South Island of New Zealand sometimes have preserved for considerable periods the bodies of their chiefs and revered dead by draining the contents of the stomach through the anus and removing the brain, in a small enclosure erected for the purpose and decorated with bird feathers and sacred carvings. The body is then very carefully dried in an oven beneath it containing special preservative woods and leaves so that the likeness of the individual is retained. It is placed in a sitting posture inside its own hut, and in the case of a chief the door is opened on occasions to enable people to gaze upon him and make addresses to him.[34]

In Mangaia Island, one of the Cook group in the South Pacific, the bodies of the dead were anointed with scented oil, carefully wrapped up in a number of pieces of cloth, and either buried in the earth within the precincts of the sacred enclosure (*marae*), or hidden away in caves which constituted the royal mausoleums of the ruling families, in which hundreds of mummies are well preserved on ledges of stalactite or wooden platforms. When the bodies were buried in the ground they were laid face downwards and tightly flexed with sennit cord, the chin and the knees meeting. The body was covered with earth and large stones were placed over the grave, which was visited periodically by relatives. Occasionally the corpse was exposed to the sun, reanointed with oil and wrapped in fresh cloth, but it was not eviscerated.[35]

In Tahiti desiccation was effected by pressing the different parts of the body, drying it in the sun by day in the sitting position, and anointing it with fragrant oils. At night it was turned over so that it might not remain long on the same side. Sometimes the intestines and the brain were removed and the cavity was filled with cloth saturated with perfumed oils, which were also injected into other parts of the body, and rubbed over the skin every day. When the muscles were completely dried up the mummy was clothed and placed in the sitting posture before a small altar at which fruit, food and flowers were offered daily by the relatives or the "chantry" priest. In this condition it was kept until it began to decay after several months. The skull was then carefully preserved by the family, and the bones and desiccated remains were buried within the precincts of the family *marae*.

When the embalmment began a special priest, known as "the corpse praying priest", interceded with the god, by whom it was thought the soul of the deceased had been required, that all the guilt he had incurred might remain with him. A hole was dug and a post was set up in it as a personification of the dead man, to remain after the mummy had decayed. Earth was thrown over it and the hole filled in to conceal and contain the evil. Taking a number of slips of the plantain leaf-stalk, the priest placed two or three under each arm of the corpse and on the breast, saying "there are your family, your child, your wife, your father and your mother. Be satisfied in the land of spirits, and look not towards those who are left in this world." Until this ceremony had been performed all who were employed in the embalmment were carefully avoided since they were in a taboo condition both as a result of their contact with the corpse and with the guilt of the sin for which he had died. At its conclusion they fled to the sea to cleanse themselves from their pollution by bathing in it, and casting the clothes they had worn into it. Having completed their ablutions they collected up a few pieces of coral from the sea and returned to the deceased, saying "with you may the pollution be", and threw the coral on the top of the hole at the grave. The bodies, however, did not long remain intact, and by the end of a year the bones had been collected and deposited either in secret caverns or in their homes, lest in time of war they should be desecrated by the victors.[36]

Images of the Dead
As in Ancient Egypt, desiccation and mummification often have been associated with the substitution of improvised portrait statues or images of the dead, either as the temporary abode of the ghost for ritual purposes during the period of mourning, or to become the surrogate of the body after the preserved tissues have decayed. Thus, in Mexico, for example, the image of a dead king was arrayed with the royal insignia and honoured with addresses and presents as though it were the sovereign himself. In the same district when a trader died away from home a figure of him was carved in wood, ornamented, and after the mourning ceremonies had been duly performed in

conjunction with it, was incinerated and the ashes were interred.[37] After a battle an effigy representing the warriors slain was burned in front of the temple and the ashes were sprinkled on the relatives while the actual bodies were buried where they died.[38]

Along the North-west Pacific coast in British Columbia portrait statues and posts have been found between the Skeena and Nass rivers, "made as life-like as possible". In one image, which originally had been clothed and ornamented, the cremated remains of the body were concealed in the trunk. At Kitzegukela on the Skeena river, the image of a man who had committed suicide was completely clothed and seated on the box containing his ashes. In his hands were the musket and bullets with which he had shot himself. In this district there are traditions of similar statues at places where men who have died on the trail were cremated and effigies have been erected to personify or commemorate their corporeal presence.[39]

Three large wooden posts representing human figures, and several subordinate posts, occur at Tununuk village, Cape Vancouver, arrayed in a row parallel to the beach and across the front of the central dwelling. These are said to symbolize people who have been lost at sea and their bodies never recovered. The top of each post was carved in the form of a human head and neck, and the one that was set up for a woman who had been buried by a landslide was covered with a fur hood. The mouth and eyes were made of ivory inlaid with wood, and walrus tusks were inserted for arms and legs.[40] The cemeteries of the villages in this district were full of carved images of this kind, some of which had wooden masks representing the human face with inlaid eyes and mouths, and votive offerings in abundance hanging from various parts of the body.

The Diegueño, who formerly lived in and around San Diego, California, at the *fiesta* of the images made effigies of eagle feathers, matting and cloth which were supposed to contain the spirits of the dead. The face was carefully constructed and the characteristic features were reproduced as closely as possible in the image. The mouth was painted red outside and black within, the teeth were shaped in pearls, and the eyes were made of abalone shell with the pupils of black wax. Bunches of eagle and of yellow-hammer feathers were stuck on the shoulders, and strings of beads and other ornaments disposed upon it. Around the neck was hung a net containing two small vessels with food and drink for the ghost on its journey to the spirit-world. As soon as the image was completed it was thought to be occupied by the spirit of the deceased, and at the end of the *fiesta*, which occupied a week devoted to ceremonial dancing, it was burned, together with offerings of blankets, clothing and other articles, in order to free the indwelling soul.[41]

Thus an effigy may be regarded as a temporary substitute for the body, providing the spirit with a habitation while the funerary rites are in progress and then discarded when it is no longer required. But in the Diegueño *fiesta* it was made to represent the likeness of the person for whose mortal remains it was the surrogate, like the portrait-statue in Egypt. Therefore, it had a vital connexion with him and the physical integument. Consequently, if the image was the equivalent of the corpse, the fact that it was burned at the end of the rite to free the soul suggests an intimate relation between the preservation and cremation of the dead. Thus, the making of mortuary effigies as the counterpart of the mummy would seem to be an important link connecting the two modes of disposal. From the prehistoric evidence interment appears to have been the original form of burial in trench graves, very frequently in the flexed or contracted position. The motive may have been partly to prevent the return of the ghost to molest the living, but also to provide him with a permanent habitation in the hereafter; though, doubtless, once the rites had been duly performed little further thought or care was bestowed upon the departed. Nevertheless, the grave was made as secure and durable as possible, and as the technique of sepulture developed, tombs became increasingly elaborate in their construction, as is demonstrated in the Egyptian pyramids and the megalithic graves, while special methods were adopted for either preserving or disposing of the body.

Natural desiccation doubtless played an important part in concentrating attention upon the continuation of human existence after death in the same physical body in which it had formerly functioned. This in Egypt led to an ever-increasing elaboration of the artificial methods of mummification to render the mortal remains imperishable, to preserve the likeness of the deceased and to restore the missing faculties by ritual devices. These attempts at preservation in a modified form have become a permanent heritage in the cult of the dead in primitive states of culture in areas as widely separated as Oceania and the New World from which regions and for this reason for the purposes of illustration most of our examples have been taken. But the labour and cost involved in the more complex processes of evisceration, embalmment and sepulture, restricted this type of burial to rulers and the privileged few who could afford the expense. For the rest of the community simpler and cheaper ways and means had to be found without materially affecting the underlying beliefs, except where two entirely different funerary traditions were maintained for rulers and commoners. Natural desiccation in dry sand or saltpetre caves could only be resorted to where the right conditions prevailed. An alternative widely adopted both in prehistoric times and in modern primitive societies has been to dry the body over a fire, or to smoke a putrefying corpse. Sometimes only the head has been preserved, or the bones have been tied up in a bundle with preservative substances and kept by the near of kin until the secondary burial. Images also have been employed as substitutes for the body, and, therefore, have been treated as the real person. To transform the effigy into the human being, parts of the corpse or the ashes of the cremated relics have been transferred to it.

THE AFTER-LIFE

The Relation of Body and Soul

The provision of substitutes treated as surrogates of the physical organism no doubt has given emphasis to the idea of the existence of a spirit or soul separable from the mortal body.

hus, like cremation with which, as we have seen, it has been
ery closely associated, it has facilitated the conception of man
s a psycho-physical duality of body and soul, each indepen-
lent of the other. As long as attention has been concentrated
n the body, its burial and preservation in an "everlasting
tomb" and imperishable mummy, the next life inevitably has
been interpreted in terms of a continuation of the present
existence. But if the life that survived the dissolution was
capable of transference to some other object, of transmigration
to another body, or of returning to the spirit-world whence it
came in the smoke of its physical integument, the way was
open for a less materialistic doctrine of immortality.

The primitive mind, however, being not prone to abstract
thought, apparently has never been able to conceive of survival
apart from a concrete entity of some kind, be it that of the
human body, an animal, a spirit or a god. Hence the prevalence
of the idea of reincarnation and transmigration, the cult of
heroes, and of an after-life lived in a terrestrial paradise or on
the isles of the blest, located often in the traditional home of
the tribe, after a brief sojourn in the vicinity of the grave during
the period of mourning and the performance of the transitional
rites. The destruction of the corpse by fire no doubt has tended
to foster the belief in the liberation of the spirit regarded as an
independent entity only temporarily housed in the body, and
of wafting it to the sky, as in the Tyrian version of the legend
of Herakles in which the hero is said to have ascended in the
smoke of his funeral pyre.[42]

Fire very frequently has been thought to be a spiritualizing
agent, and for this reason sacrificial offerings have been burnt
to liberate their vital essence. Thus, among the Semites children
were "passed through the fire" to convert their material nature
into an immaterial, just as Demeter at Eleusis endeavoured to
render the infant son of Keleos immortal by bathing him in
the fire.[43] In Brahmanic ritual in India three sacred fires were
kindled to assist the soul in its ascent to the sky, each organ
and attribute being conveyed by this means to the corresponding part of the universe.[44] In the New Hebrides the soul was

believed to rise to the sun on the fire kindled at the grave,[45] and in California the ashes of the corpses were scattered in the air to give the disembodied spirit wings so that it mounts up to hover for ever in the upper air, very much as the Diegueño effigy was burnt to free the indwelling soul.

Burial and the After-life

Nevertheless, neither mummification nor cremation can be assigned a consistent eschatological significance. Broadly speaking, it may be true to say that the preservation of the dead normally has been associated with an after-life on, or below, or very closely connected with the earth. But even so in Egypt, the classical home of mummification, when Osiris from being the Lord of the underworld was celestialized, his abode was transferred to the heavenly realms. There those whom he pronounced justified continued their former life in its fullness in the delectable Fields of Aalu, watered by the heavenly Nile, or in the celestial abode of Re where the sun never set. But no attempt was made to substitute cremation for the preservation of the body.

Similarly, while cremation sometimes has been connected with the belief that the dead go to the sun or to some other part of the sky, the correlation is too sporadic to establish a definite association between the mode of disposal and a celestial after-life. Thus, in Melanesia, where Rivers tried to bring them into conjunctions,[46] the evidence is by no means convincing. For example, in Bougainville Malaita, Shortland Island and New Ireland, where cremation is most prevalent, there are very few indications of a belief in a sky-hereafter, while in the Society Islands and the Marquesa, where it occurs, cremation is absent. In the North Pacific coast of America and the surrounding district the notion of a celestial spirit-world is well established, but it is not connected with cremation, and the Hare Indians, who burnt their dead, placed the route to the land of the dead through a subterranean region.[47] In Peru in Inca times mummification was practised but nobles and good commoners were thought to pass to a happier state in the sun, whereas bad commoners lived after death in a state of hunger and misery within the earth.

There is, therefore, no hard and fast rule concerning the treatment of the body and the situation of the abode of the dead. Nevertheless, when modes of burial begin to be stereotyped by tradition they may tend to influence beliefs about the locality and nature of the next life. Once cremation has become the established procedure, for example, the place and function of the physical remains inevitably lose their earlier significance in and beyond the grave, as all that survives of the tissues are a few ashes and possibly some bones which may have been preserved in urns or ossuaries. With the movements of peoples from one district to another the tendency very often seems to have been to regard the original home as the land of the dead whither the ghost returned at death. The belief frequently has influenced not only the mode of disposal but also such aspects of funerary ritual as the orientation of the body in the grave, and the provision made for the journey to the ancestral spirit-world, until finally the actual abode of the dead may have lost its earlier character and locality and become a distant land, either beyond the sea or in a mythical island of the blest, in the palace of the sun in the western part of the sky where light perpetual shines, or in the more sombre nether regions, often regarded as dark and sad where everything is shadowy and unreal and enveloped always in a soft cloudy mist. As these ideas have become intermingled through culture contact and other causes, a confusion between doctrine and practice has arisen, the abode of the dead frequently being a combination of the upper and under worlds, and a western terrestrial paradise connected with the sun and the horizon.

Orientation

Thus, in Western Nuerland in the Nilotic Sudan a man is buried facing east and a woman facing west, but in Eastern Nuerland both sexes are buried facing west because the Eastern Nuer came originally from the west, and it was in Western Nuerland that their ancestors were created. But they also associate the passage from birth to death with the movement of the sun across the sky. "Death follows the setting sun", the Nuer say, and because "the west is the side of death, the east is the side of life".[48] These two beliefs find expression in the orientation of the corpse, which on no account should be buried facing north or south, and in the final mortuary ceremony, four or six months after burial, those taking part in the offering of an ox to liberate the soul of the deceased must sit with their backs to the rising sun and face the direction of the setting sun.[49] The purpose of the rites is to give the dead man the full status of a ghost, and by initiating him into the spirit-world to keep him and the taint of death away from the living and their haunts.

Orientation everywhere usually denotes the route which the dead must take on leaving the body, whether it be towards the final destination of the soul or away from its earthly abode and the dwellings of the living. Thus, those Indians west of the Mississippi who are in the habit of placing the dead with the head towards the south say that they do so in order that the spirit of the deceased may go south, the land from which they believe they originally came.[50] Graves with bodies orientated to the east may be those of Christians who have adopted the traditional Christian posture with feet towards Jerusalem ready to rise at the Judgment to meet Christ on His return to the Mount of Olives.

Orientation has been more particularly observed among people who have a definite conception of the location of the after-life in some specific territory in this world, or a hypothetical land of the rising or setting sun on the horizon, which may be underground since the sun appears to sink beneath the earth in the west in the evening and to emerge again in the morning. Thus, in Indonesia the corpse is often orientated to the west because it is believed that there the underworld is entered at the "hole" where the sun goes down on the horizon to give light to it at night.[51] Sometimes the burial takes place at sunset in order that the sun may take the soul thither as it descends. The Ousun in Borneo adopt the same orientation in the belief that he underworld is in the west, which, however, is also entered through a cave.⁵² In the Malay peninsula the Jakun placed the feet towards the west, while the Mantra deposited the body in the tomb in either a sitting or standing position with the face to the west, but in the case of a child to the east.⁵³

According to the Western Samang, the lay members of the tribe go to a land of screw-pines and thatch-pines across the sea where the hole is situated into which the sun falls at night, unless by reason of their evil deeds they are compelled to turn aside northwards across the sea to a less desirable abode.⁵⁴ But the normal mode of orientation among these Negritos is with the face towards the setting sun, the region towards which the ghost is thought to journey.⁵⁵ The Kensiu in Kedah, however, bury the body with the head to the east with the result that when the soul emerges from the head it does not know the direct way westwards to the kingdom of the dead. It first goes eastwards and then flies upwards until at length it reaches its destination in the west.⁵⁶

In the south-western islands of the Malay Archipelago the usual custom seems to be to orientate the corpse in the direction of the original home of the tribe to which the dead are thought to return.⁵⁷ Thus, the Badoej adopt an east-west position with the head at the west end of the grave and the body lying on its right side so that it faces the land of the dead in the south.⁵⁸ Similarly, in British New Guinea in South Massim the body is placed on its side with the head in the direction of the legendary place of origin of the deceased's clan, while at Wamira the feet of the corpse are towards the direction whence came the clan to which it belonged.⁵⁹ In Borneo the Olo Ngadjoe lay the dead along the river in the direction of the spirit-world, Mambaroeh, which seems to be the traditional tribal home. Thus, the description of the journey made by the spirit recited by the priest at the funeral feast contains the names of various places to be passed *en route* which actually lie on the path to the cradleland of the tribe.⁶⁰ It is not improbable, therefore, that formerly the dead were taken back to the place of origin.

Status

Most of the more elaborate mortuary procedures in primitive societies are confined to the more important section of the community. The common people everywhere generally are buried immediately after death with little or no ceremony or delay. It is only the great ones who are subjected to prolonged funeral rites culminating in final or secondary burial, either at a distance in the real or assumed original home of the tribe, or in a secure and secret place, often associated with the ancestral history and land of the dead, be it in a cave, an ossuary, a remote island, or a sacred tree whence the founders of the community are thought to have emerged. The belief in human survival may be universal, but in primitive states of culture death produces no essential change in status, condition or character. Therefore, as in this life so beyond the grave only men of rank and position, or those who have shown conspicuous valour in battle, or rendered notable service to the community in some other manner, are accorded a blessed hereafter in a special paradise or Valhalla, since the next world is modelled on the pattern of existing society. The gibe "a pie in the sky when you die" as a sop for the less fortunate under mundane conditions, is certainly not applicable to the primitive conception of a future life where privileges enjoyed or denied on earth invariably are rigidly maintained in the mode of disposal of the body and in the final destination of the ghost.

Thus, in Southern Melanesia the underworld is said to be a poorer place, sad and dark, where everything is unreal and shadowy, and the dead are ethereal. It is this undesirable hereafter that is assigned to commoners in Polynesia who, according to Rivers, represent the earlier inhabitants.[61] But however it arose, a clear distinction is made in the nature and location of the after-life between commoners and rulers, the one infinitely inferior to the other. In San Cristoval the bodies of common people are cast into the sea while chiefs are interred, and some relic, such as a tooth or a skull, is preserved in a shrine in the village.[62] Sometimes the corpse of an important person is

The After-life

placed on a wooden platform surrounded by palisades until only the bones remain.[63] In the Shortland Islands commoners are interred or thrown into the sea while chiefs and their wives are burnt.[64] Among the Mafulu of British New Guinea chiefs and their families are laid in boxes or deposited in trees until the platform collapses. Then the skeleton is thrown away except the skull, and the larger bones of the arms and legs, which are interred below in a shallow grave covered with stones, kept in a box on the tree or hung up in the clubhouse (*emone*) till they are required for ritual purposes.[65] In Fiji the canoe that conveys the shades to the next life is thought to be divided in the middle, the one end (*vesi*) being reserved for chiefs, the other (*ndolou*) for commoners. On arrival at the river the shade announces his status and is thereupon assigned his proper position in the boat by the ferryman, Themba.[66]

That Fijian chiefs might be accompanied by their wives in the land of the dead, they (the wives) were often either strangled or buried alive at the funeral of their husbands, and laid at the bottom of the grave beneath the corpse. Sometimes the mother as well as the widow was sacrificed, but husbands were not killed at the death of their wives.[67] The same custom is recorded among the Sulka in New Britain.[68] In New Guinea a widow at her own request might be strangled and buried with her husband, and so acquired an honourable status in the next life,[69] very much as at the death of a Natchez chief there was considerable competition among his highest officers for the privilege of being killed at his obsequies and so to gain a place in his paradise.[70] Thus, the holocaust of wives in the royal tombs at Ur were part of a well-established tradition which has survived throughout the ages until restrictions have been placed upon the practice under the influence of higher civilizations and more humane ideas about the relations of the living and the dead.

For the vast mass of mankind, however, the spirit-world has been regarded as a mutilated existence determined by the status in the existing social structure. Sometimes bravery or cowardice has decided the fate of the soul, as, for example, among the

Haida of Queen Charlotte Islands off the North Pacific coast of America, where those who had not died as warriors went to a desolate region before they were admitted to the celestial realms of light.[71] Women guilty of infanticide and murderers of a kinsman were excluded from the Blackfeet paradise,[72] and cowards, adulterers, thieves and liars, and all who neglected their duties of life, found no admittance to the abode of bliss among the Ojibway, but were condemned to wander up and down among the rocks and morasses, and were stung by gnats as large as pigeons.[73] Only chiefs, hunters and warriors went to the Isles of the Blest reserved for this privileged section of the community,[74] just as the land of the dead beyond the mountains towards the setting sun was confined to chiefs and medicine-men among the Virginian tribes.[75]

The Ancient Mexicans maintained that men killed in war or offered as victims on the sacrificial stone, and women dying in childbirth (who were liable to become malevolent goddesses), joined the emperor and nobility in the Elysium of Huitzilo-pochtli in the eastern part of the sky where honeyed flowers and luscious fruits abounded in shady groves, and hunting was enjoyed in the parks. Dressed as warriors they accompanied the sun daily on its course and fought mock battles till it reached its zenith. Then it was transferred to the charge of the celestial women (e.g. those who had died in childbirth), who lived in the western part of the sun-house, where merchants who died on their journey also dwelt. After two years of this Elysium the souls of warriors were transmigrated into birds of golden plumage, and either returned to the earth or lived in the celestial gardens.[76] Those who were struck by lightning, drowned or died of contagious diseases went to a happy paradise (Calocan) on a mountain in the east. The rest of the people were destined to pass at death to the dreary subterranean region, Mictlan, "a most obscure land where light cometh not and whence none can ever return". There they were sunk in deep sleep, but class distinctions were maintained, the lords and nobles being separated from the commoners in the nine divisions into which it was divided.[77] At the end of the fourth year of residence in this cheerless abode the ninth division was reached, and in this its denizens were annihilated.

Duration

Although it is very rare to find no conception of a future life, endlessness is too abstract a concept for the primitive mind to grasp. Therefore, it is unable to conceive of an objective life for the dead for an indefinite period. Even when the fate of the soul is not an undesirable one and admits of a measure of idealization, it is only of temporary duration. The idea of an eternal and indestructible spirit or essence lies outside its range, which seldom extends beyond the few generations known to the individual, while the tomb is merely a habitation calculated to endure for many ages to come, as indeed it has in the case of Egyptian and megalithic monuments. But the land of the dead is the land of memory, as in Maeterlinck's fantasia, the inhabitants of which gradually pass into oblivion as the recollection of their existence becomes dim among the survivors. The holding of periodic festivals as a kind of "year's mind" has tended to prolong their survival by keeping the living in touch with them. Nevertheless, the feast of the dead and secondary burial usually mark the end of the funerary ritual, and with its termination the shades tend to pass into oblivion. In the case of commoners this is particularly apparent when mortuary rites are reduced to a minimum and the state of the hereafter is ill-defined and insecure. The distinguished and privileged classes, on the other hand, usually are assigned a position which secures for them some degree of permanence even though it may endure only for a limited period. Therefore, rank and status, together with the manner of death, determine the place in and the duration of the after-life.

Grave-goods

Closely associated with status in the spirit-world is the bestowal of grave-goods, which, as we have seen, has been a characteristic feature of funeral ritual from Palaeolithic times onwards. These gifts have generally been explained as the expression of the belief that the ghost has need of food, implements and the many and various articles lavished upon it. This doubtless is true, as is apparent, for example, in the personal necessities like rice, plates, betel-nut, money and similar articles that are laid in the ground with the Sea Dyaks in Borneo, and the baskets, swords, weaving materials, pots, jars and gongs which are placed on the surface. These unquestionably are believed to be carried into the other world "in some mystic way", as Ling Roth says, where they will be useful to the dead. The spirits of the wind, in fact, are invoked to invite the departed to come and feast on the food placed before them at the entrance of their former habitations.[78]

Similarly, the Kayans dress the corpse in its finest clothes and ornaments that he may appear to the best advantage in the next world, putting a bead of some value under each eyelid, apparently to pay for the passage of the ghost across the river of death. In the grave the body is surrounded by the most valuable personal property displayed in the most imposing manner, to indicate when possible that the deceased has been a man of wealth and position. Small packets of cooked rice and of tobacco are placed upon the coffin for the use of the soul, and hundreds of cigarettes sent by friends are hung in bundles about the low platform on which the coffin rests.[79] Among the coast Dusuns of North Borneo sometimes an open umbrella surmounts the grave to keep the spirit of the dead man dry on his last journey.[80]

In the Malay Peninsula the Sakai array their dead in their best garments, place a dagger or chopper on the breast, together with the betel-leaf wallet. As soon as the corpse is lowered into the grave tobacco and betel-nut are offered, and the furniture placed beside the body before the trench is covered up with earth. Rice and cakes are then laid on it, and these offerings are repeated on the third, seventh and hundredth days following. Sometimes, however, after leaving the body on a platform in front of the house for a day, they bury it and either burn or desert the house. Huts are constructed for the soul at the grave and filled with diminutive furniture consisting of models of

The After-life

various utensils and implements used by the deceased and placed in a soul-wallet made of fan-paten leaf.[81] This custom doubtless arose from the belief that the soul remained at the grave for a short time before journeying to its final abode and would seem to belong to the same tradition as that of the soul-chapel in Ancient Egypt. This temporary sojourn of the ghost at the place of the disposal of the body until it is dispatched at the feast of the dead coincides with the period of mourning during which the prescribed tabus have been carefully observed in respect of the grave-goods as well as of the behaviour of the survivors, since the gifts are solely for his own use. Any interference with the personal belongings of the deceased is calculated to call forth his vengeance, and, therefore, for safety's sake they should be buried with him or ritually destroyed. It is very probable, in fact, that the widespread custom of breaking grave-goods has been a precautionary measure rather than, as has been often supposed, a means of liberating their "souls".

This taboo at any rate avoids theft or disturbance inasmuch as it renders the articles useless to the living. Later it may have become interpreted in animistic terms, thereby making them of service to the dead in the hereafter. Primarily, however, it would seem more likely that the practice was associated with the sacredness of the possessions of the deceased upon which his well-being and status in the next life largely depended. As Codrington came to recognize in Melanesia, it was not just that grave-goods should accompany their former owners "in a ghostly manner", but that "they may be a memorial of him as a great and valued man, like the hatchment of old times". Similarly, his fruit-trees are cut down as a mark of respect and affection, not with any notion of these things serving him in the world of ghosts, but that they are sacred to him and so must not be enjoyed by anyone else.[82] Therefore, in Lepers' Island a man is buried with his bow and arrows and his best ornaments; but his pigs'-tusk bracelets are put on upside down. He will be known in the spirit-world to be a great man by his funerary equipment as it actually exists and not in its spiritual form as having "souls".[83] Such a belief may exist side by side with the status value of tomb-furniture, but the value attached to wealth is essentially the prestige it confers both here and hereafter, and so it becomes "the reservoir of highest good", as a sign of rank.[84] Consequently, in addition to food and drink and life-giving amulets, a lavish display of grave-goods confers status on the deceased.

Human Sacrifice

This also probably applies to the offering of human victims as an integral element in funerary ritual, notably the wives and slaves of rulers, constituting as they do an important part of their possessions. Therefore, the widow in particular, but also other members of the retinue of a chief, frequently have to accompany him to the next life at his death. In Fiji, as we have seen, the mother and wives were often strangled or buried alive at the funeral of their husbands, and generally at their own request, in the belief that both they and their husbands thereby attained a higher status in the after-life. As an alternative to the sacrifice of widows they may be treated as virtually dead, as, for example, in Eddystone Island of the Solomons, where the wife of a commoner instead of following her husband in death discards all her ornaments and wears nothing but bark-cloth, and is confined in a small enclosure inside the house. In the case of the widow of a chief she must be quite invisible and sit with her knees drawn up in the contracted position until a successful head-hunter blows the conch in the house. Food is prepared for her in another house, and she is no longer called by her name. She is forbidden to take part in festivals, and to all intents and purposes she is regarded as dead.[85] Therefore, like the rest of the property and possessions of the deceased, she has to be put out of action either permanently or temporarily as part of the death taboo, her life being bound up with that of her husband. The vigil of the widow by the grave, and the many restrictions placed upon her movements and behaviour henceforth, or for a specific period of mourning, would seem to be survivals of the belief that in death as in life she is an integral part of his personal equipment. Therefore, his status and well-being in the hereafter is in great measure determined by his mortuary retinue and the conduct of his relatives and kinsfolk at and after his decease.

THE CULT OF THE DEAD

Thus, viewed in the light of the anthropological evidence, the cult of the dead appears to have been a fundamental element in man's spiritual culture, the roots of which are deeply laid in the archaeological record, and centre in the emotions aroused by the mysterious fact of death and the nature and destiny of human beings. These found expression in the first instance in ritual acts rather than in abstract ideas. Emotional situations arising out of recurrent crises such as death and the hope of immortality require perpetual satisfaction, and it has been around these events that the cult of the dead has taken shape.

From the cradle to the grave human existence has seemed to be in a state of flux, "never continuing in one stay", a dying to be born again, exemplified in the decay and regeneration in nature. This has called forth a series of *rites de passage* at the critical junctures to obtain a fresh outpouring of life and power. By the aid of this transitional ritual from life to death, or from death to life, the tension has been relieved. Death being the gateway to the hereafter the mortuary ritual has had for its purpose the liberation of the deceased from his terrestrial existence and its associations, human and material, and the means whereby he may pass successfully through the dark and dangerous portal and be safely and securely launched on his new career.

Thus, the idea of immortality appears not to have arisen from speculations about a separable soul and phantoms of the living, as was formerly supposed, but from this ritual organization, of which it is the natural corollary. Ever-renewing life is the normal sequence of everyday experience and observation in which death seems to be an intrusion caused by violence and vengeance usually of a supernatural character; this must be overcome by revitalizing energy and life-giving agents such as red ochre, amulets, and all the ritual devices and apparatus employed in the cult of the dead to overcome the fears and contagions with which death is surrounded, and to provide for the well-being of the departed in the spirit-world, however obscure, undefined and limited the state of the hereafter may have been. In all this fear and love have been inextricably intermingled, and the conflict between the mortality of the physical body and the immortality of the body politic has been resolved by the correct observance of the mortuary ceremonial connected with the disposal of the corpse and the eschatological beliefs. Since of all the mysterious disintegrating and critical situations with which man has been confronted death has been the most disturbing and devastating, the equilibrium of the social structure has been largely dependent on the due performance of the funerary ritual. It is not surprising, therefore, that the cult of the dead has occupied such a prominent position, and played an essential role in human society from its first emergence under Palaeolithic conditions.

CHAPTER VI

The Mystery of Birth

TURNING now from the cultus that developed around the mystery of death and human survival to that associated with birth and fertility, the deepest emotions and most heartfelt needs, hopes and fears have been aroused by propagation and nutrition as the vital concern of man in all ages. As Frazer says, "to live and to cause to live, to eat food and to beget children, these were the primary wants of man in the past, and they will be the primary wants of man in the future so long as the world lasts".[1] Therefore, the promotion and conservation of life at all times has been a fundamental urge because an adequate supply of offspring and food is an essential need and a necessary condition of existence, and the production and maintenance of these two basic requirements have been the predominant concern of the human race from the Palaeolithic to the present day. But in the precarious environment in which Early Man had to engage in the struggle for survival the mysterious forces of propagation and nutrition acquired a sacred significance towards which a cautious and numinous attitude was adopted and a ritual technique developed in order to bring them under some measure of magico-religious control.

THE MYSTERY OF BIRTH IN PALAEOLITHIC TIMES

Sculptured "Venuses"

Thus, at the beginning of the Upper Palaeolithic female figurines in bone, ivory and stone, with the maternal organs grossly exaggerated, began to make their appearance in the Gravettian culture as part of the domestic equipment. The breasts are large and pendulous, the hips broad, the buttocks rotund, and excessive corpulency is suggestive of pregnancy. In these so-called "Venuses" of the squat type the face is seldom portrayed, and in that from Willendorf in Upper Austria the hair is braided like that of the head of a girl from Brassempouy in the Landes. The arms and legs are only very slightly indicated but the abdomen is prominent, and on the forearm dots seem to represent a necklace. Traces of red ochre occur in the porous limestone of which the nude figure was composed, and the emphasis clearly was on its sexual features, the rest being of little importance.

In the rock-shelter excavated by Dr Lalanne at Laussel on the Beaune near Les Eyzies in the Dordogne the remarkable relief of a nude female about 18 inches long carved on a block of stone holds in her right hand an object resembling the horn of a bison. The face is featureless, though the head is turned in profile, while the whole body had been coloured red, and all of it except the head had been polished. Two other fragmentary reliefs represent women, and a third may possibly depict the act of childbirth.[2] Another suggestion is that it represents a copulation and served an erotic purpose.[3] On this interpretation it is maintained that the emphasis was on the voluptuous character of the woman rather than on the generative maternal aspect. In support of this contention the engravings on the walls of an alcove in the cavern of Combarelles near Les Eyzies depicting male and female dancers clothed in skins and wearing tails,[4] with their faces obliterated by stalagmite, have been quoted as examples of erotic scenes in Palaeolithic art. But it would seem much more likely that they are portrayals of a masked fertility dance to control the chase like those on the walls of Marsoulas and Altamira, and on bone and reindeer horn from Abri-Murat, Abri-Mège, on a schist plaque at Lourdes, and on a pebble at La Madeleine. Moreover, it has yet to be established that the bas-relief represents a copulation. When the present writer inspected it some years ago at the house of Mme Lalanne at Bordeaux this seemed to be by no means a convincing interpretation. It may well be merely a female figure in outline resembling the other relief, or, as Miss Levy has suggested, the steatite statuette from Grimaldi.[5]

However the obscure figure is to be explained, these sculptured Venuses cannot be dismissed as "the characteristic

The Mystery of Birth in Palaeolithic Times 147

products of unregenerated male imagination"⁶ in view of their long history as an integral part of the cult of the Mother-goddess in more advanced stages of civilization. An erotic element may have been inherent in the tradition, but the main purpose has been that of the promotion and conservation of life in ever-increasing abundance mediated in and through the outward signs of maternal fecundity long before the urge of life was personified in the Earth-mother and her many and various counterparts in the composite figure of the Magna Mater of the Near and Middle East and in the Graeco-Roman world.

Like the rest of the Gravettian culture, it would seem that the Venus cult came into Europe from the east where in the valley of the Don numerous examples have been found, seven of which, skilfully carved in mammoth ivory, have come from Gagarino and one from Kostienki in the middle of Russia.⁷ At Malta near Lake Baikal, Siberia, a highly conventionalized figure occurred, and not so very far to the north-east of Willendorf on the Danube Dr Absolon has discovered the Venus of Unter Wisternitz in Moravia and the portrait statue at Vistonice modelled in ground and burnt bones mixed with fat and mud. In the Apennines another conventionalized statuette occurred at Savignano sul Panàro in Emilia, and, as we have seen, two others in the Grimaldi graves on the Franco-Italian frontier. Those from Brassempouy and Sireuil in France are rather later in the Aurignacian, suggesting that the cult took a considerable time to move as far from its base as these sites in Western Europe. Since it is also to a late Aurignacian date that the conventionalized Venus engraved on ivory from Předmost in Moravia has been assigned, the cult in Central Europe must have survived until the advent of the Solutreans.

In the light of recent evidence it would appear that it was among the hunting Gravettian communities of the South Russian steppe and Western Asia that female figurines were first fashioned as fertility charms with very considerable skill, giving excessive prominence to the sexual features. As they passed into Central and Western Europe they tended to become cruder and more conventionalized but continued to exercise the same function in relation to the mystery of birth and generation. There was also, however, a tall, more elegant, slim variety with the head clearly indicated, as, for example, in the ivory figure from Lespugne in Haute-Garonne, with a kind of loin-cloth concealing the sex organ.[8] Since some of these girdles have been decorated with cowrie and other shells as fertility amulets[9] the loin-cloth may have been depicted to stimulate fecundity.

Cowrie Shells

In addition to the squat Venuses, cowrie shells were used for amulets or ornaments by the Gravettians and in the middle Aurignacian.[10] Those at Grimaldi were associated with *cassio nufa* shell from the Indian Ocean, and, therefore, may have been brought to the Italian Riviera from India, or possibly obtained by barter since they also occur in graves in the Dordogne, where at Laugerie-Basse near Les Eyzies two sorts of Mediterranean cowries were scattered over the skeleton.[11] Shaped like the portal of birth, the cowrie was a life-giving agent which may have made its way into Europe from the East in association with the Venuses, and so was often associated with red ochre, the surrogate of blood, in the grave furniture.

Fertility Dances

It was not, however, only to revivify the dead and to make the human species fruitful and multiply and replenish the earth that the life-cult was practised. It was also employed by the Magdalenians to stimulate fecundity among the animals whereon the hunter subsisted. Thus, in a gallery of the inaccessible cavern of Tuc d'Audoubert near St Girons in Ariège, at the end of a long and narrow ascending passage, blocked by stalactite when it was first entered by the Count Bégouen and his son in 1912, two bisons modelled in clay were found, about two feet in length, leaning against a block of rock that had

The Mystery of Birth in Palaeolithic Times

Fig. 8. Dancing scene in the rock-shelter at Cogul, near Lérida, Spain

fallen from the roof. The female bison was represented as followed by the male, this suggesting a fertility motif. On the soft clay floor of the gallery were the impressions of human feet, and the incomplete model of a bison with some lumps of clay. To the right were a number of deep, rounded depressions which have been thought to be heel-marks made by dancers engaged in a fertility dance around a small hillock in the centre,[12] similar perhaps to that called the *duk-duk* in Melanesia.

Be this as it may, the numerous representations of persons dancing, apparently wearing animal masks or heads, such as the three figures masquerading in the skin of a chamois at Abri-Mège, Dordogne, and others with animal heads at Marsoulas, Hornos de la Pena, Altamira, and Lourdes, and most conclusively "the dancing sorcerer" in the case of Trois Frères near Tuc d'Audoubert, to be considered in the next chapter, show that the custom was firmly established in the Upper Palaeolithic. The practice of dancing round sacred objects, so prevalent in fertility ritual throughout the ages, and still surviving, for example, in the Maypole ceremonial, is revealed in the well-known fresco in the rock-shelter at Cogul near Lérida in Catalonia depicting a group of nine women, narrow-waisted, wearing skirts reaching to the knees, and caps but showing no facial features, dancing round a small naked male figure (Fig. 8).[13]

This celebrated scene has called forth a variety of conjectural interpretations ranging from that of a phallic cult to a gambol dance. As it now appears, incidentally in a very faded condition, a fecundity motif is suggested, though it is by no means established that the male figure has a phallic significance since the penis is not erect. The picture seems to have been the work of several Late Palaeolithic artists, executed perhaps at different times, the little dark brown male figure subsequently having been added to the representations of the black women. Even so, it is difficult to avoid the conclusion that its insertion was connected with a fertility rite in which the women were grouped round a male emblem to facilitate the production of life, however imperfectly the process of generation may have been understood.

The Aurignacians emphasized the maternal aspect of the mystery of birth and gave expression to it in their female figurines. The Magdalenians, concentrating on the magico-religious control of the chase, were mainly concerned with the cult of reproduction as it affected the maintenance of the means of subsistence,[14] and so they rarely fabricated human figurines.[15] The Eastern Spanish artists, on the other hand, at the end of the Upper Palaeolithic introduced both men and women into their vigorous and realistic schematic scenes in profusion. Thus, in the rock-shelter of La Vieja at Alpéra, between Alicante and Albacete, both male and female dancers are depicted in dark red resembling those at Cogul, and repainted at two successive epochs[16] (Fig. 9). This is essentially a hunting scene comprising some thirty goats or antelopes, twenty-six stags as well as cows, deer, moose, ibex, wild horses, wolves, and birds, combined with more than seventy human figures, mainly males, many of whom are shown with drawn bows shooting at the animals. Two of the men are quite unmistakably engaged in a dance, with legs apart showing the generative organ, and wearing a head-dress of plumes, while two of the three women are clad in skirts like those at Cogul, and one is nude and corpulent. The attitudes are those of a sacred dance rather than of the chase, though they are holding weapons. The bodily

The Mystery of Birth in Palaeolithic Times 151

Fig. 9. The "dancing chieftain" scene, a detail from a painting in the rock-shelter at Alpéra, Albacete, Spain (*after Breuil*)

proportions are fairly well preserved but the hands and faces are ovaloid and featureless. One of the women holds something in her left hand which it has been alleged is a statuette. But this is merely a conjecture as the object seemed to the present writer, when he visited Alpéra and inspected the representation, to be indecipherable.

If these eastern Spanish paintings are of Capsian origin as their technique might indicate, with possible African affinities, where similar designs occur so far south as Southern Rhodesia,[17] their precise purpose is no less obscure than their history. That they had a magico-religious significance is reasonably certain in view of their situation in rock-shelters which were shrines rather than habitations. But unlike the great caves of the Dordogne, the Pyrenees and Cantabria, where the decoration occurs in the most inaccessible recesses, they were not executed far from the profane gaze of all and sundry in mysterious darkness. Nevertheless, they must have been visited by successive generations of Upper Palaeolithic Man as some of the designs have been painted over and altered, as at Cantos de la Visera in Murcia. There a bull has been transformed into a stag, while at Minateda, between Chinchilla and Hellin, the Abbé Breuil has discovered the superposition of no less than thirteen layers of paintings. Among the reasons which took them to these unimpressive sacred places was, it would seem, the practice of a life-cult centred in the ritual dance in which men and women engaged to control the mysterious processes of birth and generation both in the human and animal species.

To the primitive mind the figure of a woman with her characteristic features given special prominence, and that of the phallus, represent the two poles of creative energy, the one feminine and receptive, the other masculine and procreative. Together they are conceived as one complete whole in the mystery of birth. The woman being the mother of the race, she is essentially the life-producer, as her male partner is the begetter. Therefore, their respective sex organs are thought to be endowed with generative power, and so they have become the symbols of fruitfulness and procreation, and employed to promote the fertility of the womb and its fecundation. In the complex process of birth, conception is the beginning and until this has been accomplished generation cannot ensue. This presupposes a union of the active and passive elements from which all life is derived, male and female, the father and the mother, brought together in a sacred conjunction in order to produce offspring.

But however essential in physiological reality the two partners may be in order to achieve procreation, the agent about whose maternal functions there can be no possibility of doubt is and always has been the woman. She is not only the symbol of generation but the actual producer of life. In the words of the writer of *The Book of Wisdom*, "all men have one entrance into life", and "in the womb of my mother was I moulded into flesh in time of ten months, being compacted in blood and the seed of man." While in primitive society there has been some

Neolithic and Chalcolithic Female Figurines 153

uncertainty about paternity,[18] this element of doubt cannot obtain in the case of the mother. Therefore, she and her organs and attributes have been the life-giving symbols *par excellence* ever since their first appearance in the Middle East and in Europe at the beginning of the Upper Palaeolithic. Her male partner in all probability was at first supplementary because his precise function in relation to conception and birth was less obvious and less clearly understood.

NEOLITHIC AND CHALCOLITHIC FEMALE FIGURINES

With the transition from food-gathering to food-production the female principle continued to predominate in the mysterious processes of birth and generation. Thus, in the Neolithic period clay and ivory figurines of the "Venus" type were in use, together with the slim variety, in the Badarian and the Amratian cultures in Egypt,[19] but elsewhere they have seldom been found in the earlier sites. Recently two have come to light in the pre-Halaf levels at Hassuna, but west of Iran it is not until the Halaf levels are reached that they become abundant.

Arpachiyah

At Arpachiyah near Nineveh at the height of the Halafian culture numerous headless clay female statuettes in the squatting posture, suggestive of childbirth, and a painted type with bent head and pendulous breasts, occur in association with spindle-whorls, cones and the bones of domestic animals. In all of them prominence is given to the maternal organs, and in some a state of pregnancy appears to have been represented. The painted examples are "steatopygous" with a garment indicated in red pigment and braces crossed between the breasts. Some have a fiddle-shaped body flat or truncated and the protuberant navel is suggestive of pregnancy. A tendency to conventionalization is a marked feature, the body often having been reduced to a peg or cone, though still showing the squatting position. Many of them quite clearly are allied to the Gravettian Palaeolithic prototypes, though often they are inferior in design and technique to the earlier examples, but they constitute an important link with the Chalcolithic female figurines in Anatolia, Crete and Aegean in Europe, and those of the Middle East, Persia and Baluchistan.[20] In Palestine at Tell Beit Mirsom, Dr Albright found a group of five statuettes representing nude women in what he describes as "the process of accouchement", having an exaggerated protrusion of the vulva region which he thinks was an attempt to suggest the descent of the infant's head at the time of delivery for the purpose of hastening parturition by magical means.[21]

Tepe Gawra

At Tepe Gawra in the Halaf deposits in the lower levels of the mound the female figurines are of common occurrence and those of males extremely rare, though the reverse is true of painted human representations on pottery and in seal designs. Nearly all are of the same general type in the squatting position, the woman holding her breasts. The heads are crudely shaped, but the facial features are sometimes indicated in paint without any attempt at modelling. A highly conventionalized "fiddle" type shows only the torso with prominent breasts and the lower part of the body exaggerated, but the arms and legs are not shown. The head is merely a short projection while the back is flat. If the stylization of this isolated example was intentional, it may have been intended to assist in parturition, as Tobler suggests.[22]

The stratified deposits of the mound have yielded an armless type without pointed knees and having prominent breasts and a painted skirt or kilt suspended from the shoulders by two straps between the breasts. There are also indications of tattoo marks or cicatrices. Fattening of the buttocks, distention of the abdomen and protuberant navels are not characteristic features of the figurines at Gawra as elsewhere, and the erect type is unknown in the mound. In the 'Ubaid period two are so stylized as to be little more than cones, and except for the breasts they give little indication of being human figures at all. Most, however, are either of the pointed knees, decorated variety with arms encircling the breasts, or without arms and showing a skirt held by straps. Both belong to the lowest levels. Only the fragment of one male statuette has been found with a spot of paint at the end of the phallus.[23]

Tell Hassuna and Al 'Ubaid

At Tell Hassuna near Mosul the clay figurines of the "Mother-goddess" type conform to those found at Arpachiyah, though the largest has an unexplained excrescence on the left thigh, and one of the truncated arms is missing.[24] The excavations at Tell Chagar Bazar in North Syria have revealed naturalistic terra-cotta figures wearing turbans and seated on circular stools, as if in parturition. Several are painted with simple bands around the neck, arms, and legs, or breasts. These marks might represent tattooing, clothing or ornaments.[25] In the Tell Al 'Ubaid settlements from below the flood deposit the earliest of the Ur female figurines have been recovered. Some of them are greenish as a result of the overfiring of the clay. Others are much lighter, but both represent the slender type painted in black and red with wigs of bitumen applied to the head. The heads are elongated and grotesque, but the bodies are well modelled with feet together and hands at the waist, or holding a child to the breast, or sometimes resting their hands on their hips. Bands and stripes are painted on the nude body to indicate ornaments or tattooing, and the pubes and division between the legs are depicted by linear incision.[26] Male counterparts have been found at Abu Shahrain, also with a monstrous head and having much the same posture though less skilfully modelled with flattened shoulders.[27]

Warka

In the mound of Warka at Uruk the female figurines resemble those at Ur in form and ornamentation with black paint. One has a cylindrical body, a splayed base with the division between the legs marked by incision and wing-like arms. The heads are again monstrous with a snout and gashes in strips of clay for eyes, and wearing sometimes a peaked head-dress. Others in contrast are equally small and devoid of features except for a large nose. Across the shoulder and under the right arm a diagonal band has been painted in some of the examples.[28] Between the C and D levels of the Anu Ziqqurat a very small nude female figure in translucent stone, excellently modelled with arms bent at the elbows and clenched fists,[29] was doubtless employed for amuletic purposes.

Susa

In Iran similar painted figurines with conical heads have been recovered from Juwi,[30] where on one of them what seem to be cicatrices are shown as at Ur and Gawra.[31] In the earliest settlements at Susa (A) figurines of women were modelled in clay, the eyes and breasts were rendered by dabs, the nose and brows by thick rolls struck on the flat slab, and an incised triangle.[32] In the first Elamite period (c. 2800 B.C.) a statuette was found on the Acropolis on which one of the splayed hands is placed on the stomach and the other is shown holding the breast.[33] In another figurine with a cylindrical body the hands are clasped, the head appears to be covered with a turban, the eyes are indicated by incised lines, and two bracelets are shown on each wrist;[34] very much as in a later example, now in the Ashmolean Museum in Oxford, in addition to a turban and bracelets, a necklace of two strings of large beads is shown with a rosette pendant in the middle. Another necklace passes across the chest.[35] In the proto-Elamite period the use of necklaces in this type of figurine was an established feature.[36]

Anau

At Anau in Transcaspia the terra-cotta figurines found by Pumpelly were fragmentary, but in all those of females the breasts were clearly marked, and in most of them also the navel. A necklace ornament is represented on several torsos,[37] but the head is indicated by a projection of the nose and by small depressions of the eyes.[38] The hips are strongly developed, but the legs are brought together in a point and the generative organs are emphasized.[39] From the adjacent ruins now called

Neolithic and Chalcolithic Female Figurines 157

Ghiaur Kala, the ancient Merv, on the Acropolis naked figures have been found painted in black, red and yellow, and a female relief standing in a long robe with neck ornaments, holding a mirror in the right hand before the breast. The left hand is placed lower down but the head is missing.[40]

Baluchistan

In South Baluchistan in the Kulli culture, established in Makran before 3000 B.C., a number of clay figurines of women have been discovered which finish at the waist in a splayed pedestal. The arms are bent with hands on the hips, and while breasts are usually shown they are not unduly exaggerated. The faces are grotesque caricatures with the eyes fashioned from pellets, and the hair is elaborately dressed and kept in place by a fillet, or plaited. The ornaments which adorn the head include oval pendants resembling cowrie shells, while on the arms and wrists are bangles. Or, again, in the Zhob valley sites the same type of female figures recur with necklaces, large and beak-like noses, hooded heads, exaggerated breasts, circular eye-holes, and slit mouths and bangles.[41] These are so uniform in style and features that Sir Aurel Stein conjectures that they "might have been intended to represent some tutelary goddess".[42] That they had a fertility significance is shown by the representation of a phallus carved in stone at the mound of Mogul Ghundai near the left bank of the Zhob river south-west of Fort Sandeman, and at the neighbouring mound of Periano-Ghundai on the right bank of the river, where a vulva is depicted with great prominence.[43]

The Indus Valley

In the Indus valley terra-cotta female figurines have been discovered in considerable numbers at Harappa and Mohenjo-daro, the majority of which are nude except for a small skirt secured by a girdle round the loins; they have a large fan-shaped head-dress and pannier-like side projections having a black stain which seems to have been made by smoke. Therefore, the inference is that they were used as lamps or incense-burners in the practice of a cult connected with the Mother-goddess. At Mohenjo-daro they occurred at all levels, frequently in a mutilated condition, in the streets and in the dwellings, painted over with a red slip or wash doubtless to enhance their life-giving potency, as in Ancient Egypt, Mesopotamia and Malta.[44] They were adorned with quantities of jewellery which included bead necklaces with pendants, ornamental collars, armlets, bracelets and anklets. Some in the higher levels were seated with hands clasped round the knees, roughly modelled and with no ornaments. Others were in postures which suggest that they were engaged in a ritual dance, such as is represented on a faience plaque.[45]

That they were sacred images is beyond doubt, and, as Sir John Marshall says, it is probable that "they represent a goddess with attributes very similar to those of the great Mother Goddess, 'the Lady of Heaven', and a special patroness of women, whose images are found in large numbers at so many sites in Elam, Mesopotamia, Egypt and the Eastern Mediterranean area."[46] Dr Mackay may also be correct in thinking that they were household deities kept in a niche in the wall in almost every house in the Indus valley cities, just as today in India the Mother-goddess is the guardian of the house and village, presiding over childbirth and daily needs.[47] If this be the correct interpretation of this type of figurine, whether she was associated with a male partner—as in her later developments both in India and elsewhere—is not clear. Figures of male gods, frequently horned, recur in the Harappa culture,[48] but they are not prevalent and seldom are brought into conjunction with those of goddesses. On pottery they are extremely rare and, unlike the skirted female statuettes, are entirely nude, though on one of the male figures red lines on the arms and neck probably represent bangles and a scarf necklace.[49]

The three-faced male god from Mohenjo-daro sitting in the attitude of a *yogi* with arms outstretched and covered with bangles, and the chest with triangular necklaces or torques, like the figurines from Kulli and Zhob in Baluchistan, is

Neolithic and Chalcolithic Female Figurines 159

surrounded by four animals—an elephant, tiger, rhinoceros and buffalo—with two deer beneath his throne. A pair of horns crowns his head, and there is either a phallus or the end of a waistband between the legs.[50] That this is a prototype of the Hindu god Shiva as Lord of the Beasts and Prince of *Yogis* is unquestionably suggested by the form and symbolism.[51] Moreover, on several seals a similar figure occurs associated with the sacred *pipal*, or fig-tree, and cult animals like the Lord of the Beasts in Minoan Crete, and with Cybele the Anatolian Mother-goddess.[52]

Phallic Emblems

There is also evidence of phallic emblems, or *lingas*, in the form of realistic models of the male generative organ, together with *yoni*, or female vulva,[53] used probably as life-bestowing amulets, as among Saivites in India today. The more conventionalized resemble very closely *linga* from Mogul Ghundai in Baluchistan,[54] *yoni* bases having been used sometimes to symbolize the union of the two organs.[55] Some of the larger cones, however, that have been found at Mohenjo-daro in ordinary dwellings do not appear to have been *lingas*, their smooth worn bases suggesting rather that they were grinders. Nevertheless, there is every probability that many of the finished cones showing no signs of polishing were in fact phallic emblems.[56]

At Harappa a number of limestone conical *lingas* have been recorded, some of which are in the form of chessmen in chalcedony, carnelian, lapis lazuli, alabaster, faience, paste, shell, ivory and terra-cotta, as well as in limestone.[57] A conventionalized example in yellow sandstone with finely cut coils and necklaces may have had a *yoni* base, and six occurred in an earthware jar with some small pieces of shell, a unicorn seal, stone pestles and a stone palette. Some miniature conical baetyls have a sort of ring round the body which has been regarded as a possible indication of a *yoni*.[58] Large undulating rings of stone are thought to symbolize the female principle,[59] and to these may be added miniature imitation carnelian rings of the same class, and other small undulating rings of the same kind which fit exactly on a base taken to be a *linga*.[60]

In the worship of Shiva today the *linga* is the most popular object of veneration, the pouring of libations over them and anointing them with butter being a universal practice throughout India. It would seem that this phallic symbolism is very deeply laid in the prehistoric substratum of Hinduism in the Indus valley civilization, going back to the third millennium B.C. in the form of huge cone-shaped *linga* and *yoni* rings, often wavy along the edge like the modern Hindu counterparts, and various much smaller varieties less than two inches high, though some of these may have been used as "chessmen" in board-games. Behind this phallic cult was the mystery of birth, and the predominance of female figurines over male in the earliest levels of all the cultures in which they occur in the Ancient Middle East, from the Eastern Mediterranean to the Indus valley, shows that attention at first was concentrated on the feminine aspects of the process of generation.

There can be little doubt that they represent a deity responsible for the bestowal of life, probably the Mother-goddess herself whose emblem, the dove, is of frequent occurrence in the Indus valley cities, though in this early Indian civilization her functions were confined apparently to this world, and not, as elsewhere, also to the care and renewal of the dead. At Anau, for instance, the earliest figurines were found in the graves of children buried under the floor of the house,[61] suggesting that they were deposited there to facilitate their rebirth. At Mohenjo-daro, Harappa and Chanhu-daro, as in Baluchistan, like the Hindu Mother-goddess, they were connected essentially with household shrines. But they were also emblems of the tutelary deity guarding the portal through which life emerges into this world as well as protectors of the house, village or city over which she presided. Whether or not she was associated with a male partner, such as the horned-god depicted on the seals, cannot be determined with any degree of certainty. Be this as it may—and this will be considered later[62]

Neolithic and Chalcolithic Female Figurines 161

she was by virtue of her functions destined to become the consort of the vegetation god.

Anatolia, Cyprus and the Cyclades

In western Anatolia, Cyprus and the Aegean, female figurines with marked genitalia and painted ornamentation occur in considerable numbers. Those in stone in Khirokitia sometimes afford no indication of their sex, but in the Erimi period in Cyprus the terra-cotta figures are true to type and they are frequent on the local red-ware, indicating the introduction of a life-giving cult in the Mother-goddess tradition in a fairly early phase of the Neolithic period.[63] Myres, in fact, suggested that Asia Minor and Syria constituted the cradleland of the emblems of the "Great Mother of Asia", which he described as "the earliest 'ideal type' in history, and the earliest cult of which we know the meaning as well as the symbol".[64] This, however, ignores the Palaeolithic "Venuses" as the prototype of the Neolithic comparable figurines, and until we know more precisely what lies behind the recent evidence from Arpachiyah, Samarra, and Tell Halaf in the fifth millennium B.C., the first civilization in Susa in Elam, and the latest discoveries at Mersin in Cilicia of an even greater antiquity, we are not in a position to determine the origin of the cult centred in the mystery of birth and the Earth-mother from whose womb all life proceeded and by whom it was nourished and sustained with the aid of the emblematic figurines modelled in clay or carved in stone, often highly conventionalized and worn as amulets.

At the first city of Troy (*c.* 3000 B.C.) she seems to have been portrayed sculptured in low relief flanking the gateway, her heart-shaped human face accentuated by the hair having been indicated by a series of small holes. To the left of the face is the shaft of a staff or sceptre with a spherical head. Below the face to the right is further carving which may be that of an arm or a hand.[65] At Thermi the clay figurines and phalli are later than the conventionalized stone statuettes, while in the Cyclades elegant figures in marble appear as importations from Asia

Minor, together with the "fiddle idol" type in the oldest cemeteries (i.e. the Pelos group). In the poorer graves at Antiparos the crudest and most conventionalized occurred, but where any attempt had been made to fashion a figure in the marble, special attention had been paid to the vulva triangle, and in one figure the sitting posture was indicated. From Amorgos came a female torso with the arm of another person round her back, and in some of the graves were single marble legs. The head invariably was "pointed like the blade of a stone implement", and everywhere there was an excess of female figures over male. From this it is concluded that it was a goddess who was worshipped.[66]

Crete

That Neolithic Crete was an Anatolian province, as Evans affirmed, is shown by the clay figurines from Knossos which include all the principal types found in South-east Europe and the Aegean basin—the so-called steatopygous variety of obese females, those in the squatting attitude, and the flat fiddle-shaped types, all of which, as we have seen, were so widespread and recurrent throughout the Middle East, in Anatolia and Northern Syria.[67] In the earliest Neolithic deposit at Knossos with only one exception all were of the squatting or seated "Venus" kind. In the succeeding period in Crete, Anatolia and the Cyclades the extended stylized figures became prevalent as Western Asiatic and Anatolian influences increased, bringing with them transitional forms, especially in Central Crete, where attempts were made to reproduce facial features.

THE MOTHER-GODDESS

The Great Minoan Goddess

Since it is impossible to dissociate these figurines from those that appear in the sanctuaries of the Great Minoan Goddess, it can scarcely be mere coincidence, as Evans has pointed out, that all the various centres in which the emblems occur eventually became seats of the Mother-goddess cult in its manifold forms and nomenclatures.[68] But that Crete was its original

The Mother-goddess

ome, as has often been contended, is now less probable, owever much it may have been its area of characterization. hus, it seems to have flourished at Arpachiyah a thousand ears before it was established in the Aegean. Moreover, the louble axe, formerly supposed to have been a Cretan innova- ion, is now known to have been a cult object, together with the dove as a symbol of the Mother-goddess, among the Arpachiyahians and elsewhere in the Ancient Middle East in the Chalcolithic period. It was from Asia Minor that the earliest Neolithic influences were felt in Crete about 4000 B.C., and from this centre the Goddess symbolism almost certainly was introduced.

Once established on the island it soon became a dominating force, and the Cretan claim to have been the cradleland of the Phrygian Mysteries of the Great Mother cannot be lightly dismissed.[69] From Middle Minoan times she was worshipped as the Mistress of Trees and Mountains and Lady of the Wild Beasts. In association with her youthful male partner she represented the life-giving principle in nature and in man, until eventually on the Greek mainland her functions and attributes were assumed by a number of goddesses. Thus, Athena, once an Earth-divinity, acquired her snake and bird emblems;[70] Artemis her wild creatures, forests and streams,[71] while Aphrodite took over her doves who became her divine son and the dynamic embodiment of her own functions.

It was in her role of the Earth Mother, the Mountain Mother and the Goddess of Vegetation, that the Minoan Mother was represented in her figures in clay and porcelain with out- stretched or uplifted arms, often holding or encircled by snakes, clad in a skirt with flounces and wearing a high crown, sometimes accompanied by a priestess or facsimile of herself, together with the double axe and horns of consecration and votive garments[72]. On some of the seals and signets she is represented as seated beneath her tree receiving offerings of the first-fruits of her bounty, or in later Minoan scenes (*c.* 1500 B.C.) as the hunting Goddess accompanied by lions and with a spear in her hand, or replaced by a pillar or mountain standing between rampant lions. At Knossos she is herself elevated on a mountain wearing the typical Minoan flounced skirt, holding a lance or sceptre and flanked by lions.[73] To the left is a shrine with "baetylic" pillars and horns of consecration—the symbols connecting her with plant and animal life. Before her stands a male divinity descending from the sky and accompanied by lions.[74] At Hagia Triada a female of gigantic stature is depicted between two smaller females before a shrine,[75] and everywhere the Goddess predominates in Cretan worship, the young male, when represented at all, always being subordinate and later in time than the Great Minoan Mother.

When the "Lady of the Mountain" made her way from Western Asia through the Eastern Mediterranean to the Aegean area she retained her position and life-giving functions which, as in Mesopotamia, extended to the land of the dead. Thus, the Temple Tomb in the glen above the Palace site at Knossos, which corresponds in essential details to the temple of Aphrodite, "the Lady of the Dove", described by Diodorus as the legendary tomb of Minos in Sicily,[76] was a temple of the Goddess with the double axe and horns of consecration in the upper sanctuary leading to the sepulchral chamber. This was a ritual pillar crypt used as a shrine in her honour as the guardian and reviver of the dead.[77] At Hagia Triada the sarcophagus in a kind of chamber-tomb ascribed to the Late Minoan II and III is ornamented with scenes depicting an altar with horns of consecration, an olive-tree with spreading branches, a pole painted pink with a double axe and a bird, a priestess with a vessel of offerings, a libation jug and a basket of fruit. Then follows the sacrifice of a bull; the blood, it seems, being collected in a pail while a priestess clad in the skin of a victim offers libations at an altar. Behind the bull is a figure playing the double pipes (Fig. 10).[78] Various interpretations of the pictures have been given, but the emblems suggest the cult of the Goddess in a funerary setting with her priestesses as the officiants in a sacrificial oblation on behalf of the deceased, perhaps with the blood flowing down to the earth through

Fig. 10. Cult scene on the Hagia Triada sarcophagus in Crete

bottomless vessels as an offering to Mother-Earth as the ultimate source of rebirth.[79]

The Maltese Goddess Cult

In Malta obese female figurines of Western Asiatic type with Tell Halaf and Arpachiyah affinities are prevalent. Thus, from Hagia Kim have come a number of headless corpulent statuettes in the sitting posture with the legs folded towards the left and the hands resting on the thighs often showing traces of red pigment. The sex is not always at all easy to determine, but a woman clearly is indicated in the case of a figure with breasts, covered by a garment, resting on the upper part of the thighs, and clad in a flounced skirt which conceals what seems to be a stool. In another in a similar position the pigmented line of a necklace can be discerned, while in a standing naked female the breasts and abdomen are pendulous, the right hand resting on the right thigh, the left across the abdomen.[80]

At Tarxien a headless very corpulent statuette in the sitting posture has the hands resting on the thighs towards the genital organ,[81] and this attitude is repeated in a small clay model which is unmistakably female with the right hand pointing to the very clearly marked vulva.[82] In a small headless female sitting figure the knees are drawn up against the chest, and the pendulous breasts touch the thighs,[83] while on a fragment of a clay female figure found among the Neolithic debris the sexual triangle is shown by a deep incision.[84] A female torso of lightly baked red clay from Mnaidra has very large and protruding breasts resting on an immense projection from the abdomen which may suggest pregnancy.[85] The abdomen also is very prominent in another torso from this site, though the breasts are small in this case.[86]

The occurrence of a considerable number of both male and female figures suggests that in Malta the Goddess was associated with a partner in the guise of either a husband or son, as in the Eastern Mediterranean. This also may explain the temples having been built in pairs sometimes with a double shrine. Thus, outside the double chapel at Borg en Nadur a crude phallic figure was found in limestone with incised lines, probably of Neolithic Asiatic origin, and used to express the male procreative aspect of deity,[87] the female counterparts being employed as life-producing emblems. Therefore, in them emphasis was given to the maternal organs.

At the Hal-Saflieni Hypogeum near the Tarxien megalithic ruins, clay and alabaster figures of the naked steatopygous type, comparable to those from Hagiar Kim and the Tarxien temples, have been discovered, together with a perfectly baked clay model of a woman lying asleep on a couch on her right side with the head resting on her arm supported by a pillow.[88] As Zammit suggests, this may indicate that the Hypogeum was used for the practice of incubation in the consultation of oracles, with cubicles for devotees who slept there to have their dreams interpreted by the priests in the service of the Goddess, since emblems of her cult abound in the sanctuary. The breasts of the sleeping figure are large and prominent, the abdomen is transversely grooved and the hips are enormous. Above the flounced skirt the body is naked, and conforms in all essentials to the Tarxien and Hagia Kim type. With it was a similar terra-cotta model, very fat, naked to the waist and showing the remains of red pigment. It is lying on its face, and although the head is missing the pillow remains.[89]

Doubtless before it became an ossuary[90] this great sanctuary

The Mother-goddess

in the third millennium B.C. was the scene of a complex and composite cultus which included a variety of life-bestowing rites, sacrificial, votive and oracular, centred in the worship of the Asiatic Goddess. From the Near East came religious beliefs and practices deeply laid in the Tell Halaf culture which as they passed along the Mediterranean littoral and the hinterland of South-west Asia Minor and Thessaly developed the maternal features differentiating the Maltese Goddess cult from that of the Aegean, with its sepulchral emphasis. In the main court at Hal Tarxien she reigned supreme with her colossal statue standing over seven feet high, arrayed in a fluted skirt and having pear-shaped legs. In attendance were her priests in long skirts and short wigs like Chaldaean officials, offering before the statue burnt sacrifices on the near-by altar, and pouring the blood into a cylindrical stone vessel with a hollow base, decorated with pit marks on the outside and a deep cavity at the top to receive it, while incense was burnt in the cup-shaped cylindrical tops of pillars.[91]

The Iberian Goddess Cult

With the spread of Neolithic culture to the west, the cult of the Mother-goddess from its centre at Malta radiated its influence to the Iberian peninsula, where in Almeria it recurred and found expression in the hundreds of female figurines in the megalithic tombs and huts at Los Millares. So plentiful were they, in fact, that, as at Mohenjo-daro in the Indus valley, it would seem that they must have found a place as part of the regular equipment of every household. They are not as excessively corpulent as the Maltese figures, and often they are stylized almost beyond recognition. Some in Almeria and Portugal are mere outlines of human figures in stone without any faces, others are bone or ivory cylinders, schist plaques or bovine phalanges decorated with what have been described as "owl eyes" (Fig. 11). At El-Garcel in south-east Spain a small fiddle-shaped "idol" characteristic of the eastern Mediterranean Goddess tradition has been found, and similar examples have recurred at El Castillo near Pavia, Alemtejo, in

Portugal.[92] The schist plaque, however, is typical of the south-western province, and when it is not of common occurrence in Almeria a few incisions suffice for arms. The facial features are indicated by a few incised lines or carved knobs. In this area anthropomorphic designs for the most part are confined to figurines made from knuckle-bones or long-bones.[93]

Since El-Garcel with its slag of copper ores and the coastal Almerian province were colonized by Mediterranean mariners having Near East affinities, it is not surprising that the Goddess cult made its way into Western Europe by this route, probably about 2700 B.C. Thence it spread to the south-west of Spain and Portugal, where the marble cylindrical idols with incised face and eyes became a characteristic feature, distinct from the phalange figurines in Almeria. Flat stone and phalange examples recur in the collective tombs on the plateau of Granada in the neighbourhood of Guardix, Gor and Gorafe.[94] Similar designs appear incised on croziers and plaque idols in the Palmella graves in Portugal in addition to phalange and Almerian statuettes. On the Portuguese highlands schist and marble figurines are among the funerary furniture in the slab-cists,[95] and on the east coast of Spain phalanges recur sporadically in Catalonia.[96] But the farther from the great centres in the south the poorer the emblems of the Goddess become, suggesting that although the cult persisted in the hinterland and the north, only a few cherished symbols survived in the process of diffusion, thereby corresponding to the devolution of the megalithic monuments with which it was closely associated.

Statue-menhirs

That the worship of the Mother-goddess was an integral element in the megalithic culture is shown by the recurrence of its symbolism in menhir-statues in Brittany, the Paris Basin, the Marne and the Channel Islands, while the Abbé Breuil has claimed to have found the face and features of the Goddess in the highly conventionalized "buckler" and "octapus" patterns carved on the slabs of the tomb on Gavr'inis in Southern Morbihan. Be this as it may, the figures with breasts

The Mother-goddess 169

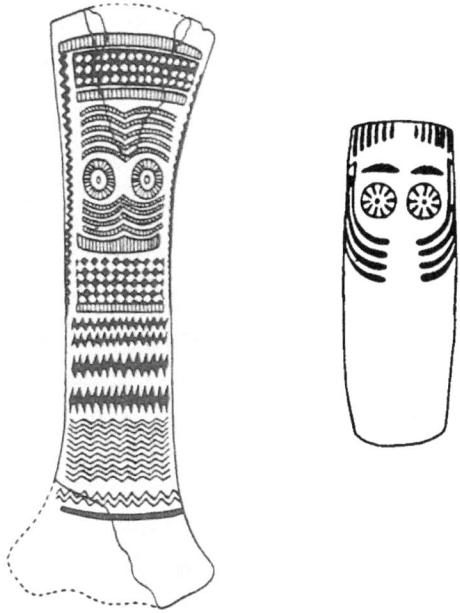

Fig. 11. Owl-eyed female figurines, Almeria, Spain

and necklaces discovered in Aveyron, the Tarn and Gard, and in Guernsey, leave no doubt about their being emblems of the cult. Thus, the Breton tomb designs conform to the Goddess tradition in respect of the maternal symbolism and schematic representation of human features, the general affinity being with the menhir-carvings of the south of France and Guernsey, the Seine-Oise-Marne (S.O.M.) cists, and the prehistoric tomb-sculptures and schist plaques of Spain and Portugal.[97]

In the Channel Islands the statue-menhirs appear to be an integral part of the earliest megalithic culture, the links being closer with the Iberian Atlantic littoral than with the south of France.[98] That known as "La Gran'mere du Chinquière", now standing at the gates of the churchyard of St Martin's, Guernsey, is a rectangular granite pillar 5 feet 6 inches high, terminating in a human head carved out of a block having a massive chin, arched eyebrows, oval eyes, a broad nose and deep upper lip. Two slight elevations from the side of the statue suggest arms and hands, and in the centre are two breasts close together in high relief with a suggestion of nipples, surmounted by a circular groove. Lower down is a girdle in the form of a horizontal band running round the stone. The ornamentation about the head and shoulders may have been intended to depict a tightly fitting head-dress with a row of protruding curls and a fringe across the forehead. Four bosses under the chin may be an ornament of some kind.[99] The predominant feature, however, are the breasts, as in other statue-menhirs, and the carved head reminiscent of the Corsican statuettes with rudely carved facial features but no sexual organs.[100]

In the churchyard of S. Marie-du-Câtel in Guernsey there is a statue-menhir of local granite which formerly was buried within the chancel an equal distance from the north and south walls, about a foot below the surface. It had been placed on its left side, lying east and west. The front was nearly flat except for two projecting breasts close together, one of which has been broken. At the side of the boulder two shoulders are indicated, and the portion corresponding with the head is dome-shaped. On each side of the head, extending from the forehead to the breasts, are two ridges raised a little above the surface of the stone, which may have been intended to represent a head-dress or tresses of hair. Whether or not it ever contained facial features which have been destroyed deliberately can only be conjectured by signs of hammer and chisel marks on what should be the face.[101] In any case, it was an attempt to model a human figure in the round with a collar above the breasts like the goddesses in the cists of the Seine and Oise valleys, as, for example, at Bellehaye, near Boury in the department of the Oise, where two hemispherical breasts occur only three-quarters of an inch apart with a collar above about 15 inches in length formed of three U-shaped bars.[102]

A similar statue-slab of a female divinity armed with an axe was used as a lintel in a corbelled megalithic tomb at Collorgues in Gard on which, however, face, arms and fingers are sculptured in relief,[103] and in the chalk country of the Marne on the walls of the artificial caves in the valley of Petit Orin, the conventionalized figure of the Goddess is carved or sketched

The Mother-goddess

in charcoal, bearing sometimes an axe, guarding the antechamber of the tomb.[104] But in these grottoes the face with eyebrows and wedge-shaped nose is emphasized at the expense of the breasts that appear only in one instance. In Brittany there is one long-cist with sculptured breasts at Tressé, Ille-et-Vilaine,[105] but the centre of the Goddess cult in Northern Europe was in the Paris Basin and the S.O.M. culture.

The Goddess Cult in Britain and Northern France

In England a fat figurine of a pregnant woman carved in chalk has been recovered from a ritual deposit at Grime's Graves in Norfolk with a chalk phallus carved on the left side, and an "altar" in front composed of blocks of flint in the form of a triangle with a chalk cup at the base opposite the Goddess. Upon the "altar" were seven deer-antler picks.[106] At Maiden Castle a headless conventionalized torso has been found, perhaps skirted, having two holes at the base for the insertion of legs, and from Windmill Hill a female figurine, together with phalli carved in chalk, have been recovered.[107] With the possible exception of alleged examples of phalli from Trundle, Whitehawk Camp, Blackpatch flint-mines and the Thickthorn long barrow,[108] and the employment of a phallic symbol in the central ceremony when the ashes of the dead were placed in an urn in Pond Cairn, Glamorgan, in the middle of the Bronze Age,[109] these generative symbols are unknown in the British Isles. Like clay female figurines, they are of very infrequent occurrence in the Neolithic culture in Western Europe, just as clay statuettes are confined to the fortified camp at Fort Harrouard on the downlands of northern France,[110] unless the example recovered by Déchelette from La Grotte Nicolas, Gard, be accepted as a genuine figurine.[111] The closest affinity of the Grime's Graves statuette is with the Palaeolithic "Venuses", and as the others from Britain and Northern France cannot be equated with the Iberian technique, they would seem to belong to the Eastern Mediterranean goddess tradition, where the mystery of birth appears to have most deeply impressed the mind and imagination of Early Man.

CHAPTER VII

Fertility and the Food Supply

So intimate appeared to be the relation between the processes of birth and generation and those of fertility in general that the two aspects of the same "mystery" found very similar modes of ritual expression under prehistoric conditions. As we have seen, food and offspring always have been the first need of the human species, as, indeed, of other organisms, and around these essential requirements a magico-religious cultus has developed to increase and control the supply.

PALAEOLITHIC HUNTING RITUAL

Thus, in the Upper Palaeolithic it has been estimated that four-fifths of the representations in the parietal art are of animals, presumably because they constituted the principal means of subsistence and so had a unique status and importance in the economy. Unlike an increase in the human population which raised the problem of providing an adequate food supply in a struggling Palaeolithic community, the greater the number of edible animals available the higher the standard of living for Early Man. Therefore, rites of increase, comparable to the Intichiuma ceremonies among the native tribes of Central Australia,[1] doubtless were of common occurrence in the cave sanctuaries, as is suggested by the representations of a male following a female in erotic fashion at Tuc d'Audoubert,[2] the numerous zoomorphic figures showing the conjunction of animals in various similar attitudes, often superimposed for magical purposes in the same style, as in the contemporary group of engraved animals at Teyjat in the Dordogne, or the stag's horn added to a hollow in the rock at Niaux near Tarascon-sur-Ariège, indicating that certain spots were considered to be charged especially with sacred potency which could be brought into operation by the masked dancers in animal disguises.

Increase Rites

In most instances the animal dances were connected with the designs executed on the walls of these deep and tortuous mysterious caves, often in nooks and corners, or in the most inaccessible or obscure positions, like the fine painting of a woolly rhinoceros high up on the left-hand wall at the end of a very narrow crevice at Font-de-Gaume, near Les Eyzies, drawn apparently by the artist standing on the shoulders of a companion. To reach the clay bisons 758 yards from the entrance at Tuc d'Audoubert the services of a boat, as has been pointed out, were required, while at the neighbouring cave of the Trois Frères, the three young sons of the Count Bégouen, when they first entered it, had to worm their way through a very small passage leading out of the little cave called Enlène until they reached an alcove on the right-hand side adorned with the engravings of a lion. Beyond this lay a small chamber covered with engravings of a great number of animals, and at the end of a winding passage opening out into a kind of window, about 12 feet above the ground, was the figure of a man with a human face and long beard, the eyes of an owl, the antlers of a stag, the ears of a wolf, the claws of a lion and the tail of a horse (Fig. 12) engraved on the rock wall just beside the window.[3] Whether or not this strange masked figure was the representation of the arch-sorcerer, or shaman, embodying the attributes and functions of the animals it portrayed, as Bégouen suggests,[4] a cult is indicated in which human beings and animals were brought together in a mystic communion with the source of providential bounty in a joint endeavour to conserve and promote the food supply. The emphasis clearly was on fecundity for the purpose of securing an abundance of the species on which man depended for his means of subsistence.

The mysterious forces of nutrition and propagation being sacred and the centres of emotional interest and concern, a reverent attitude was adopted towards them which found expression in a ritual technique to bring them under some measure of supernatural control. To eat is to live. Therefore, the main link between man and his environment was food; for, as Malinowski has said, "nature is his living larder".[5] Before the adoption of agriculture and herding, when a precarious existence was eked out on the chase and edible fruits, roots and berries, the animal and vegetable species which formed his staple diet acquired a sacred character and significance. With this he endeavoured to establish efficacious relations through a prescribed ritual procedure performed by experts in carefully secluded sanctuaries set apart for the purpose in awe-inspiring surroundings and conditions calculated to produce a sense of the numinous.

The Control of the Chase

Propagation was not, however, the only end in view in the practice of hunting magic. The animals had to be procured as well as to be rendered prolific. So to the cavern sanctuaries the Palaeolithic ritual experts repaired to set in motion powerful supernatural forces to control the fortunes of the chase. Thus, for example, in the great caves in the Garonne valley—those at Niaux, Portel, Montespan, Tuc d'Audoubert and Trois Frères—a very considerable number of the paintings and drawings of animals have spears and arrows drawn on their flanks in the region of the heart. At Niaux, just over half a mile from the entrance, three small cup-like hollows were cleverly utilized to represent wounds by drawing round them the outline of a bison and marking the cups with arrows in red ochre. In front of an outline figure of an expiring bison with its legs drawn up close to the body are circles and club-shaped designs depicting missiles (Fig. 13).

When in 1923 M. Casteret first explored the cave of Montespan near the château of the celebrated Marquise in the Haute Garonne, after swimming for nearly a mile in the icy water of a subterranean stream which filled part of the tunnel, and through a siphon, he found in the gallery over twenty clay models of wounded animals. These included the figures of a number of felines riddled with wounds, and raised on a platform in the centre a figure of a small headless bear $3\frac{1}{2}$ feet long

Palaeolithic Hunting Ritual

Fig. 12. "The Sorcerer" in Les Trois Frères, Ariège, France

and 2 feet high, holding the skull of a young bear between its paws. Against the walls, which are decorated with engravings, were three larger models, 5 feet long, apparently lionesses, and a model of a horse's head, while part of the body of a woman lay on a clay hillock. On the floor the design of a horse showed thrusts in the neck and marks made by spears were visible on the neck and chest of the bear, and on the breast of one of the lionesses. In another gallery having a very low roof is the representation of a small horse falling backwards covered with a coating of stalagmite. At the end of the passage there is a scene which Bégouen thinks depicts a corral surrounded with palisades into which wild horses are being driven by darts and stones.[6]

In this sanctuary the rites appear to have been concentrated on the killing of animals in the chase rather than on ensuring an ample supply of them. Thither the sorcerer resorted doubtless before a party set out on a hunting expedition and pierced the images with a spear as he uttered the magic spell that was destined to produce the reciprocal effect upon the prey. That the same model was used for this purpose time after time is shown by that of the headless bear and those of some of the felines being covered with spear-marks, though often fresh ones may have been made if and when the efficacy of the magic declined. At Marsoulas, also in Haute Garonne, a series of polychromes with spear-markings have been painted one above the other as if they had been constantly renewed, an existing drawing having been modified according to the purpose required. In a small recess at Trois Frères the head of a lion engraved on stalactite had been redrawn three times in different positions, and the tail once shown as straight was subsequently rendered as curling. Judging from the number of arrows engraved or painted on it, it must have been in constant use as a magical effigy.

Sometimes—for example, at Tuc d'Audoubert—only particular parts of an animal, such as the head or horns, were depicted, as in the case of the conventionalized figurines discussed in the last chapter, since for the purposes of magical control these sufficed as efficacious symbols to convey the spell on the prey. In the cave known as Pech-Merle at Cabrerets in the valley of the Lot near Cahors in Corrèze, the Abbé Lemozi has detected representations of mammoth and cattle without eyes and ears, which he thinks have been deliberately portrayed in this manner for the purpose of depriving of sight and hearing their counterparts in the chase, thereby rendering them an easy prey to the hunters.[7] Whether or not this be the correct interpretation, that many of the animals do lack these organs was clear to the present writer after a recent visit to this very fine cave. But since headless figures of women also occur on the roof of the galleries at Pech-Merle, it may be that, like the female figurines lacking heads or faces, for purposes of the magic art these appendages were felt to be superfluous. In any

Fig. 13. Dying bison and claviform designs in Niaux, Ariège, France

case, it was to control the chase that they were executed, sometimes with consummate artistic skill, as at Altamira and Font-de-Gaume; at other times merely in outline or in part, as at Tuc d'Audoubert, Enlène and Cabrerets, or even in conventionalized geometric patterns, as at Marsoulas and on bone tools and Azilian pebbles.

In the hall and gallery at Lascaux near Montignac on the Vézère, horses are represented with missiles directed towards them, striking them, or superimposed on them. There are no indications of actual wounds, however, except in the relatively late scene depicting a hunting tragedy, in the most secluded subterranean "crypt" reached by a hazardous descent of some twenty-five feet. There occurs the stylized figure of a man with a bird-shaped head who apparently had been killed by a bison, portrayed with its flank transfixed by a spear exposing its entrails as it was about to fall to the ground, like a gored horse in a bull-fight. To the left is a woolly rhinoceros, painted in a different style, which seems to be slowly moving away after perhaps having ripped up the bison. A little lower down in front of the man is a bird on a pole, rather like an Egyptian ceremonial stave. Behind the rhinoceros below the tail are six black dots arranged in two rows.

In this remarkable fresco an accident in the chase appears to have been recorded. A Late Magdalenian hunter wearing a bird-mask, and possibly carrying a bird-pole, is represented as having been gored by a bison he had wounded; if the woolly rhinoceros has not been superimposed subsequently on the rest of the group, it then ripped open the bison with its horn.[8] The Abbé Breuil has conjectured that the scene is a votive painting to the deceased hunter who, he suggests, may have been buried in the cave.[9] This awaits confirmation. As Windels has pointed out, in view of the magical potency assigned to cave-paintings, it seems hardly likely that a tragedy of this kind would been given graphic portrayal.[10] An alternative interpretation would be that it has a more sinister motive, having been executed with malicious intent to bring about the destruction of the hunter. But against regarding it as a product of black magic is the fact that the death of the hunter is shown as having been avenged on his slayer by the rhinoceros. If, therefore, its original purpose and meaning remain obscure, there can be little doubt that the "problem picture" was delineated in this very difficult and dangerous "crypt" of the cave because for good or ill it was there that great potency could be put into operation in the control of the chase and the fortunes of the hunters.

More accessible on the left-hand side of the main hall is a mythical animal with a massive sagging body, oval rings on the flanks, and two long horns projecting from the forehead and terminating in a tuft. It is possible that it represents a masked sorcerer in a spotted skin of some *Bovidae* impersonating an ancestral spirit believed to be responsible for fertility and success in the chase. Since disguises and masks have been thought to confer supernatural power, Palaeolithic ritual experts appear to have clad themselves in the skins, horns and tails of animals to acquire the attributes and potency of the species they venerated and regarded as standing in a close relation with the food supply on which they depended for their subsistence. This strange figure, not very accurately described as of "unicorn" type, appears to be a mythical or sacred animal, resembling ancient Chinese paintings of horses with short legs and sagging barrel-like bodies, and does not correspond to any known species. Therefore, its reproduction, and possibly impersonation, was doubtless for the purpose either of veneration or f destruction, if the large oval spots on the flank can be interpreted as wound marks. In another group at the end of the axial passage a horse is depicted falling over a precipice or into a pit, and the tectiform and other magical signs, which frequently appear on the paintings, may indicate traps, unless, as Breuil suggests, they are local tribal marks.

Hunting Art and Ritual

In spite of the conjectural character of much of the symbolism, there can be little doubt that resort was made to these great cavern sanctuaries before setting out on hunting expeditions and for the performance of food-producing ceremonies analogous to those known as Intichiuma among the Arunta tribe in Central Australia. There at such sacred spots as Emily Gap near Alice Springs some of the rocks are believed to be full of the spirit-parts of animals awaiting reincarnation, and adorned with drawings of the totems.[11] Each local group has its own totemic signs and paintings preserved in places which are taboo to women, children and uninitiated men. Some are still painted and re-painted as part of the fertility ritual, and, as at Gargas, Castillo, Pech-Merle, Trois Frères and Altamira, in the Franco-Cantabrian Palaeolithic caves, include designs of stencilled human hands, the meaning of which remains obscure, though at Gargas mutilation suggests that the sacrifice of fingers was practised as a propitiatory life-giving rite.

Many of the Australian zoomorphic and phytomorphic paintings are merely outlines of animals and plants in charcoal or red ochre, or conventionalized drawings, often very difficult to decipher, and geometrical figures without apparently any definite meaning, though probably they are derived from zoomorphs of totemic origin.[12] Among the native tribes of the north-west, realistic drawings of animals occur in the rock-shelters in white pipe-clay, charcoal and red or yellow ochre, together with representations of mythical heroes connected with rain and fertility; as, for example, Katuru or "lightning man" at Kalurungari on the Calder river, and Wond'ina at the Kobudda shelter, Walcott Inlet—the ancestor responsible for rain, the increase in nature and of spirit-children. Some are also mischievous spirits who are on the warpath at night to lure away the souls of the unwary.[13] But, as in the Palaeolithic cave ritual, the main purpose of the art is to promote plenty by contributing towards the fertility of the species on which the people depend for their food supply.

Among the Australian aborigines the performance of Intichiuma is a collective responsibility and co-operative effort. Each totemic clan exercises its functions for the benefit of the rest of the community since the sacred species is either taboo or may be eaten only very sparingly by those who are responsible for its increase. The representation of so many different varieties of animals in the same cave is not indicative of a totemic organization of Palaeolithic society, as each totem presumably would have had its own sanctuary; even though, as Breuil has pointed out, the bones of the animals depicted in the caves are absent from the midden-heaps.[14] But whether or not anything that fairly can be described as totemism was practised in connexion with the Palaeolithic designs,[15] it seems to have been the duty of ritual experts to carry out food-producing rites in the seclusion of the remote sanctuaries on behalf of the group, probably at set seasons and on specific occasions.

The figures of the masked dancers in animal disguises suggest the existence of a cult in which the hunter would appear to have impersonated the "spirit" of the animals he embodied, and to have dramatically represented in a series of ritual actions a rehearsal of that which it was earnestly desired should be accomplished in the chase. The will to live as a primary emotion was discharged by anticipatory rites as a pre-presentation of a successful hunt. To these actions a magical efficacy was given not because "like produces like" but because a ritual that involved a more or less realistic reproduction of some practical activity established the *ex post facto* idea of "sympathetic" causation. Thus, the original re-enactment was given a secondary interpretation in magical terms. The primary function, however, was to give expression to a vital impulse, the desire to act discharging itself on the symbol, the ritual being the vent of pent-up emotions and activity.[16] The purpose of the actions performed and of their representation in visual form was to secure the prey, to gain control over the food supply, or to establish a "mystical union" with the source of bounty through ritual efficacy, and to relieve the tension in a precarious situation amid all the hazards of the chase and the vagaries of unpredictable events.

In a great sanctuary like Lascaux, Niaux or Les Trois Frères, the ceremonies must have involved an organized effort on the part of the community in a collective attempt to control natural forces and processes by supernatural means directed to the common good. The sacred tradition arose and functioned, it would appear, largely as an economic ritual to maintain the food supply. This became an integrating dynamic which afforded strength and power to the members of the group to enable them to cope with the perplexities and hazards of everyday life, and established a bond between man and his bewildering environment. Moreover, the community was thereby resolved into a co-operative fellowship in which each individual directly or indirectly played his part for the benefit of the whole under the leadership and direction of ritual experts who were responsible for the actual performance of the prescribed ceremonial at the appointed times and places in a representative capacity.

THE VEGETATION CULTUS IN THE ANCIENT NEAR EAST

With the transition from hunting and food-collecting to the cultivation of edible plants and/or the breeding of flocks and herds, the ritual control of fertility and food-production was concentrated on the crops, the sequence of the seasons and the breeding and rearing of cattle, sheep and goats rather than on the precarious conditions of the chase, even though hunting often lingered on side by side with husbandry and domestication. Nevertheless, under the influence of these new ceremonies, social structures and religious organizations began to emerge adapted to the requirements of an agricultural or pastoral mode

Fertility and the Food Supply

of life, and those of "mixed farming" when cultivation was combined with stock-rearing and hunting.

In the Fertile Crescent this became apparent in the fifth millennium B.C. when food-production began to supplement and supplant food-gathering in Tells like Sialk on the western edge of the arid Iranian plateau, Qalat Jarmo on the Kurdish foothills to the east of the Tigris, Hassuna in Assyria, Merimde north of Cairo to the west of the Nile Delta, and at Badari and Deir Tasa in Middle Egypt, and in other similar favourable localities in the Ancient Near East. At first in the oases hunting and fishing usually were combined with tilling the land, growing grain and keeping a few sheep or cattle. But as the chase dropped more and more into the background, until finally it was abandoned as a means of subsistence in the agricultural or pastoral communities, the fertility of the soil and the succession of summer and winter, spring-time and harvest, together with the associated pursuits, became the centre of interest and of the ritual organization. Under these conditions the regular growth of the crops was a matter of no less vital concern than had been the hazards of the chase. Consequently, at the critical seasons an emotional reaction called forth a ritual response to ensure success in the food-producing activities at their several stages by overcoming the unpredictable elements in the situation which lay outside human control. Thus, when the ground was prepared and the crops were sown, and later when the harvest was gathered, a ritual technique was devised for the twofold purpose of overcoming sterility and promoting fertility in man, beast and the crops, around which a mythology developed in terms of a death and resurrection drama.

In prehistoric times the Nile valley was divided into a number of small city-states which before the beginning of the Dynastic period consisted of administrative nomes, each deriving its name from its ensign or standard. As these clan symbols often took the form of animals, such as the falcon or the ibis, and other sacred objects which were regarded as divine, sometimes they have been interpreted as totems. But in the Egyptian sources there are no indications that they stood actually in a totemic relationship to the clans or nomes, or were associated with such characteristic features as exogamy or rites of increase and tribal unity. They were essentially local gods who ruled the nomes and who gave to the nomarchs as the chief of the clans their authority, until at length when the nome became a kingdom and the nomarch a king, he was then regarded as the son of the god who exercised his rule and functions by virtue of his divine status.

The Divine Kingship in Egypt

The last of these primordial god-kings was "the Horus", a sky deity of the falcon clan in predynastic times who was alleged to have conquered the Delta and set up a single line of kings with a centralized administration. From the earliest times he was depicted as a bird, and Hierakonpolis in the third nome of Upper Egypt became the predynastic centre of his worship and clan. Other Falcon-gods, however, were identified with him, and when the Lower Kingdom conquered Upper Egypt his cult was established at Behdet (Edfu). Henceforth Horus often was called Behdety, "He of Behdet", and with the union of the country as a single nation the Behdetite was the predominant figure in the kingship accomplished by a ruler; this ruler may have been Narmer identified with the traditional Menes,[17] whose Falcon-god Horus was a sky-god who became incarnate in the person of the Upper Egyptian king and bestowed upon him his Horus-name.[18]

The Cult of Osiris

In the Eastern Delta at Busiris (Per-Usire or Djedu), the capital of the ninth nome, the cult of Osiris was established at an early date. It is possible that originally it was associated with a deified civilizing king who became the centre of a death and resurrection cultus before Osiris developed into a composite figure as the Lord of the dead, the God of vegetation and the personification of the fructifying waters of the Nile, and his sister-wife, Isis, personified his royal throne. Exactly how and under what circumstances Horus became identified with the son of Osiris is still a matter of debate, but however this is to be explained, very early in the Dynastic period the pharaohs reigned as the Osirian Horus conceived by Isis when she hovered over the mummy of her murdered husband. According to one interpretation, the struggle between Horus and his Uncle Seth, the perpetrator of the crime against his father (Osiris), was a re-enactment in myth and ritual of the conflicts of the predynastic Horus kings before the nation was unified in a single ruler with divine prerogatives. Thus, Osiris, on this hypothesis, may have been a prehistoric nomadic chief or leader who introduced agriculture among the indigenous people in the Eastern Delta, and eventually came to blows with their ruler Seth when the intruders penetrated up the Nile as far south as Abydos. If Osiris was killed in this campaign, his son Horus may have rectified the position, and the episode eventually was immortalized in tradition in terms of a death and resurrection myth and ritual in which the culture hero, Osiris, played the leading role as the dead king, and his son Horus as the living king.[19] Alternatively, Osiris may have been the personification of the life-giving waters of the Nile and of the renewal of vegetation through the annual inundation rather than an historical character.

The Solar Theology
Both of these suggestions can claim support from the Pyramid Texts, which constitute the chief original sources of information on this complex problem, dating from the Fifth Dynasty (c. 2580 B.C.) when the solar theology had become predominant at Heliopolis. It was under the influence of the Heliopolitan priesthood that the solar line of kings was equated with Re, the Sun-god, and then associated with Osiris. Thus, in their Ennead, Osiris was represented as the son of Nut the Sky-goddess and Geb the Earth-god, and given a place in the sun by descent from Atum-Re, the head of the pantheon as the dead king, while the living pharaoh was Horus "the seed of Geb".[20] From prehistoric times Heliopolis had been a solar

The Vegetation Cultus in the Ancient Near East 185

centre, and in the Fifth Dynasty it became the recognized home of the Re-cult with its temple, the "House of the Obelisk", erected on the primordial hill—the "sandhill"—which was supposed to have emerged out of the waters of Nun at the creation, on the top of which Atum first appeared in the form of a phoenix.[21]

Under the influence of this Heliopolitan solar cult the victorious kings of Upper Egypt identified the Falcon-god Horus with Re in the composite deity Herakhite, "Horus of the Horizon". This opened the way for them to be declared the sons of Re. In the Second Dynasty the second king, Re-neb, had been given a Horus-name, though it was not until the Fourth Dynasty that the Heliopolitan kings Khafre and Menkaure (the builders of the second and third pyramids) actually assumed the title "son of Re". In the middle of the next century each king built a temple for the worship of the Sun-god in conjunction with the royal residence on the margin of the desert. By the Sixth Dynasty (c. 2440–2250) the title had become universally adopted, and with the Osirianization of the solar cult at Heliopolis the living king was equated with Horus, the posthumous son of Osiris. As a result of this synthesis, as at death every pharaoh was Osiris, so he reigned in the guise of Horus who had been established in the throne by the decree of the gods when his father Osiris was vindicated by the Ennead.

By virtue of all these converging traditions and mythologies handed down from remote prehistoric times, the pharaoh became the epitome of all that was divine in the Nile valley, and exercised his functions in relation to all the gods he embodied. Foremost among these being Re, the personification of the all-enveloping glory and power of the Egyptian sun, and Osiris, that of the life-giving waters of the inundation. As Breasted has pointed out, these two great phenomena of nature, the Sun and the Nile, made the most profound impression upon the ancient Egyptians, and the gods discerned in these two insistent features of the country dominated religious and intellectual development from the earliest times.[22] Upon both of them, taken together, the remarkable fertility of the oasis depended.

It is hardly surprising, therefore, that the solar and Osirian cults acquired a vegetation significance even though neither Atum-Re nor Osiris was actually a vegetation god. Thus, the Sun-god standing at the head of the Ennead, in his various aspects, manifestations and capacities was the creator and begetter of life. Osiris, though not the personification of the earth, was immanent in the annual sprouting of vegetation and the growing grain and in the rising waters of the Nile, as well as the bestower of life beyond the grave. In the Mystery play performed at the accession of Senusert I to the throne in the Twelfth Dynasty about 1900 B.C. but containing much earlier material,[23] he is identified with the barley and the emmer that nourishes the gods in heaven and man on earth, having made the corn from "the liquid that is in him".[24] This belief, like so many other prehistoric religious ideas and practices, lingered on until the Ptolemaic period and found expression in the watering of figures of Osiris made of earth and corn in order that the grain might appear as sprouting from his body. These "Osiris gardens" were symbolical of his resurrection in the later Mysteries, but, nevertheless, they suggest his association with the germination of the grain in a vegetation capacity which occupied such a prominent place in popular practice from very early times in the Nile valley.

In the official calendar, however, the Harvest Festival was dedicated to Min, who as a sky- and fertility-god was established at the dawn of Egyptian civilization about 3500 B.C.,[25] and was regarded as the power immanent in the grain which was cut at this season. In the New Kingdom the ceremonies that culminated in the reaping of a sheaf of emmer by the pharaoh were performed with all the signs of rejoicing rather than of lamentation, such as would have been appropriate if the killing of the corn-spirit had been involved. The ithyphallic statue of Min was carried in procession on poles by priests beneath a canopy preceded by a white bull, the sacred animal of Min, and followed by bundles of lettuce, his plant. The king walked immediately behind the bull in front of the image, and on arriving at the temple of Min in the presence of the god and of his bull he reaped the sheaf of spelt "for his father".[26] Since in the Middle Kingdom Min was regarded as a form of Horus, the son of Osiris,[27] Gardiner is probably correct in assuming that the pharaoh in this ritual act impersonated Horus and in this capacity reaped the emmer for Osiris.[28] Therefore, as Min (whose generative powers were embodied in his sacred bull) personified the fertility of the fields, the beasts and vegetation, and was brought into relation with the reigning sovereign as the living Horus, the king exercised his functions at the Harvest Festival to secure a plentiful supply of crops in the ensuing year.

The Annual Festival

In the Spring Festival, celebrated during the latter part of the month of Khoiakh in honour of the death and resurrection of Osiris, an effigy of the dead god (Osiris) cast in a mould of gold in the form of a mummy was filled with a mixture of barley and sand, wrapped in rushes and laid in a shallow basin. For the next ten days (12th–21st) it was watered daily and then, on the 21st of Khoiakh, it was exposed to the sun just before sunset and sent on a voyage until on the 25th of the month it was buried in a coffin and laid in a grave.[29] On the last day of the festival (30th) the interment of Osiris was enacted, coinciding with the cessation of the inundation and the sprouting of the newly sown grain, symbolized later in the Ptolemaic temple of Isis at Philae by the representation of the stalks of wheat growing from the mummy of the dead god watered by a priest from a pitcher. Before the bier the *crux ansata* is figured as the symbol of life, and the inscription records that "this is the form of him who may not be named, Osiris of the mysteries, who springs from the returning waters".[30] Moreover, it was on this last day of the rites that the *Djed*-column was raised by the king and the priests as a symbol of the god's resurrection,[31] thereby showing how very intimately the annual renewal in nature was related to the resuscitation of Osiris and the kingship, fertility and the food supply, both of which were so dependent upon the rise and fall of the Nile.

The Sacred Marriage of the King and the Goddess in Mesopotamia
In Mesopotamia, on the other hand, the unpredictable behaviour of the Tigris and Euphrates in contrast to the uniformity of the inundation in Egypt, and the variability of the climatic conditions, created a very different religious and social structure and ritual order. The country was divided into a series of city-states, as in Greece, loosely bound together to meet the needs of recurrent emergencies and governed by either a secular ruler or by the high priest of the city-god. Instead of being the consolidating centre of the entire nation like the Egyptian throne, in Mesopotamia the royal office was confined to the local seat of administration and subordinate to that of the hierarchy. Even after Hammurabi had unified the state in the empire in the second millennium B.C. and made Babylon the capital with its chief god Marduk the head of the pantheon, the king had to deliver up the symbols of his office to the high priest every year at the Annual Festival and be reinstated by him, acting on behalf of Marduk.

Such an act of royal humiliation would have been unthinkable in Egypt, where the pharaohs reigned as gods incarnate, firmly established as the dynamic centre of the whole structure of society and the bestowers of the vital forces of the earth in the annual flood of the Nile. In Mesopotamia kings were human beings who had been chosen by the gods to act as their servants on earth, and to be the instruments of the Mother-goddess (Inanna or Ishtar), who chose the ruler to be her bridegroom in a sacred marriage. In Egypt the queen was visited by her royal husband in all his divine majesty and glory to beget an heir to the throne. In Mesopotamia at the Annual Festival the king in the guise of Tammuz, the generative force in nature and the husband-son of Ishtar, engaged in a sacred marriage with a priestess, personifying the Mother-goddess, to renew vegetation and fecundity in the spring. In this union she rather than the king was the active partner.

The Dying and Reviving Year-god in Western Asia

While Osiris was at once a dead king, the lord of the netherworld and the author and giver of the life of the grain personified in the fructifying waters of the Nile, Tammuz, "the faithful son of the waters that came forth from the earth" (*Dumu-zi*), was a suffering god dependent upon the Goddess, Ishtar, his mother-consort. This youthful Dumu-zi, or "true son", died annually in the course of the normal rotation of the seasons, and passed into the land of darkness and death from which for ordinary mortals there was no return. From the Tammuz ritual texts it would seem that Ishtar descended into the underworld to seek her husband where he was held captive,[32] like Marduk in the "mountain",[33] invoking him by all his titles, and declaring that she had decked herself like a cedar to make glad the heart of him, her child, her beloved, who had passed over the river, so that "the noble cedar-tree was delivered from prison". It is possible, as Professor Hooke has suggested, that since the cedar-tree does not belong to the Mesopotamian plain, this is an ancient myth and ritual which the Sumerians brought with them when they migrated from the highlands lying to the north-west of Mesopotamia, before the theme was elaborated in the Babylonian New Year Festival.[34]

Be this as it may, throughout the ancient world, in Mesopotamia, Anatolia, Syria and Greece, the seasonal decline of nature was interpreted in terms of the vegetation year-god dying and reviving in the cycle of the crops as the child of the Mother-goddess who was the source of all life. The suffering and resurrected god in Mesopotamia though youthful was a mature figure, restored to fulfil his nuptial relations with the goddess in order that nature's prolific fertility might be insured. Adonis, the Syrian "Lord" (*Adon*), died at midsummer, and, unlike the vigorous youthful Tammuz, he personified the all too brief spring vegetation that passed away like a shadow "dead ere his prime", when his virility was poured out under the pine-tree. Similarly, Kore, the daughter of the Earth-Mother Demeter, the maiden of the meadows whose abduction by Pluto caused the flowers in the fields to wilt, and man and beast to become sterile, symbolized the sudden end of the fleeting loveliness of a Levantine or Hellenic spring.

The Mesopotamian suffering and resurrected god, on the other hand, was the archetype of the recuperative powers of the Euphrates valley when it was flooded by the revitalizing waters of the two rivers in the later winter transforming the parched desert into a fertile oasis. But this inundation never inspired the dwellers in Mesopotamia with the same confidence in the cyclic sequence of the seasons that prevailed in Egypt, where the never-failing waters of the Nile gave a sense of assurance in a static cosmic order. The Babylonians were too much at the mercy of the vagaries of an uncertain rainfall and of the incalculable floods of the two great rivers.[35] Therefore, in this region it was not easy to harmonize in a stable ritual order the life of the community with that of the natural environment. Consequently, the suffering god who reflected these conditions was a complex figure with peculiarities of his own which differentiated him from the other comparable deities in the Fertile Crescent, Western Asia and the Aegean.

Thus, this figure did not fulfil Frazer's conception of the "dying god" as a generalized spirit of fertility dying to rise again. His relation to Inanna, or Ishtar, was quite different from that of Osiris to Isis. He was never a dead god who lived and reigned in a posthumous son like Horus and his earthly manifestation, the reigning pharaoh. Having been restored from the land of the dead in the fullness of his virile manhood, he was responsible for the revival of the new life springing forth from the parched ground in the spring and autumn. Therefore, his restoration as the "resurrected child" of the Goddess was celebrated annually with appropriate rejoicing, just as his descent was greeted with bitter lamentation and wailing.[36] The triumph, however precarious, was more enduring than in the Aegean, but it was never extended to man beyond the grave as in Egypt, where Osiris bestowed immortal life on those who were found to be "true of heart and voice" at the judgment. In Babylonia the renewal of life in nature did not carry any such implications in respect of the hereafter which remained a semi-conscious existence in a "land of no return".

Therefore, whereas in Egypt the Osirian Festival was held in honour of the death and resurrection of the god personifying the emergence of life from death in all its ramifications, the Annual Festival, or *Akitu*, in Babylon in the month of Nisan centred in the liberation of the captive god, Marduk, the re-enactment of the creation Epic (the *Enuma elish*), the humiliation and reinstatement of the king, and his ritual marriage with the Goddess in his Tammuz capacity to renew the processes of vegetation, to secure the fertility of the land and to determine the destinies at the beginning of the New Year.[37] Although many of the details of this complex ritual are obscure, the central position of the king as the chief actor in the role of Marduk is clear. It might, therefore, seem paradoxical that at a crucial point on the fifth day of the Festival he was conducted to the shrine of the god and there before the statue of Marduk he was stripped of his royal insignia, struck on the cheek by the high priest, forced to his knees and made to declare that he had not been negligent regarding the divinity of the "Lord of the lands", or of having destroyed Babylon. He was then reinstated on the throne, the regalia were restored to him, and his face was again struck in the hope of drawing tears as a propitious omen, indicating that he was regarded with favour by Marduk, whose goodwill he enjoyed.

Precisely what happened after this humiliation of the king can only be conjectured, as the texts fail at this point. From a commentary, however, it appears that the suffering god (Marduk) having been confined in the mountain—that is to say, held captive by the forces of death—was liberated and resuscitated, apparently by the New Year rites then in progress of which the rehabilitation of the king was the crux. Thus, on the eighth day the restored sovereign, holding his sceptre in his hand, conducted the statue of Marduk in a triumphal procession to the *Bitakitu*, or Festival House, outside the city, to "fix the destinies" in a chapel dedicated to Nabu, the son of Marduk, who had rescued his father from the mountain.

There the victory of Marduk over Tiamat, the leader of the forces of Chaos in the creation story, was celebrated at a great banquet before a return was made to the city for the consummation of the sacred marriage in the *Esagila*, enacted by the king and the priestess in a chamber (*gigunu*) on one of the stages of the ziggurat—which may have been decorated with greenery[38] —in order to restore the fertility of the fields, the flocks and men after the blight of winter or summer.

Thus, the New Year Festival in Babylon was a ritual enactment of the death and resurrection of the god who was the embodiment of the conditions of fertility, even though Marduk was never conceived as a single cosmic power like Re in Egypt, any more than the monarch was the dynamic centre of the social structure in Mesopotamia. Neither the king, the government nor the gods had an assured and completely secure position in an immutable order with the same deity as the unchanging transcendental unifying principle, as in the Egyptian solar theology or in the Osirian Horus relationship of the pharaohs. Nevertheless, in the background of the New Year rites, long before the creation story had taken its later shape around the very ancient seasonal ritual going back to Neolithic times, *rites de passage* were held to effect the transition at the critical stages of each new season.[39]

That the sacral kingship played a significant part in these rites is beyond doubt, though exactly how it functioned and exercised supernatural control over the processes of fertility is by no means easily determined. We know that in the Ancient Near East the institution was regarded as the very basis of civilization, so that, for example, an ancient Sumerian epic affirmed that "kingship descended from heaven" as a gift of the gods, both before and after the Flood in the third millennium B.C.[40] Therefore, it was of divine origin just as in the Nile valley with the unification of Egypt under one pharaoh the throne acquired a sacred status as the dynamic centre of the nation by appointment of the gods who became incarnate in the reigning sovereign. Moreover, because he personified the fructifying waters of the inundation containing all the

otentialities of life, the king was the god who brought fertility) Egypt. In this capacity he was the "herdsman of every one, ithout evil in his heart", whom the Sun-god "appointed to be ıepherd of the land, to keep alive the people and the folk".[41]
nd the first responsibility of the herdsman was to maintain he food supply. Therefore, he produced the life-giving waters and at the Harvest Festival presented to the gods the sheaf of grain which symbolized the fruits of the earth and the fertility of the land.

In Mesopotamia, "mother earth" rather than the sun and the rivers was the inexhaustible source of new life. Consequently, the power manifest in fertility in all its forms was personified in the Goddess who was the incarnation of the reproductive forces in nature and the mother of the gods and of mankind. It was she who renewed vegetation, promoted the growth of the crops and the propagation of man and beast. In her Inanna-Ishtar guise her marriage with the shepherd-god Dumu-zi or Tammuz, who incarnated the creative powers of spring, was held to symbolize and effect the renewal of life at the turn of the year, delivering the earth from the blight of sterility.

In the prehistoric background of this death and resurrection drama the struggle between the two opposed forces in nature, those of fecundity and barrenness, was enacted by human beings with whom the conflicting powers were identified. From time immemorial the king or chieftain was believed to exercise supernatural control over the processes of fertility by virtue of his identification with the creative forces in nature. Thus, in Sumer the king was *Dumu-zi*, and his marriage with the priestess of Inanna was an act of renewal recreating "the life of all lands".[42] This beneficent gift, however, was only bestowed after the perennial struggle with the malevolent hosts of primeval chaos had been successfully accomplished, which involved the imprisonment of Marduk in the role of Dumu-zi-Tammuz in the mountain of death, the humiliation of his earthly counterpart, the king, and the descent of Inanna-Ishtar into the underworld, in which the populace joined at the New Year Festival in Babylon when the annual rescue and re-marriage were re-enacted in the *Akitu* drama. Thus, the suffering and reviving god theme was developed from a prehistoric *rite de passage* centred in and around the emotional situation arising out of the sequence of the seasons and the renewal of the life of nature in the spring.

Whether or not this involved the killing of the king to revivify the natural processes and promote the welfare of the community, as has been conjectured, the mysterious powers of fecundity were related to the virility of the occupant of the throne, which in ancient agricultural society often required the ritual renewal of the king, either annually or at stated periods.[43] In Egypt, for example, the very ancient *Sed*-festival was held periodically on the first day of spring (i.e. the season of "the Coming Forth"), either thirty years after the accession of the pharaoh, or at shorter intervals, to confirm the reigning sovereign in his kingdom by a ritual rejuvenescence.[44] This included his sitting alternately on each of two thrones to symbolize his rule over Upper and Lower Egypt, crossing the temple court ceremonially to assert his power over the entire land, and the reception of the sceptre, flail and crook of his office in the chapel of Horus of Libya. These insignia eventually he offered to the jackal-god Upuaut of Situ. While the symbolism is obscure, and it is by no means clear whether it was the death and resurrection of Osiris that was impersonated, as Gardiner maintains,[45] and Griffiths and Frankfort deny,[46] the festival in any case was closely associated with the periodic resuscitation of the king in his divine capacity.[47]

Similarly, from the Ras Shamra texts, it would seem that in Syria in the middle of the second millennium B.C. a fertility cult of the dying and rising vegetation-god was established in which a ritual renewal was held perhaps every seven years. Here, again, however, the evidence is very uncertain, the texts being fragmentary and their decipherment incomplete. Nevertheless, the central theme appears to have been the struggle between life and death in nature in which a number of gods and goddesses, such as Aleyan-Baal and his enemy Mot, lord of the underworld, play their familiar roles in a vegetation drama,[48] though t may not have been an annual death and revival of the god of fertility that was celebrated in the liturgical rituals.⁴⁹ In these texts drought and famine seem to have been represented as seven-year scourges rather than seasonal phenomena. It was, however, the death of the god that caused the languishing of the earth which lasted for seven years.⁵⁰ Therefore, apparently the Ugaritic Baal was a fertility but not a seasonal god who seems to have undergone considerable modification if the Ras Shamra ritual was a Canaanite version of the Tammuz-Adonis cult, having perhaps affinities with the Egyptian Sed-festival. That the theme was very deeply rooted and firmly established in Syria is shown by the persistence of the cult of Adonis with its germinating seeds sown in "gardens", coupled with wailings for the young god and the wilted plants, and all that these observances involved.

THE CULTUS IN THE AEGEAN

The Minoan-Mycenaean Goddess of Vegetation and the Young Male God

In the Eastern Mediterranean, as we have seen, the Mother-goddess became the principal object of worship, especially in Cyprus and Crete, where her emblems and adjuncts abounded —the snake, dove, double axe, horns of consecration, obese figurines, mountain, tree or pillar. While she was primarily concerned with birth and maternal functions, as the Earth-mother she was also the Goddess of vegetation, with or without a male partner. Thus, in a group of Minoan-Mycenaean signet rings the vegetation cycle is represented in a series of cult scenes portraying the Mother-goddess in a variety of settings. A Late Minoan ring now in the Ashmolean Museum at Oxford, which may have come from the Vapheio Tomb at Mycenae, shows a kneeling woman bending over a large jar with her left arm, bent at the elbow, resting on the rim. Her head is inclined forward supported by her left hand in an attitude of mourning. Above her are the eye and ear symbols, and a little to the left in the air is a small rigid male figure holding an oval object that looks like a bow. Below is a richly dressed female figure with wavy hair, thought by Evans to b the Mother-goddess, while the male figure he took to be th "boy-god" as a youthful archer (Fig. 14).[51] Professor Persso thinks the scene has a funerary significance, the vessel being o the type used in pithos burial, and the theme that of sorro over death. The object next to the jar he interprets as a elliptically rounded stone with the leafless branches of a tre or bush behind it, symbolizing, as he suggests, the dyin vegetation in winter and man's sorrow and lamentatio "associated with the bleak world of nature gone dry and desiccate".[52]

On the Vapheio signet a mourning scene is represented in which the Goddess in a flounced skirt assumed apparently the role of the *Mater dolorosa* bowed in grief in the attitude o lamentation over a kind of miniature temenos. Within the sacred enclosure stands a narrow baetyl with a small Minoan shield hanging beside it; above, the Goddess is represented as a branch in leaf. To the right of her is a similar female figure, presumably the Goddess again in an upright position about to receive the fruit of a tree from a sanctuary containing a sacred pillar, and extended to her by a young male attendant whom Evans equates with the Cretan Zeus in a Tammuz role.[53] If the enclosure is a tomb containing a phallic stone, as is probable, the scene is brought into line with the grave of Attis in Phrygia and of Zeus at Knossos.[54] The mourning, therefore, may refer to a Minoan version of the suffering goddess theme in Western Asia and the vegetation cycle, the coming of spring being expressed in the budding leaves and ripening fruits. This is confirmed by the scene on a gold ring in the Museum of Candia, showing the sacred tree in an enclosure with scanty foliage. The stem is grasped by a woman with both hands, and on the left is an almost identical female figure in a flounced skirt with naked upper body and prominent breasts with her back to the tree and her arms extended to a third identical woman. In the fields are chevrons.[55]

Here the barrenness of winter gives place to the epiphany of the Goddess in its spring setting like that reproduced on a ring

The Cultus in the Aegean

Fig. 14. Minoan Goddess scene on a signet ring, Ashmolean Museum, Oxford

from a cist in a small tomb where an orgiastic dance in a field of lilies by four female votaries in typical Minoan garments is portrayed. Above the chief worshipper in the centre is a small female figure apparently rapidly descending, and to the left a human eye, which may symbolize the Goddess regarding the ecstatic dance being performed in her honour at the renewal of life in the spring, of which the snake by the side of the central figure below the eye is an emblem.[56] The bull which occupied such a conspicuous position in the Cretan "circus scenes"[57] may also have a fertility significance as a potent image of the reproductive force in nature in the spring festival[58] in which the king-god played the leading part, in conjunction with the Goddess as his consort, in the slaying of the Minotaur to overcome death and renew life.[59]

Zeus and Demeter

The function of the youthful male was to revive the life of vegetation in the annual cycle of the seasons, whereas that of the Goddess was to give birth to life of which she was the ultimate source and the generative force. Unlike her male partner she did not die to rise again, being the Earth-mother bringing forth vegetation as her offspring. With the development of agricultural society the "boy-god", however, becam the Sky-father who fertilized the Earth-goddess by pourin upon her the fertilizing rain from heaven. Thus, in Greece, a will be considered in the next chapter,⁶⁰ the Indo-Europea sky-and-weather-god, Zeus, consorted with goddesses an mortal mistresses in his capacity as the head of the Olympia pantheon. Among these were the chthonian Demeter, th Earth-mother, whose daughter, Kore (Persephone) was th Corn-maiden embodying the ripe grain annually gathered a the time of harvest. That Demeter inherited the attributes of th Minoan Goddess can hardly be doubted. Whether or not i was her marriage with Zeus "to make the fields wave with yellow corn" that was celebrated in her mysteries at Eleusis, as Frazer maintains,⁶¹ is less certain, though one of the purposes of the rites apparently was to secure the fertility of the crops and maintain the vegetation cycle, at any rate in the earlier developments of the cultus. Thus, it is not improbable that it arose from a very ancient agricultural festival which Nilsson suggests celebrated the bringing up of the threshold corn from the silos where after the harvest in June it had been stored to ripen until the seed-time in October. During the four months when it was below ground the fields were barren and desolate, withered by the scorching sun. Once the autumn rains began, ploughing started and the fields soon became green again in the mild winter with the crops ripening in early spring, about February or March. It was then that the annual commemoration of the dead, the Anthesteria, named after the flowers that appeared at that season, was held in Athens and the Lesser Mysteries of Demeter at Agrai, a suburb of the capital. Attendance at these rites was a preliminary to initiation at the Greater Mysteries at Eleusis in the autumn when the time of sowing was approaching and the seed corn was brought up from the silos, symbolizing the ascent of the Corn-maiden.⁶²

This interpretation of the origin of the Mystery makes it essentially a corn festival and Demeter a corn-goddess. The precise meaning of *de* in her name is in dispute and could ignify "corn" or "earth", but while at Eleusis she was primarily he giver of the grain, she was also the goddess of vegetation. As the personification of the fertile soil she was the Earth-mother whose daughter Kore later became confused with Persephone, queen of Hades and wife of Pluto, whose name connected her with Pluton, a god of the fruits of the fertile soil. Thus, Kore was transformed into Persephone and made responsible for sending up the new crops from below ground by her annual return from the nether regions. This gave the earlier agricultural rites a deeper meaning, associating them with the death and resurrection theme. But exactly how this was given ritual expression in the Mysteries can only be conjectured from the relatively late sources of information.

According to the post-Christian writer Hippolytus, the *mystae* in the Telesterion at Eleusis, at the supreme moment of initiation on the twenty-second day of Boedromion, sitting on stools covered with sheep-skins in darkness and complete silence, suddenly beheld the reaping of an ear of corn in a blaze of light, and heard the announcement of the birth of a divine child, Brimos.[63] Whether or not this had anything to do with a sacred marriage between Zeus and Demeter, symbolized by the union of the hierophant and the chief-priestess in their respective roles, is a matter of debate. While Hippolytus seems to have confused the Phrygian Attis rites with those of Demeter, if a corn-token was one of the sacred objects revealed it would be in accordance with the vegetation setting and circumstances of the Eleusinian Mysteries. The germinating ear was at once the symbol of the harvest of the grain and of the purpose of the Mysteries to secure a joyful resurrection of the initiates in the delectable meadows of Persephone, secured by means of a protracted series of purifications, processions, sacred utterances, the sacrifice of oxen and possibly a bull-fight.[64]

Furthermore, as the marriage of Zeus with goddesses in Greek tradition was an expression of the ancient belief in the union of heaven and earth whereby the earth was fertilized, a sacred alliance of this nature would be a normal and fitting conclusion of the Harvest Festival as in Mesopotamia and elsewhere in the Near East. This is confirmed by a passage in Proclus in the first century A.D., amended by Lobeck, in which the worshippers are said to have gazed up to the sky and cried aloud, "Rain (O Sky), Conceive (O Earth). Be fruitful."[65] This formula, as Farnell has pointed out, "savours of a very primitive liturgy that closely resembles the famous Dodenaean invocation to Zeus, the Sky-god, and Mother-earth; and it belongs to that part of the Eleusinian ritual *quod ad frumentum attinet*".[66]

Here, again, there are grounds for thinking that the same theme which prevails in the seasonal drama in the Ancient Near East recurred at Eleusis, and in combination with the more orgiastic Thraco-Phrygian Dionysiac,[67] the birth of a divine child (variously called Zagreus, Dionysos, Domophoon or Iacchos) appears to represent the fruit of a sacred marriage of the Sky-god (Zeus) and the Earth-goddess (Demeter), enacted by the hierophant in the capacity of the heavenly creator and the chief-priestess impersonating Demeter. The royal character of the ritual is suggested by the representation of the torch-bearers in the official robes of the high priests on a vase of the fifth century B.C. in the museum at Eleusis. The hair is wreathed with myrtle and tied at the forehead with a broad fillet, the *tout ensemble* giving the appearance of a king. The hierophant, the torch-bearer, the herald and the other principal officiants were members of the ancient Eleusinian families of the Eumolpidai and the Kerykes, to whom application had to be made for initiation. Therefore, while the Mysteries were open to all who could speak or understand Greek, and had not been polluted by blood-guilt or similar taboos, the rites were the hereditary possession of a priestly caste who may have been of royal descent.

Similarly, in the iconography on reliefs in the sacred precinct of Mycenaean origin, the mission of Triptolemus, the hero of agriculture and one of the princes of Eleusis, is depicted going about the earth in his chariot teaching men how to till the soil under instruction from the Goddess, reminiscent of the Osiris-Isis myth. In his raised left hand he is shown holding a sceptre nd seated on a magnificently carved throne drawn by winged ragons. In his right hand he holds the ears of corn, and looks ttently at Demeter in an attitude suggestive of listening to her nstructions. On a later plaque, dedicated to the gods of leusis by the priest Lakrateides, he is represented seated on throne transformed into a chariot and holding out his left and to receive the corn from Demeter, who sits in front of im with Kore behind holding torches. Close to her is Pluto ith the royal sceptre as king of the underworld, and to the ight an unnamed god on a throne and a goddess with a ceptre. At the back is the upright figure of a young man arrying a torch, probably Eubouleus, one of the youthful leusinian king-gods to whom it is dedicated.[68]

On a red figured vase from Rhodes, now in the museum of stanbul, the Earth-goddess is shown rising from the ground nd lifting a cornucopia on the top of which sits a male child hom she presents to a goddess with a sceptre, standing to the right. To the left of Demeter is a figure, possibly that of Kore, and above her head is Triptolemus in his winged car.[69] Nilsson identifies the child with Ploutos,[70] the fruit of the fields and representative of vegetation, while Triptolemus was the revealer of the secrets of Demeter, the promoter of agriculture, and the bestower of beneficent bounty, who invariably stands by the side of the divine pair, the Corn-mother and Earth-goddess, and her daughter the Corn-maiden.

THE VEGETATION CULT IN NORTH-WEST EUROPE

As the Goddess cult was diffused from the Mediterranean through Spain and France to Brittany, Britain, the S.O.M. region and Scandinavia, to what extent the vegetation cycle was retained is progressively less apparent the farther it spread from its original cradleland in the Near East and the Aegean. Its chief emblems, as we have seen, unquestionably persisted throughout the megalithic region in such forms as the baetylic pillar, the sacred tree or pole, the snake, the dove, the bull, *Pectunculus* shells, female figurines sometimes in association with male statuettes, and representations and carvings on tombs of the tutelary divinity who presided over the occupants in th French graves. Professor Persson has compared with simila scenes on Minoan-Mycenaean gold rings two figures of a ma and a woman beside a boat on a rock engraving in the provinc of Bohus in Sweden, and on another in the same area of a ma and a woman embracing on a ship with a tree over them possibly in process of marriage.[71] These, he maintains, are no isolated instances of such similarities in which can be detecte the vegetation seasonal theme and its ritual expression. Thus he equates with Aegean counterpart figures on Scandinavia rock engravings dressed in ancient skins with horns and, as h believes, with tails, and decapitated bodies, or bodies wit amputated limbs.[72] Whether or not Nerthus, the Norther Goddess of vegetation, was associated with the seasonal ritua cycle, the magico-religious control of the processes of fertilit in nature in its traditional Asiatic and Minoan-Mycenaea setting hardly can be excluded altogether in these more remot regions in North-west Europe. Thus, the procession of Nerthus in her wagon around the land, recorded by Tacitus,[73] is remarkably reminiscent of the progress of Cybele in her car drawn by oxen in the Roman ecstatic rites,[74] and of our own May Day revels.

Aegean Influences in Wessex
In the British Isles the vegetation cult of the Neolithic peasantry was overlaid by that of the sun and the heavens under Indo-European influence, introduced into the religion of the Beaker folk by their contact with the Battle-axe warriors in Central Europe. This becomes apparent in their great British sanctuaries at Avebury and Stonehenge in Wessex. As will be considered in the next chapter, both of these temples appear to have been dedicated to the worship of a sky-god. Nevertheless, the recent discovery at Stonehenge of engravings of a hilted dagger and a flanged axe with Mycenaean affinities on one of the horseshoe trilithons (No. 53), and similar axe-carvings on several of the sarsens of the outer circle, may indicate that the cult of the axe had penetrated to Britain from the Aegean not

later than about 1470 B.C.[75] Indeed it is possible, as Mr Atkinson suggests, that between 1500 and 1400 B.C. the sarsens were erected and the blue stones rearranged by the Wessex chieftains under the inspiration of Mycenaean builders in a co-ordinate effort demanding great skill and ingenuity; of one of whom, he conjectures, Silbury Hill near Avebury may represent the cenotaph.[76] Whatever may be the precise significance of these latest discoveries at Stonehenge, they are another indication of a link between the Wessex culture and Mycenaean Greece from about 1500 to 1300 B.C.[77]

The source of the gold ornaments and the gold-mounted amber disks in Wessex graves would seem to have been the Aegean, just as the blue glazed beads worn by Wessex chieftains were of Eastern Mediterranean manufacture. That some of the British axes were inspired by metal Minoan *bipennes*, or their derivatives, is not improbable,[78] or that bronze axes with side-flanges were imported from the Eastern Mediterranean via Spain.[79] From about 1600 the amber route constituted another important highway between the Baltic, Central Europe and the Aegean, and along it, and the Atlantic maritime route, ideas and cult-practices as well as commodities passed to North-west Europe, which included the Goddess tradition. With it may have come the vegetation rites associated with the seasonal cycle. In Wessex, like cremation, they seem to have been an intrusive element in the Early Bronze Age, if the open sanctuaries were connected primarily with the worship of the Sky-god rather than with that of the Mother-goddess. Nevertheless, since the solar cult in its long and complex history was so intimately associated with fertility, it would not be difficult for rites of this character upon which the livelihood and prosperity of a pastoral community depended, to be resuscitated under Aegean influences at Stonehenge and elsewhere, in a seasonal ritual celebrated at the summer solstice to make its flocks and herds multiply and to renew the generative forces in nature.

CHAPTER VIII

The Sky-religion

IF Early Man in his struggle for subsistence projected his religious consciousness primarily into the symbolic objects and emblems connected with the principle of fecundity, he also appears to have been aware of a transcendent power external to the world, directly or indirectly governing its processes, and having his abode in the sky.

THE IDEA OF GOD
Animism and Polytheism
Under the influence of the evolutionary thought that predominated at the end of the last century, a unilineal development of religion was postulated proceeding in an orderly sequence from animism through polytheism to monotheism. Thus, Tylor defined religion as "a belief in spiritual beings" arising, as he affirmed, from mistaken inferences from observation of such phenomena as dreams, trances, visions and death, transferred to the natural order. In this way, it was supposed, the sun, stars, trees, rivers, winds, clouds and mountains became animated by a soul or spirit and behaved like men or animals, the indwelling spiritual beings controlling the events of the material world and of man's life here and hereafter.[1] As human qualities were applied to them divine society and government were modelled on human society and its constitution with great gods and lesser spirits corresponding to chiefs and kings and their officers, and assigned their respective functions in a polytheistic pantheon of departmental deities.

The hierarchy of higher gods reigned in the sky in heavenly splendour and sent down rain to nourish the earth unless they were moved to wrath in which event they manifested their divine displeasure in the agonizing terror of the thunderstorm, the devastating hurricane, or the consuming fire. Rivalling in power and glory the all-encompassing Heavens was the Sun, rising anew every morning and passing into oblivion in the underworld in the evening, giving light and life to the living and the dead, and often becoming incarnate in the occupant of the throne on earth. Sometimes the Moon was his satellite, or the order might be reversed, the Moon taking precedence of the Sun. But whatever status was accorded to them, the various members of the polytheistic hierarchy were regarded as a development of animism, very much as in the world's assembly of great gods, chiefs, benefactors and other beneficent ancestors were among the deified heroes raised to divine rank and status after their death and duly venerated and propitiated as immortals.[2]

Therefore, from animism as "the minimum definition of religion" the development of the idea of deity proceeded in an orderly manner either, as Herbert Spencer stressed, from the deification and propitiation of the illustrious dead,[3] or, as Frazer maintained, by a supposed craving for simplification and unification reducing to a limited pantheon the gods believed to control the several departments, attributes and aspects of nature. "Instead of a separate spirit in every individual tree, they came to conceive of a god of the woods in general, a Silvanus or what not; instead of personifying all the winds as gods, each with his distinct character and features, they imagined a single god of the wind, an Aeolus, for example, who kept them shut up in a bag and could let them out at pleasure to lash the sea into fury." By a further generalization and abstraction "the instinctive craving of the mind after simplification and unification of its ideas" caused the many localized and departmentalized gods to be deposed in favour of one supreme creator and controller of all things. Thus, it was contended, as polytheism evolved out of animism, so monotheism emerged from polytheism when at length one solitary Deity was conceived as the sovereign lord and maker of heaven and earth.[4]

Supreme Beings

That such a neat and tidy theoretical interpretation of the development of theism was untenable became apparent when Andrew Lang called attention to the fact that so far from monotheism being the final product of an evolutionary process, among such very primitive people as the Australian aborigines tribal High Gods, or Supreme Beings, are neither spirits, ghosts of the dead nor departmental gods carried to the highest power.[5] While often they may stand aloof from everyday affairs, they are the personification and guardians of the tribal ethic. Having given the tribe its laws and instituted the initiation rites for the purpose of inculcating right conduct in society, the rules of which are handed on from generation to generation in these solemn assemblies over which they preside, they retired to dignified seclusion in the sky. So transcendent are these remote deities, in fact, representing the highest expression of supernatural power and will, primeval and beneficent, the guardians and givers of the social, ritual and moral orders, that Tylor and his followers dismissed them as importations by Christian missionaries. It has now been established, however, largely through the indefatigable researches of Pater Wilhelm Schmidt and his collaborators, that they constitute a genuine feature of uncontaminated primitive religion recurrent among such aboriginal people as the native tribes of Australia, the Fuegians in South America, the Californian tribes in North America, and certain negritos and other negroids in Africa and elsewhere.[6]

Whatever may have been their origin, these High Gods do in fact stand alone, head and shoulders above all secondary divinities, though certainly not to the exclusion of the lesser spiritual beings, totems, culture heroes and localized gods to whom popular worship is directed. Sometimes they have become so otiose that they are little more than a name, or, as in Central Australia, the personification of the bull-roarer, the thunderous booming of which is regarded as the voice of the god, at any rate by the women and uninitiated.[7] But although they are liable to become obscured in their lofty celestial eclusion, they stand on a plane by themselves, having greater and ider significance if a less clearly defined sphere of influence han that of the other divinities and spirits. Moreover, they eem to represent the ultimate moral value of the universe so ar as the primitive mind conceives such a reality.

Thus, Professor Evans-Pritchard records that among the uer in Nilotic East Africa, God is *Kwoth*, a being of pure pirit, and because he is like wind or air "he is everywhere and)eing everywhere he is here now". He is far away in the sky et present in the earth which he created and sustains. "Everything in nature, in culture, in society and in men is as it is because God made it so." Although he is ubiquitous and invisible he sees and hears all that happens, and being responsive to the supplications of those who call upon him, prayers are addressed to him and sacrifices offered to avoid misfortunes. Since God can be angry he can and does punish wrongdoing, and suffering is accepted with resignation because it is his will, and, therefore, beyond human control. But the consequences of wrongdoing can be stayed or mitigated by contrition and reparation, prayer and sacrifice.[8]

Such a conception of Deity, which is almost indistinguishable from that which obtains in the higher monotheisms like Christianity, Islam or Judaism,[9] is a religious response to the notion of divine Providence more fundamental than any gradual development from plurality to unity. It is a spontaneous, purposive functioning of an inherent type of thought and emotion; an evaluation of the *mysterium tremendum*, rather than speculation about souls or the universe. Indeed when the mind has reflected upon the animation of nature and arrived at conceptual ideas about spirits and organized pantheons the Supreme Being not infrequently has been left vaguely in the background. Therefore, so far from animism and polytheism passing into monotheism as a result of abstraction and generalization, simplification and unification, speculation about nature and its processes and man and his constitution appears to have led to the peopling of natural phenomena with a multiplicity of spirits, tutelary divinities, departmental gods and culture heroes in such profusion that the remote High God often has retired into the background.

The Universality and Antiquity of the Sky-god
This is not to suggest that a "primeval monotheism" once obtained, either as the result of a special divine revelation or of particular psychological processes and reactions which disappeared in the later stages of the development of any particular religion. The belief in High Gods among low races cannot be described as a true monotheism, since in addition to the transcendent Sky-god a number of particular lesser spirits of the air and of the earth, immanent in natural phenomena or growing out of the social, economic and cultural environment and the psychological concomitants of its organization, coexist with the Supreme Being and standardize behaviour by supernatural sanctions in which he is only remotely concerned. Pater Wilhelm Schmidt and his collaborators, it is true, have endeavoured to maintain that an exclusively monotheistic conception of Deity obtained in a hypothetical *Urkultur* at the threshold of human history, of which the Pygmy tribes, the Bushmen, the Ainus, the Tierra del Fuegians and the Kurnai, Kulin and Yin tribes of South-east Australia are modern representatives. But apart from the anthropological difficulties which the *Kulturkreise* method of ethnological analysis encounters in the determination of the origins and development of human institutions and beliefs, the available archaeological evidence affords little or no support for such a contention.

So far as the existence of Supreme Beings is concerned, the only possible indications of such a belief in Palaeolithic times are a few small oval pendants of bone and stone, perforated at one end, found at Laugerie-Basse and at Laugerie-Haute near Les Eyzies in the Dordogne,[10] identical in shape with the bull-roarer. Similar objects in bone have been discovered in a Magdalenian site at Saint Marcel, Indre, with markings not unlike those on Australian churinga,[11] and at Pin Hole cave at Cresswell Crags in Derbyshire in association with implements of a Mousterian type which apparently had survived in the

Gravettian phase at the beginning of the Upper Palaeolithic. Since the sacred bull-roarer and stone churinga figured prominently in the cult of the High God in Australia and elsewhere,[12] the occurrence of the mystic object in Upper Palaeolithic deposits could suggest that the belief in High Gods may have been a feature of the religion of the Gravettians and the Magdalenians in Western Europe. This is as far as the archaeological evidence takes us, and it must be recognized that a few very hypothetical pendants in a relatively late phase of the Palaeolithic is extremely insecure ground on which to build a far-reaching hypothesis concerning the beliefs that may have obtained at the emergence of the human race.

Nevertheless, the existence of a sky-god is so firmly established and deeply rooted in the history of religion from Neolithic times onwards, that this transcendental aspect of Deity may well go back to a very early period prior to the rise of the higher civilizations in the Near East. If in fact "bull-roarers" really were the outward and visible sign of the belief under Palaeolithic conditions, since they would have had to be made of wood to fulfil their functions in producing the weird thunderous noise which has been interpreted as the voice of the god, they could scarcely have survived the ravages of time any more than have other implements in wood. Thus, they cannot be expected to throw much light on the problem. The most that can be concluded from the pendants is that the sacred object may have existed and reproductions of it in more durable material were made and worn as amulets because of its sanctity, however and whenever the concept of Deity may have arisen in the religious consciousness of primeval man.

THE SKY-GOD IN THE NEAR EAST

The Sky-religion in Egypt

When the existence of an extra-mundane divine power was established and made the source of universal creative activity centred in the god of the sky, the various aspects and attributes of nature were related to him, directly or indirectly, as the head of the pantheon. Everywhere the same linguistic root connects the heavens, the clouds and the rain with their personifications in the Sky-god and his manifestations in the revivification of nature, the thunder and the storm. As Zeus, or Dyaus Pitar, among the Indo-Europeans was primarily the god of the sky and of the weather, known under a number of names, before he assumed the functions of the various gods whom he assimilated, so in Egypt the Falcon-god Horus is represented in the Pyramid Texts as the source of life and death, of rain and of celestial fire, thereby indirectly connecting the reigning pharaoh in his Horus capacity with an ancient predynastic Supreme Being[13] as well as with the son of Osiris, when the Sky-god had been replaced by the Sun-god as the Creator of the world.

The many forms in which the Sun-god was represented in the Egyptian texts are doubtless survivals of an earlier cult of the omnipresent Sky-god brought into conjunction with the all-prevailing solar worship in its many manifestations. As Breasted has pointed out, "the all-enveloping glory and power of the Egyptian sun is the most insistent fact in the Nile valley",[14] and it is hardly surprising that the ancient Egyptians saw the solar deity in different, doubtless originally local forms. Flying across the heavens like a falcon in his daily course, he was known as Harakhte, the "Horus of the Horizon", who with three other local Horuses constituted the Four Horuses of the eastern sky, represented as "four youths who sit on the east side of the sky, with curly hair".[15] In the morning he came forth as Khepera, a winged beetle rising in the east, and flying across the sky with outspread wings, the solar disk on his head, until he tottered down to the west as an aged man, Atum, as he appeared at Heliopolis, having run his daily course.

As head of the Egyptian pantheon, in his composite form Re combined all the forces of nature, and at Heliopolis before the First Dynasty he was conceived as the sun in the sky manifest in the solar disk. Horus became his son, and as the solar cult predominated after the unification of Egypt by the victorious Upper Egyptian kings (who personified the Sky-god Horus and came under Heliopolitan influence) Re became

upreme among the gods, absolute in his control of the Nile
alley, the ally and protector of the throne. Thus, in addition
) his being the source of life and increase, he was a divine
·ng, Re-Atum the self-created Creator, Re-Harakhte the
outhful god on the eastern horizon, and eventually at Thebes,
Amon-Re, the "king of the gods", worshipped in great magnificence at Karnak and Luxor. These aspects of deity, together
with Ptah, the "Great One" of Memphis, in due course were
blended not in a single monotheistic god but in three independent divinities with the same nature.

Thus, the Egyptians arrived at a conception of a universal
God without abandoning their polytheistic tradition, except
for the very short interlude in the Eighteenth Dynasty when
Amenhotep IV (Ikhnaton) transferred his allegiance solely to
Aton, an ancient god of the air and light, known also as
Show, and set up a new hierarchy and temple organization.
Karnak and the other temples of Amon-Re were closed, and
the names of all the gods erased from the monuments. The
capital having been removed from Thebes to Amarna in
Middle Egypt and renamed Akhetaton, "the Horizon of
Aton", the sole God of heaven and earth was there worshipped
by his royal son and embodiment as the creator and sustainer
of all things with altars in the open air. All anthropomorphic
and theriomorphic images were rigidly excluded, the only
symbol employed being that of the solar disk with emanating
rays.[16] But although the monotheistic movement was in line
with the new imperial power of the State, it made no permanent impression on the nation. Therefore, in the confusion that
followed the death of Ikhnaton in 1350 B.C., the dispossessed
Amonite priesthood regained its power, and the old régime
was restored with a new line of kings.

In the ancient world the ephemeral Aton cult of Amenhotep IV was the only attempt to reduce a pantheon of
polytheistic deities to a single all-embracing heavenly Creator.
Thus, even Yahweh among the Hebrews, until the end of the
Exile in the sixth century B.C. was primarily the God of Israel,
an essentially exclusive God with a localized sovereignty in the

land of his own choosing for the people with whom he stood in a covenant relationship. Indeed Ikhnaton, notwithstanding his fanatical zeal for the exclusiveness of Aton, apparently never tried to introduce the cult outside Egypt, except for erecting a temple in Nubia in a town he renamed Gematon. Where he differed from his immediate predecessors, who already had recognized the universality of Amon-Re, was in eliminating the syncretistic nature of Re as a blend of the deified sun, the horizon and the falcon, "Re-Harakhte of the two horizons rejoicing in his name of Show, who is the Aton". But, while the Aton was proclaimed to be the one and only God, for the Egyptians in general he was the actual heavenly orb as the ancient Sky-god was the falcon regarded as the manifestation of the power of the sun in the expanse of the sky.

Originally Horus was "the lofty one" (*Hrw*), and his association with the sun was subsidiary to his primary function in his Sky-god capacity.[17] Aton, on the other hand, was the material sun as it appears by day during its journey from the eastern to the western horizon, and his worship was so essentially centred in the solar disk that it was no more concerned with life on earth than with that in the hereafter.[18] Therefore, unlike that of Osiris, it made no popular appeal, having little or nothing to offer the toiling masses in this world or in the next life. It was confined to the pharaoh and his family, notwithstanding the universal supremacy of the Sun-god's dominion and his life-giving power emanating from his beneficent rays which shone upon the whole earth. For as Amenhotep IV declared, "there is no other that knoweth thee save thy son Ikhnaton". Thus, Atonism was destined to suffer the fate of the worship of all High Gods who became divorced from human affairs and the fundamental needs of mankind at large, expressed and made efficacious in an accessible cultus. To fulfil these requirements the Sky-gods and goddesses of the Egyptian solar cycle were brought into relation with the Earth-gods of the Osiris cycle and the cult of the dead so that the beneficence of the celestial realms through their agency might be bestowed on the earth in fruitful seasons with abundance of corn and

ine, destroying the forces of evil and giving immortality and
esurrection to the dead.

The Babylonian Triads

n Mesopotamia the assembly of gods in the sky was the highest
uthority in the universe determining the course of events on
arth. Under the leadership of Anu, the god of heaven, the
osmic order as an organized whole was established out of
haos and anarchy. His name, in fact, in Sumerian was "the
ky", and the high esteem in which he was held as the most
potent force in the cosmos long after his cult had fallen into
obscurity suggests his great antiquity going back to prehistoric
times. He is not mentioned, however, in the Sumerian lists,
and it is not until the time of Gudea, king of Lagash (c. 2060–
2042 B.C.), that his supremacy is affirmed and maintained
throughout the subsequent records of Babylonian religion. In
the "An-Anum list" in which the Sumerian and Akkadian
designations of the god of heaven are equated, his genealogy is
given under a series of names, and "the twenty-one parents
(i.e. ancestors) of Anu" accord with his descent from Apsu,
the god of the subterranean ocean, and Tiamat, the primeval
Chaos, in the Creation Epic.

Both he and the Storm-god, Enlil, the second member of the
Great Triad of deities, were described as "king of the gods",
and the kingship on earth was represented as a divine gift or
invention with the royal insignia resting "before the throne of
Anu".[19] But neither Anu nor Enlil nor the rulers (*lugal*) on
earth, occupied the unique position of the Sun-god and the
pharaoh in Egypt. As in the heavenly pantheon the Triad
were the leaders of the assembly, so in the Mesopotamian city-
states the kings were their servants, rising and falling with the
fortunes of the cities over which they ruled. Thus, although
"kingship came down from heaven", it resided temporarily in
five or six Sumerian centres with local dynasties subject to the
vicissitudes of hegemonies established by conquest.[20] Even
when Hammurabi unified the State into an Empire and made
Babylon the capital with its chief god Marduk (who inherited

the status and so many of the attributes and functions of Enlil) as the head of the pantheon, it was merely a temporary stability that was attained. The earlier Sumerian Triad (Anu, Enlil, and Ea, or Enki) with their respective priesthoods were only partially eclipsed, each continuing to rule over one of the three divisions of the universe, heaven, the air and the waters. Therefore, even Marduk was never regarded as the creator and source of all the other gods like Re or Ptah in Egypt.

Instead of the Creator emerging by a self-creative act from the primeval waters of Nun, in Mesopotamia, it was out of a state of chaos that the male and female progenitors, Apsu and Tiamat, brought forth their progeny, and, according to the original version, apparently the earth was created by Enlil before he was replaced by Marduk.[21] Eventually the kingship was established on the earth by the gods as an emergency measure before and after it had been destroyed by the Flood. The legendary "divine shepherd" *Dumu-zi* (Tammuz), under the designation of the "fisherman", alone continued the antediluvian régime in the Second Dynasty of Erech, between the god Lugal-banda and Gilgamesh in the traditional King-list. The Shepherd *par excellence* of Babylonia, however, was the historical Sumerian ruler Lugal-zaggesi, who claimed to exercise his sovereign rule over Mesopotamia under the sanction o Enlil, and when he was conquered by Sargon of Akkad the victor called himself "he who rules the Four Quarters". His son Naram-Sin assumed the title "king of the Four Quarters", which was also borne by the great gods, Anu, Enlil and Shamash (Uru), the Sun-god.[22] But it was not until Marduk was exalted over all the other gods by Anu and Enlil, and Babylon was declared to be the head of all the cities with Hammurabi as its ruler, that the kingship was brought into relation with a supreme deity at all comparable to Re and Osiris in Egypt. Even so, although Marduk was regarded as the Creator of mankind and king of the pantheon, it was only in a restricted sense that he had exercised his creative functions long after the universe had come into being when the gods were in conflict against Chaos.

The Sky-god in the Near East

Indeed in this pre-cosmic battle it was Ea, the god of water, originally Enki, the third of the Triad, who countered the threat to Tiamat and Apsu by casting a spell upon the waters and establishing a magical circle, before the gods conferred upon Marduk their collective power.[23] Moreover, he formed man from the blood of Kingu, the leader of the forces of Chaos,[24] and on the instructions of Ea Utnapishtim built his ship to save the human race from utter destruction during the Flood which Enlil had caused with that end in view.[25] Ea, in fact, was much more beneficent to mankind than either Anu or Enlil, and when Marduk attained supremacy he consulted his father (Ea) and sought his co-operation in the exercise of his office, as the source of wisdom and magical knowledge unrivalled among the gods. Upon his divinatory powers protection against the hostile supernatural forces depended, so that Ea became the patron of exorcists and was assigned his portion of the heavens whence he determined and controlled human destinies.

In a second Triad in the early god-lists Adad, or Hadad, the Storm-god of the air, is combined with Shamash, the Sun-god, and Sin, the Moon-god, also called Nannar in the Sumerian lists, the son of Enlil and the father of Shamash. It was Sin who both fixed the calendrical sequence of days, months and years and ordered the fertility of cattle. His son Shamash, the Utu or Babbar of the Sumerian lists, turned his "radiant face" upon kings and gave them the laws of good government. His special function being to uphold truth, order and justice, like that of Maat in Egypt, the daughter of Re, by whom the gods were said "to live", both he and Adad were concerned with oracular divination. They were, in fact, "lords of Oracles", and to their sanctuaries recourse was made to inspect the portents.

In his wider aspects, however, Adad was essentially an atmospheric High God whose cult extended throughout the Near East—in Mesopotamia, Syria and Palestine, and among the Hittites—under a variety of names (e.g. Addu, Resheph, Rammon and Teshub). Like Zeus, he was the god of the thunderstorms, and therefore his symbol was lightning, held in his right hand, and in his left hand an axe. In view of his destructive properties he was an object of fear, but combined with Shamash he was a god of justice whose sacred animal the bull was often associated with the sun in Syria.[26] This dual title was borne by some West Semitic kings who were said to give "his thunderings in the heaven as Adad so that the whole land trembles at his thunder".[27] Originally, however, Adad seems to have been primarily a sky-god connected with rain, the weather and the atmosphere, controlling the omens in the heavens, and as such readily acquired a solar relationship like most ancient deities of this nature.

Rain being the essential and most urgent need in parched arid regions, it was to those powers who controlled the elements that man turned in the first instance as the ultimate source of life and fertility. Therefore, it is not surprising that in the background of almost every prehistoric pantheon there is the figure of the Sky-god, however obscured it may have become in the process of solarization. Thus, Adad, like Horus and Min in Egypt, was a heavenly Being—the Power of the Sky—with his celestial bull, his thunderbolt and axe or hammer, who combined weather and fertility functions with those of the solar and storm divinities, and the attributes of the various gods associated with them.

THE INDO-EUROPEAN SKY-GODS

The Indo-Iranian Sky-gods

Amid all the vicissitudes of the Sky-god sometimes he retained his earlier supremacy in the physical universe and in the highest heaven, or he became incorporeal outside and independent of the world, as in the case of Varuna in India, whose name occurred with those of Mitra, Indra and the Nasatya twins, in a treaty between the Anatolian Hittites and the Mitanni in Syria about 1400 B.C.[28]

In prehistoric times the Aryans of India must have been very closely associated with those of Iran, even though they may not have been in actual historical contact with each other; the Indo-European cradleland towards the end of the third

The Indo-European Sky-gods

millennium B.C. having been somewhere between the Danube and the Oxus, not improbably on the steppes east of the Caspian Sea. This common home is reflected in the Iranian mythology but not in the hymns of the Rig-veda, the earliest Hindu texts which cannot be later than the middle of the second millennium B.C. (c. 1500), notwithstanding the recurrence of Iranian names in India and implied references to Persia in the Vedic literature.[29] This may have been an intentional repression, as the two sections appear to have been in a state of hostility for a very long time. Thus, in the earliest Indo-European religion only the gods of the sky, the wind and the sun, together with a sun-cult were recognized. To these the soma-cult was added by the Indo-Iranians. There was a tendency for an abstract quality to be associated with each god. Thus, Varuna was a heavenly god who upheld and regulated the moral cosmic order, like his Avestan counterpart, Ahura, who was also the supreme guardian of the moral law and of the cosmic order, symbolized in Rta. But when the Indian and Iranian groups broke asunder and developed their respective cultures the abstract deities, instead of being known as *daiva* gods as heretofore, were called in Iran *Asura*.[30]

In India, Varuna originally was the all-encompassing sky who supported heaven, earth and the air, bestowed rain, and whose Sanskrit name may be equated with the Greek *Ouranos* (sky).[31] In this capacity he was a heavenly monarch living in a golden abode in the sky, and became associated with Mitra, a solar god of light. The mighty warrior Indra, the god of thunder, had his headquarters in the atmosphere, between the sky and the earth, and Agni, the god of fire, was as all-pervading as the wind. Behind all these celestial gods was the old Indo-European Dyaus Pitar, identical with the Greek Zeus and the Roman Jupiter, the sky- and weather-god who eventually found a home on the Capitoline Hill at Rome in the temple in which an ancient boundary-stone open to the sky had been venerated from time immemorial. As the personification of the heavens Dyaus Pitar was the source of the fertilizing rain and also of the thunder, and in his paternal capacity he was united with Prithivi, the earth, as the universal parents. But he was only vaguely conceived in the Rig-veda, and very seldom appealed to, having been displaced by the nature gods and goddesses.

Thus, it was the all-encompassing Varuna taken in conjunction with Rta, "the right order", who in Iran eventually emerged as Ahura Mazda, the Wise-lord of the Avesta. But although in India the conception of Deity started from much the same presuppositions as those which prevailed in the Ancient Middle East, with the sky and the earth assuming their customary roles in the process of reproduction, the movement in Vedic tradition was towards a monistic unification of the universal cosmic order. When in due course the institution of sacrifice replaced Varuna and the nature gods under Brahmanic influence between 800 and 600 B.C., Prajapati became the Lord of Reproduction and the personification of the creative principle, at once creator and creation. As the ruler of the macrocosm and microcosm he pervaded all things, and through the universal cosmic and moral order (Rta) he fulfilled his operations as an immanent dynamic process permeating all things. By his primal sacrifice at the hands of the gods the phenomenal universe came into being as so many parts of his body, Prajapati having reproduced himself by means of a golden egg from which emerged the neuter impersonal creative principle Brahman operative in the sacred utterance (Veda) and in cosmic activity (Rta), generated by the sacrificial ritual. It was this creative process that was renewed by the priests, "the sacrifice being the god Prajapati at his own sacrifice", and by this offering the whole creation was resolved into a unity sustained by the rite.[32]

The merging of one divinity into another was the inevitable result of the cosmic principle expressed in terms of Rta and Varuna as the unifying element in nature and man, and of the various aspects of the universal order. When under Brahmanic influence the neuter Brahman emerged as the first-born of All, and in the Upanishads became the divine principle identified at once with the entire universe and the transcendent self

(Atman) of man, the ancient gods of the sky and of the earth were retained as aspects and attributes of the Absolute. Although the worship of the Vedic gods and the ritual order went on little changed in India among the masses, the One Ultimate Reality was resolved in Universal Being, expressed in the Upanishadic equation *tat tvam asi*, "That Thou art", centering in the unchanging, unknowable, actionless Brahman set over against yet pervading the unreal phenomenal world in a perpetual state of flux—the essence of all that is "unmoved, yet moving swifter than the mind", and like the air supporting all vital action.[33]

In Iran, on the other hand, against this monistic interpretation of the Ultimate Reality lying behind the world of phenomena and the desire to escape from the cycle of existences, the earlier polytheism moved in the direction of a monotheistic or dualistic totality of the one all-wise Lord Ahura Mazda, as the only God. To him the other *daevas* and *ahuras* were subordinated without losing all their primitive meaning and significance, since they became aspects of Ahura Mazda, modalities of his action. The struggle between good and evil, light and darkness, so fundamental in the magico-religious cult of Early Man, continued; but it was welded together into a single conflict in which God and man played their respective roles. Like Varuna, Ahura Mazda was the all-encompassing, all-wise, omniscient, governor of the universe and the actions of mankind, the embodiment of the "right law" (*Asha*). As Good Mind he was the Father of Reason, revealing himself to man and helping man to fulfil his proper vocation on earth, upholding the "Best Mind" (virtuous action), the Creator of Right, acting directly through the mind. In the Gathas he is the Eternal Being, who can be perceived only in thought, but his governance of the universe is apparent to all—the Good Architect whose sovereign righteous rule will be vindicated when the renovated world will be transformed at the end of the present age.[34]

When Mazdaeism began to spread throughout the Persian Empire, Ahura Mazda was represented on the royal

Achaemenian tombs and monuments at Persapolis by a winged disk out of which arose the head and shoulders of the Wise Lord, symbolizing how he reigned in the sky and enfolded and protected with his wings the earth and its ruler. Often he was surrounded by divine assistants who had been worshipped originally as polytheistic nature gods, and now engaged in the primeval struggle between the forces of good and evil under one or other of the twin spirits, Spenta Mainyu or Angra Mainyu.[35] As the oldest Avestan texts date back only to Zarathushtra, what lies behind his reform can only be conjectured. Nevertheless, this symbolism in Egyptian iconography belongs to the beginning of the monarchy in the fourth millennium B.C., where, as we have seen, the sky was represented by the outstretched wings of Horus. Indeed it seems that in some respects Zoroastrianism was not so much a break with the past as a determined effort to reassert the old Asura religion by ridding it of all *daivic* contaminations and pantheistic developments in order to restore the supreme Sky-god Varuna, now called Ahura Mazda, to his earlier position, and raising him to a unique level as an ethical monotheistic Deity. This would make him comparable to Yahweh in the neighbouring and contemporary post-exilic Jewish community which became part of the Persian Empire at the end of the sixth century B.C.

As Dumézil has shown, the structure of Indo-European society was reflected in its pantheons, and as an abstract entity tended to become associated with each god in the divine hierarchy, Zarathushtra succeeded in making Ahura Mazda the ethical Deity *par excellence* among the cattle-rearing farmers, who were beset by the marauding Turanian nomads from the north, regarded as the followers of the forces of evil intent on capturing cattle for sacrifices to their *daevas*. Against them Zarathushtra fought his holy wars, and it was as a result of his victory over them that the new faith was established on firm foundations. The good life was identified with agriculture on earth and the reign of the Wise-Lord, the Father of Good Mind, in the heavenly realm, with the long history behind the tradition going back in all probability to prehistoric times and he worship of the Supreme Being as a tribal All-Father and uardian of the law of right conduct. Through Judaism it assed to the West and influenced Christian thought and heology, particularly in its eschatological aspects.

Zeus and the Olympian Divine Family
On the northern grasslands stretching from the Lower Danube eastwards along the north side of the Black Sea through southern Russia, and north and east of the Caspian Sea, the ancestors of the Indo-European peoples were still in the Stone Age, pasturing their herds on the steppe, before they separated in two groups about 2000 B.C. and dispersed into India and the Balkans, the pastures of Thessaly, and the verdant hills of Italy, where they became ancestors of the Greeks and Romans, speaking an Aryan type of language. Driving their herds before them, on the northern borders of Greece they settled under the shadow of Mount Olympus before they invaded the Aegean fortresses such as Tiryns and Mycenae. With them they brought their gods who were essentially the mountain deities of the Indo-European polytheistic tradition, as the Hebrews carried into Palestine Yahweh their god of the sacred mount, Horeb or Sinai.

At the head of their pantheon stood the great Sky-god whom they had worshipped on the grasslands under a variety of names, such as Dyaus Pitar, Varuna, and finally was known as Zeus, "the sky". On the summit of Mount Olympus he dwelt in his cloud palace with the lightning in his hand, ruling his *comitatus* like a Nordic chieftain. If in the Homeric tradition he reigned supreme in his heavenly kingdom organized on the model of a human clan, each of his retainers controlled as his own a realm of nature or of the affairs of men, though Zeus retained his position as their permanent overlord. But being primarily and originally the god of the sky and the weather, his proper home, and that of the rest of the Olympians, was in the heavens in contradistinction to the chthonians, whose domain was on and below the earth, being the gods of the indigenous population before the arrival of the Indo-European and Achaean invaders in the second millennium B.C. In the celestial realms with which Olympus was equated Zeus was the Supreme Deity ruling among the immortals as the "father of gods and men", "of broad vision" (i.e. all-wise like Varuna and Ahura Mazda), and all-powerful over heaven and on earth.

On the plains of Thessaly, however, the Homeric Olympian mythology developed in a feudal society where feasting, fighting and hunting were prominent features of everyday life, especially among the Nordic chieftains and their vassals. Therefore, the gods are represented as conquering chieftains, royal buccaneers. As Professor Gilbert Murray says, "they fight and feast, and play, and make music; they drink deep, and roar with laughter at the lame smith who waits on them. They are never afraid, except of their own king. They never tell lies, except in love and war."[36] In Greece they were conquerors rather than creators, and divided the spoils of war among themselves, and lived on the revenues.

But the Homeric tradition was only one strand in the complex Olympian pattern. Not only was the sky-and-weather-god endowed with the character of the society in which he held dominion. But other legends grew up around Zeus which had little to do with his original nature and attributes, such as the Cretan story of his birth. In this myth he is very unlike the Olympian heavenly chief. Rather than being the Sky-god *par excellence* of the Homeric tradition he was the son of Rhea, the consort of Kronos and the Cretan counterpart of the Anatolian Mother-goddess, Cybele. After his birth he was hidden in a cave in the mountain called Aigaion and suckled by a goat, and, according to one curious tale, fire issued from it every year when the blood from the birth of Zeus streamed forth, suggesting, as Nilsson says, that "this child is the year-god, the spirit of fertility, the new life of spring".[37]

This Cretan Zeus was a much more primitive figure than the Indo-European Sky-god, embodying the processes of fecundity on earth rather than renewing them by sending the italizing rain from the heavens. Nevertheless, as the Aryan-chaean and Aegean aspects of Greek religion fused they ound a common centre in "the father of gods and men" and he syncretistic Zeus came to occupy a position in the cultus s comprehensive as that of the Magna Mater in the Graeco-oman world. It is hardly surprising that a deity equated with he sky and made responsible for the weather should be iden-ified with the god of fertility, ensuring abundant crops as well s the increase of flocks and herds. Such coalescence, as we ave seen, had frequently occurred in the Near East, in Asia ˙nor, Egypt, and in the Indo-Iranian region, and it recurred n Greece when the cultus of the Indo-European invaders ombined with that of the Aegean basin. Then without essen-˙ally changing his character and status the indigenous vegeta-on deity became Zeus, but he continued to exercise his unctions without any substantial change, while Zeus remained he head of the pantheon and took over a number of offices, aspects and attributes beyond the range of his original nature as sky-and-weather-god, the cloud-gatherer, the rain-giver, the thunderer, and the chief of the Olympians.

Thus, before he attained his exalted position, in the Hesiodic tradition he is represented as having had to overthrow the Titans, an earlier group of gods from whom he was himself descended through his father, Kronos. This may be a reflection of an historical situation when the Olympian Sky-religion defeated the chthonian indigenous cult of the soil but incor-porated much of the chthonian tradition, as the human race was thought to have imbibed a Titanic element in its essential ancestral history in combination with the divine nature derived from Zagreus-Dionysos. This dual character of the historic Zeus is revealed in his celestial aspects and attributes brought into relation with his connexion with the fertility of the earth and of vegetation the rain-producer when the invaders had to live on the produce of the soil on settling in Greece; very much as Yahweh acquired a vegetation cultus after the conquest of Palestine by the conglomeration of Hebrew tribes.

The Sky-father and the Earth-mother

The various unions of Zeus with Earth- and Corn-goddesses —Hera, Dione, Demeter, Semele and Persephone—suggest that in the background of these traditions lay the widespread conception of the marriage of Heaven and Earth in which he played the role of the Sky-father. When the local legends were correlated in the Epic literature one of the brides was exalted to the status of the official wife (i.e. Hera) of Zeus, while the rest were regarded as his mistresses, in accordance with the custom that prevailed in the Greek States where such irregularities were generally accepted.[38] Thus, he was accredited with a considerable illegitimate offspring, partly divine when born of goddesses, and partly human when their mothers were mortal women. But in prehistoric times it would seem that the Sky-father-Earth-mother fertility ritual was enacted, doubtless by human instruments and agents of the respective god and goddess, to enhance the fecundity of the soil and the reproductive processes in nature generally.[39]

In the Aegean the youthful male god was subordinate to the Mother-goddess who gave birth to all life, human, animal and vegetable,[40] until with the fusion of the Olympian and the chthonian cults the Sky-god became supreme as the chief deity of the dominant invaders with their Indo-European background. Henceforth Zeus played the leading role, and his consorts were relatively minor figures, so that it is often difficult to determine to what extent they were his wives. Even the cult of Hera, concentrated on the life and function of women and marriage, had little or nothing to do with that of Zeus, and her union with him was merely the result of her having been the chief goddess and in consequence a fitting partner for the chief god in spite of his previous nuptials with earth-goddesses like Demeter, Semele and Themis.[41] But neither was Zeus always the Sky-god, nor did he always marry an Earth- or Corn-goddess.[42] Taking over the functions of local lesser divinities he was a syncretistic figure as he was much married to a variety of subordinate wives, and had contracted unions with innumerable concubines and mistresses. Nevertheless, he etained his position of supremacy, paramount in nature, in he control of human life and its affairs, until in classical times e became for poets and philosophers the concept of deity ı its abstract ethical and universal evaluation, either as a antheistic principle or as the omnipotent and omniscient ivine ruler of the universe.

The Scandinavian Heavenly Deities

he Indo-Europeans living originally in nomadic pastoral ommunities in a steppe country, unlike settled agriculturists, ad always worshipped the Sky-father rather than the Earth-mother as their supreme god. Indeed as Childe has pointed out, no Earth-goddess is traceable in their language,[43] and female figurines were not prominent among them. But in Northern Europe, as in the Aegean, the Sky-god was often associated with the Earth-goddess as his consort, and the marriage of Zeus and Hera had its counterpart in Scandinavia. Thus, Othin (Woden), who in the early developments of Teutonic religion probably was a Sky-god, was the husband of Jörd, the Earth-goddess and mother of Thor, the thunder-god.

According to the Prose Edda, composed by Snorri in the twelfth century A.D., Othin was at once the All-Father, a divine king who came from the Black Sea, where as Asgard he was the chief of the city, a great warrior, conqueror, culture-hero and magician who taught by means of runes and spells. Among his children, Thor in addition to being the thunderer was a god of fertility who sent the showers to fertilize the ground and produce "the fair fruits of the earth", being the son of Jörd, the Earth-mother. When he blew into his red beard the thunder was heard, and his hammer was the lightning-bolt. To wield it with deadly consequences he put on iron gloves and clasped about him his "girdle of might", holding "the rod of power" wherein lay the magical strength of Othin. As he drove in the heavens in his wagon drawn by he-goats the thunder rolled, and such was his power and prestige that in Norway and Iceland he was worshipped as the beneficent Supreme God with aspects and attributes not unlike those of

Zeus. But like Indra he was the personification of strength and might, equipped with thunder-bolts as the thunder-god; the protector of mankind against his demonic adversaries. In fact, behind the two figures may stand a common hero of Indo-European tradition who has assumed a variety of forms in the process of diffusion from the transcaspian cradleland to India, the Eastern Mediterranean and Scandinavia, very much as Nerthus, the oldest Norse goddess of fertility, and the Phrygian Cybele, were local expressions of the universal Magna Mater.

The occurrence of small hammer-shaped amulets of amber, bone or stone, comparable to the almost identical hammers of Thor found in viking graves and to the symbols cut in runic stones, suggests that the lightning cult associated with Thor is of prehistoric origin, like the closely related cult of the double-axe in the Aegean and the Near East which recurs in Scandinavia. Thus, in Denmark frail ceremonial axes decorated with gold were used as votive offerings in the Bronze Age, and in a grave at Kivik in Skane two axes were engraved on each side of an altar, and in the scene of a procession men are depicted carrying axes of the same shape, together with solar symbols and pictures of ships.[44] In Iceland a bronze disk representing the sun was set on a chariot with six wheels and on the axles, doubtless depicting the horse-drawn chariot in which Sol, the sister of the Moon, drove across the sky by day. The Sun, however, was female in Old Norse mythology, and Snorri makes her one of the group of goddesses known as *asynja* who, although equal with the gods, were not in the same category as Othin the All-Father, Thor the Almighty and Frey the world's god. Sol, no doubt, was worshipped from very early times as the prehistoric solar symbolism indicates, but little or nothing of importance can be extracted from the mythological literature concerning the origins of the cult. The fire-festivals, however, which have been a prominent feature in Scandinavia and elsewhere in Europe at the summer solstice,[45] are probably relics of the magical rites performed at this season to assist the sun at the critical turning-point in its annual course along the heavenly road.

Sky-worship in Wessex

n the British Isles, as we have seen,[46] the Mediterranean megalithic cult so closely associated with the Earth-mother, death and rebirth, was fused with the Indo-European sky and solar religion at the beginning of the Bronze Age when the Beaker folk with their Battle-axe cultural affinities transformed the Avebury complex of monuments into sanctuaries open to the sky which culminated in the great stone circle on Salisbury Plain. Without endorsing the elaborate astronomical speculations which have been made in connexion with Stonehenge, that in this remarkable temple a celestial and solar ritual of some kind was practised can hardly be doubted, directed in all probability to a Sky-god comparable to Varuna, Zeus and Jupiter.

Thus, its orientation seems to have been aligned on the rising sun at midsummer, since on the summer solstice the sun rises so very near the peak of the Heelstone, even though the central line of the Avenue is not the point of sunrise, as Sir Norman Lockyer contended, because it is not visible from the centre of Stonehenge. Nevertheless, it seems that the monument has been intentionally arranged in relation to solar alignments connected with the solstices.[47] If this be so, it would appear to have been erected primarily for the performance of rites at seasonal festivals, probably associated with the rising and the setting of the sun in the north-east and the south-east respectively, as the alignments suggest, unless they were employed merely to fix the time of the festival.

In any case, whether or not Stonehenge was actually a Sun temple, unquestionably it was an open sanctuary characteristic of the Indo-European worship of the Sky-god, planned and erected in relation to celestial phenomena. Only a very intensive religious motive could have produced such uniquely elaborate and extensive cult-centres as Avebury and Stonehenge of which the simple stone circles were pale reflections. That these circular megalithic monuments are almost exclusively peculiar to Britain and Brittany, and in the case of Stonehenge underwent so many reconstructions from the Late Neolithic

(c. 1900–1700 B.C.) to the end of the Bronze Age (c. 1300 B.C.), shows the vigour and vitality of the cultus in this region, under the supremacy of the Breton-Wessex chieftains who were largely responsible for the maintenance and development o Sky-worship in its central sanctuaries in Wiltshire.

CHAPTER IX

Prehistoric Religion

FROM the foregoing survey of the archaeological data it has become apparent that prehistoric religion centred in and developed around the three most critical and perplexing situations with which Early Man was confronted in his every‑ day experience—birth, death and the means of subsistence in a precarious environment. The pressure of events in the external world and in human affairs, the perpetual struggle for existence and survival here and hereafter, the innumerable frustrations and awe‑inspiring experiences, often completely outside his control and comprehension, created, it would seem, a tension for the relief of which ways‑ and means had to be found. When life depended largely on the hazards of the chase, the vagaries of the seasons and so many unpredictable and un‑ toward circumstances and events, the emotional strain must have been endemic. And once a ritual technique had been devised to sublimate the stress, it became established and developed indefinitely to meet every new demand and maintain the equilibrium in an expanding social structure and religious organization.

THE RITUAL CONTROL OF NATURAL PROCESSES

Thus, the religious consciousness was projected into whatever natural force or process or object it identified with the sacred. A symbol as the image or mental reflex of instinct may arise spontaneously, as Jung maintains, independent of conscious volition, as in the realms of dreams, visions and hallucinations. This type of human experience has found expression in animistic and theistic interpretations of natural phenomena, so that the mysterious sacred power has been equated with parti‑ cular species of animals and physical features such as mountains, rivers, the wind, the sun, the moon and the constellations. It has also been associated pre-eminently with life-giving processes—fecundity, maternity and everything connected with generation and birth—and with the disturbing and disintegrating phenomenon of death. Natural forces and events, in fact, have been so overwhelming that they have appeared as many different supernatural powers and principles at work in a variety of ways, good and bad, beneficent and malevolent. Consequently, as many symbolic images of divinity have been devised as different sacred identities have been established, each duly equipped with its appropriate ritual techniques in the form of a cultus designed to bring under control and to make efficacious the forces with which the symbols are associated.

In their several capacities these transcendental entities have been regarded as belonging essentially to the "other world" which mysteriously imposes itself on this world and its events. Therefore, the religious reaction is not just a mental reflex of instinct arising purely spontaneously as a product of a "psychological machine", as Durkheim contended; merely a product of society which has "all that is necessary to arouse the sensation of the Divine in minds by the power it has over them; so that to its members it is what a god is to its worshippers".[1] While it is true that religion has emerged within society and that it functions as an integral aspect of its structure enabling human beings to live together in an orderly arrangement of social relations, and to make their own life and characteristics explicit through a social medium,[2] it is very much more than the evaluation and personification of the organization of the community. The totem, for example, is not just "the clan itself personified and represented to the imagination under the visible form of the totemic animal or vegetable", as Durkheim contended, any more than religion is only "a unified system of beliefs and practices relative to sacred things" which "unite into one single community all those who adhere to them".[3]

That the discipline has arisen very largely in relation to such practical problems as the maintenance of the food supply has been demonstrated in this volume,[4] and unquestionably it has united individuals and groups into stable social structures in

The Ritual Control of Natural Processes

higher unity to preserve a state of equilibrium; but behind and over and above the "collective representations" it has imposed on the members of a social group there has always been apparently the conception of a transcendental order external to man and society associated with abnormal, unpredictable, inexplicable and mysterious occurrences, objects and processes in the universe and in human experience. This is of the very essence of religion at all times and in all states of culture. Indeed, so far as this aspect of the discipline is concerned, religion may be described as the recognition of and the endeavour to establish and maintain beneficial relations with the supra-mundane sacred order manifesting itself in the universe and controlling its processes and human affairs, whether collective or personal. This found expression in a technique which aimed at establishing through ritual institutions an efficacious relationship with the source of life and power, of abundance and well-being at the heart of all existence, to overcome the disabilities of death, sterility and the ills to which mortal flesh is heir, as well as of producing stability and equilibrium in the body politic. By means of symbols, rites and dances human energies have been directed into new activities which have exercised an integrative function in society by enabling man individually and collectively to meet his crises with confidence, trust and hope by assimilating life-giving strength, allaying his fears and renewing his aspirations.

Thus, at critical junctures alike in the career of the individual from the cradle to the grave and its aftermath, and in the sequence of the seasons, especially at the turn of the year, the chances and changes of this mortal life have been unified, controlled and fortified by supernatural forces believed to govern the course of events and human destinies. Under Palaeolithic conditions, discharge of emotion and longing was centred on the food supply, birth and death. Therefore, it was in relation to these precarious phenomena that a ritual cultus developed to give effective expression to the most urgent needs of a tense situation fraught with such serious dangers, difficulties and consequences for all concerned. In respect of the food supply the position was complicated by the fact that a feeling of kinship existed between man and the animals which had to be hunted. Indeed, since they constituted a vital aspect of a providential bounty and beneficence of the world and its processes, they acquired a divine character and significance, being the primary source of the means of human subsistence. Consequently the necessity to kill and eat them was in conflict with the sense of kinship with them, and of dependence upon their goodwill and continuance. It was apparently out of this contradictory situation and its emotional tension that the cultus of the caves emerged.

The Nature and Function of Symbols
Thus, in the seclusion of these numinous and inaccessible Palaeolithic sanctuaries hunting magic to secure success in the chase was combined with fertility rites of increase and masked dances to establish and maintain a right relationship with the sacred species. To follow Lévy Bruhl and explain this behaviour as the result of a "prelogical mentality"[5] is a misconception of what he calls the "Law of Contradiction" and the "Law of Participation". On his hypothesis everything is permeated by forces, influences and actions which, though imperceptible to sense, are so real that all things are fused and no distinction is made between this world and the "other" world; "to what is actually present to sense, and what is beyond". Therefore, all the objects and entities of the natural order are not divided from one another, but are so united in a bond that each participates in the other, making it what it is not and enabling the same entity to be simultaneously in many places. Consequently, in totemic society a man imagines himself to be his totem, or under Palaeolithic conditions assumes animal disguises, as in the figure of "the Sorcerer" at Les Trois Frères, or in that of a masked dancer at Lourdes and elsewhere.

But while it is true that both primitive and prehistoric peoples not infrequently have regarded themselves as an animal r bird, or even an inanimate object, and equated natural henomena with divine beings and activities, it cannot be aintained that "the law of contradiction" and the laws of nagic are thereby excluded from their mentality. The identification of the symbol with the thing symbolized is the result f the introduction of a third term in the equation. In the case of the totemic relationship the union is achieved by the supposition that the human group participates in the spiritual nature of its sacred ally from whom it is descended, and it is this common element which effects the bond between them, making them what otherwise they would not be. Among the Nuer, in fact, the links between a lineage and its totem is the tutelary spirit of the lineage associated with the totem. The natural species is not identical with a spirit except in relation to its lineage. Similarly, when the relationship is represented by a material symbol the symbol is regarded and treated in the same way as the spiritual entity it symbolizes, not because it is thought to be other than it actually is but because it has acquired a spiritual quality which does not belong to it in its own nature without changing its outward and visible form and character.[6]

This sacramental conception of symbolism does not contravene either logic or the "law of contradiction". It merely presupposes the existence of an extra-mundane spiritual world standing against and in a particular relation with this world over which it exercises some measure of control. This is a fundamental religious assumption at all times and in all states of culture, however crudely and naively, or mystically and metaphysically, it may have been expressed and interpreted. In its prehistoric mode of expression it lay behind the ritual control of natural processes and events, the kinship with the animal creation and the mimetic dance in which animal disguises were a prominent feature. When a ritual expert arrayed himself in the skin and antlers of a stag, or in the feathers of a bird, and imitated the behaviour of the species he personified, he did so in the belief that for the time being, and for the prescribed purpose, he was what he represented himself to be, and in that capacity he did not imitate but he actually did what he set out to do. He caught and killed his prey; he made the copulation of male and female effective in the reproduction of offspring; he established a sacramental relationship between man and the providential source of his food supply.

Totemism and the Sacred Dance

That this involved the practice of totemism is not very probable since, apart from the archaeological objections that have been considered,[7] in its more developed forms the institution involves a social and religious structure which is not likely to have prevailed in Palaeolithic times. In practice it is a particular and specialized system of economics with its own technique for the supernatural control of the food supply and the elaborate kinship organization of society it entails, presupposing a long process of development. Although it is of frequent occurrence in primitive states of culture, its absence among such very rudimentary peoples as the Veddas of Ceylon, the Punan of Borneo, the Andaman Islanders, the Pygmies of the Congo, the Bushmen of South Africa, as well as the clanless inhabitants of the North-west Pacific coast of America and the low Brazilian tribes in the southern half of the New World, shows that it is by no means universal in distribution or a constant feature in primitive society.

Nevertheless, it was from the sense of kinship with the animal order which the archaeological evidence establishes beyond reasonable doubt to have been a characteristic feature of Palaeolithic ritual and belief, that totemism in due course arose and developed as a dominant socio-religious institution in many parts of the world. This is most apparent in the sacred dances and their mimetic representations when those who took part in the rites, with the aid of masks, antlers, skins of animals and feathers of birds, and appropriate realistic gestures, identified themselves with the species they believed themselves to have become through a process of "participation". Thus, a realization of unity and kinship with the source of the food supply was attained, and the emotional desire for life in greater abundance given expression in mimetic actions to bring about the longed-for results, uniting in the closest bond of kinship those who took part in the rites by virtue of their all sharing in a common life-principle and the joint effort to secure the end in view. From such fundamental concepts as these, deeply laid in the cult of Early Man, totemism in all probability developed as a socio-religious institution.

In the Nile valley it would appear that Upper and Lower Egypt, unified as a theocratic State under a single divine ruler, emerged from a multiplicity of clans with their heraldic ensigns regarded as a sacred emblem and rallying sign, such as those of the falcon, the elephant, the cow, the serpent and the ibis. These survived in the Dynastic period after the clans and independent city-states had become administrative districts, or nomes, each having its own distinctive standards, towns and chief cities. In fact, some of the prehistoric ensigns which gave their name to the clan and the capital city remained in use until the end of Egyptian civilization,[8] having developed into local ancestral animal deities; later they sometimes occupied very prominent positions in the national pantheon. Thus, Amratian representations of a pole with cow's horns and a head on top may have had a quasi-totemic significance before they became the emblems of the fertility-goddess, later identified with Hathor and the other goddesses who subsequently were confused with their prototype the Mother-goddess, the nourisher and protector of the living and the dead, like the totemic supernatural ally.[9]

FERTILITY AND THE MYSTERY OF BIRTH AND GENERATION

Cow-symbolism

In the Late Predynastic Age in Egypt and at Al'Ubaid on the Euphrates the Mother-goddess appears in a new guise identified with the cow. In this Hathor form her advent seems to have coincided with the rise to power of the Falcon clan, which eventually unified the "two lands" under its own ensign, and soon she became the predominant deity, assuming many and various roles.[10] It may have been under the influence of the peoples of the Western Desert who had domesticated cattle at a very early period that the Mother-goddess as Neith was first conceived as a cow,[11] or, as Hornblower believes, the symbolism may be of Mesopotamian origin.[12] In any case, Hathor emerged from the Stone Age as a female divinity with the solar disk on her head between two cow's horns, or as a cow wearing the solar disk and two plumes between her horns; the Hathor cow-head going back to the Gerzean period and recurring in Amratian rock-drawings in Upper Egypt.[13] Later her horns were worn by Isis in conjunction with the lunar disk, and in the Dynastic epoch she became the universal Mother-goddess worshipped throughout Egypt with Denderah as the centre of the cult. At Heliopolis she was made the wife of Re, and so became the mother of Horus, her name signifying "House of Horus". In this synthesis, typical of Egyptian mythology, her relation to Horus was at once that of mother and wife, while as Cow-goddess she was also his nurse. Thus, from a prehistoric zoomorphic origin a series of life-giving and life-sustaining deities emerged (especially in the seventh and twenty-second nomes of Upper Egypt and in the third nome of Lower Egypt) in which cow-symbolism was a dominant feature with shrines extending to Nubia, Syria and Sinai.

In Egypt, however, as we have seen, the function of the mother-goddesses was that of the reproduction of life. In Mesopotamia, on the other hand, they were regarded as the actual source of life to the living and the dead, exercising their creative operations in association with a male partner. At Al 'Ubaid, for instance, the goddess subsequently known as Nin-Khursag, "she who gives life to the dead", was the guardian of the fecundity of the fields and of the cattle they sustained, and from her was drawn the "holy milk" which nourished the sacred herd of the temple dairy at Lagash.[14] Not only was she the mother of the gods, but kings were "fashioned" in her womb, who pray to her that her gracious influence may be withdrawn from their enemies "so that birth may cease in their lands". Her usual symbol was the cow, and as is indicated

Fertility and the Mystery of Birth and Generation 237

on the seals, stone vases and limstone reliefs, she presided over the sacred farm at Al 'Ubaid, which provided the holy milk destined for the nourishment of kings and priests; very much as the members of a totemic clan were sustained by the totem, of which the cow and its symbolism seem to be a development adapted to the conditions of a pastoral society and brought into relation with the earlier cult centred in the mystery of birth and generation. If, as Gadd suggests, the hooped door-posts and lintel of the cow-byre in the form of a moon-crescent symbolized the fertility god of Ur, the Bull, upon whose union with the Goddess all increase depended, then it seems highly probable that the divine nuptials of the Cow-goddess Nin-Khursag and the Moon-god of Ur were celebrated annually in the customary manner and for the usual purposes of renewing the life of nature at its source.[15]

The cult of the cow which has occupied such a conspicuous place in Brahmanic Hinduism certainly was not introduced into India by the Aryan invasion in the second millennium B.C. since it is foreign to the Rig-veda. The first prohibition of cow-killing occurs in the comparatively Late Atharva-veda, which betrays signs of contact and admixture with non-Indo-European influences. In the earlier Vedas the sacrifice of cattle to Indra, Varuna and other deities was enjoined though it is said to be abhorrent to public opinion, suggesting that already they were regarded as sacred animals by the non-Aryan population as in Western Asia and Egypt, where, as we have seen, the bull and the cow were venerated as an integral element in the Goddess fertility cult. It would seem, therefore, that cow worship in India arose in the indigenous Dravidian civilization when with the development of agriculture the cow as the source of milk needed for sustenance became essentially the sacred emblem of fertility hedged round with taboos, so that even in the Rig-veda under pre-Aryan influences the epithet *aghnyax*, "not to be killed", was assigned to it.

While the Vedic Indians were meat-eaters and engaged in agriculture, like their predecessors they were primarily a pastoral people with milk and its products as a very important element in their staple diet. While the ox, the sheep and the goat were killed for food, and, like the horse, as sacrificial victims, the cow acquired an increasing sanctity by virtue of its being the source of the milk supply. In Indo-Iranian times it was treated with care and respect, milked three times daily and kept in a stall during the night and when the sun was at its height. Bulls and oxen used for ploughing fertilized the land by their droppings, and so played their part in the cultivation of the soil. The bull, therefore, became sacred to Shiva, a non-Vedic god, who before he acquired a destructive character when he was identified with Rudra, a minor Vedic storm-deity, may have had a fertility significance if the figure of the three-faced god at Mohenjo-daro with its horned head-dress was in fact his prototype, Pasupati,[16] the Lord of Beasts, and possibly a male partner of the Mother-goddess. Be this as it may, the cult of the bull is established beyond reasonable doubt as a feature of the Harappan civilization which in due course became a dominant element of non-Vedic origin in Brahmanism. Though no trace occurs of cow-worship in the Indus religions notwithstanding the numerous female figurines already reviewed,[17] bull-worship seems to indicate that some form of veneration of the Mother-goddess was an integral aspect of the Harappan household cult, similar to that which prevailed in Western Asia and in Palaeolithic Europe. The closely related phallic symbols were another pre-Aryan element destined to play an important role in post-Vedic Hinduism in the same context.

Generation and Maternity

Therefore, it may be concluded that in the prehistoric background of the ancient civilizations the religious preoccupation largely was concerned with fertility and the ever-present pressing problem of subsistence coupled with the mysterious phenomena connected with birth and generation, upon which the survival of the race also depended. The will to live finding expression in a variety of symbolic actions and objects—dances and mimetic rites, masks and other disguises, female figurines, phalli, realistic and stylized zoomorphic and anthropomorphic

esigns and tectiforms—is the most insistent and recurrent fact
n prehistoric religion. The underlying principle in all and
undry is fecundity in its manifold forms conceived as a
ynamic spiritual force and process manifest in the duality of
ale and female brought into conjunction for the procreation
f life.

HE GODDESS CULT

At first it would seem to have been maternity that held the field. The life-producing mother was the central figure in reproduction in the human and animal world alike, and then extended to the vegetable kingdom when Mother-earth became the womb in which the crops were sown. With the establishment of husbandry and domestication, however, the function of the male in the process of generation became more apparent and vital, however dimly it may have been recognized in food-gathering communities. The Mother-goddess, therefore, was assigned a spouse to play his role as the begetter, even though, as in Mesopotamia, he remained the servant or son of the Goddess. But at length he became the co-equal, and eventually the predominant, partner in the sacred marriage, when the Sky-father contracted his alliance with the Earth-mother, or the pharaoh as the incarnate son of Re visited his queen to beget an heir to the throne.

In Crete, nevertheless, the Goddess retained her former position, for in the Minoan civilization she was clearly the chief anthropomorphic object of worship, either depicted alone or in association with her priestesses and her most characteristic emblems and accompaniments—doves, lions, snakes, the double axe, shells, horns of consecration, the sacred tree and the mountain on which she often stood. Indeed throughout the Eastern Mediterranean and the Aegean the cult of the Mother-goddess predominated, and to fertilize the Earth-mother the virility of the sacred bull may have been poured out sacrificially on the horned-altars in Minoan sanctuaries, especially at the spring festival. But she herself never was adorned with horns nor represented as suckling her offspring. In short, in Crete she did not assume the role of the divine cow and its symbolism.

On the mainland Zeus took the guise of a bull to carry off Europa to Crete, where she became the mother of Minos. His wife Pasiphae in her turn concealed herself in the effigy of a cow to have intercourse with the bull with which she had become infatuated and so conceived the Minotaur. Here there would appear to be a survival of a symbolic ritual marriage to a sacred bull and of the kind of mimetic dance portrayed in a Palaeolithic engraving of a man and woman clothed in skins with tails in the cave of Combarelles in the Dordogne.[18] The classical Moon-goddess Selene, the daughter of the Sun, with whom Pasiphae is connected by her name, was figured as a cow-goddess with horns, and in the legend the bull was the universal god of the sky and of fertility.[19] This association with the moon brings Pasiphae into line with the Goddess cult in the Near East, where the goddess of fertility was so often a lunar deity, perhaps because in arid districts the moon stimulates the dew and so promotes the growth of vegetation, just as the Earth-mother was thought to be fertilized by the rain bestowed upon her by the Sky-father. Therefore, to promote fertility in nature the life-giving forces had to be made operative through a ritual re-enactment of the act of copulation between the Goddess and her spouse symbolized by the cow and the bull, the earth and the sky, the moon and the sun.

Under this imagery the myth and ritual of the fertility and vegetation cult in Asia Minor, Syria, Babylonia, Egypt, the Eastern Mediterranean, Crete and the Aegean developed. In the Minoan-Mycenaean region the figures of gods are of very infrequent occurrence while those of goddesses abound. Indeed everywhere that of the universal Mother lying behind the various emblems and localizations of maternity predominates, representing the mystery of birth and generation in its manifold aspects and attributes. But closely associated with the Goddess was the young male god as her brother, spouse or son, brought together in a nuptial ritual in relation to the annual cycle of vegetation in the agricultural calendrical sequence in which the king and queen were cast to play the leading roles, either in a divine capacity, as in Egypt, or as servants of the Goddess, as in Mesopotamia.

With the concentration of creative energy in the male principle as the begetter, the Goddess tended to lose in some measure her dominance and prestige, but the Asiatic cult persisted in its diffusion from the Near East to Britain and Scandinavia, in association with the megalithic civilization. Centred in the sacred isle of Malta with its great temples and its colossal image of the obese Mother clad in a fluted skirt, it spread through Spain and along the Atlantic littoral to its Palaeolithic cradleland in Western Europe, to carry on and develop the ancient tradition of the "Venuses" and the decorated caves and rock-shelters under megalithic conditions. Thus, on cave walls and in adjacent shelters in the Iberian peninsula are to be seen paintings of ritual significance of wild animals and episodes of the chase which may be of Palaeolithic descent, combined with those of domestic cattle, sheep and goats, and pastoral scenes, while the owl-face of the Millares Goddess may be derived from Capsian conventionalized designs. In Brittany, the Paris Basin and the Channel Islands the statue-menhirs with their "cupolas" bear witness to the persistence of the cult in a relatively late stage of its diffusion in Northern France, where it had acquired essentially a funerary content.

THE CULT OF THE DEAD

Palaeolithic

The extension of the life-giving process to the dead which, as has been demonstrated, has been one of the earliest features of prehistoric religion, could hardly fail to bring the mystery of death into relation with that of birth and fertility. At first apparently it sufficed to lay the body to rest in a carefully prepared grave and to provide it with the implements and food offerings required in the after-life. The head seems to have been regarded as having special potency, and so was preserved for ritual purposes and the brain extracted and eaten to imbibe its magico-religious qualities. Usually, however, the body was buried whole and entire in a position suggesting sleep, sometimes, as at La Ferrassie in the Dordogne, protected with slabs of stone on which, in this case, were markings suggestive of female symbols and heads of animals.[20] But the head of the male corpse appears to have been severed after death.

In the Upper Palaeolithic, in addition to the extended position and that of sleep, flexing was adopted, perhaps to prevent the return of the ghost. But that the renewal of life was the predominant motive is shown by the presence of such vitalizing agents to reanimate the body as red ochre, shells and occasionally horns or tusks. Dismemberment was rare, though the nest of skulls at Ofnet shows that the practice of decapitation survived in the Mesolithic period, coupled with the ornamentation of the skulls with cowrie shells and burial in red ochre, suggesting that they were honoured trophies preserved for veneration rather than cannibalistic relics. Whether or not any such interpretation is to be placed on the painting of the hunting tragedy at Lascaux remains to be determined. If the mortal remains of the luckless hunter killed by the bison should be revealed in the "crypt" of the cave, the Abbé Breuil's suggestion that the scene represents a votive picture would be substantiated in some measure.[21]

While the available data are still very incomplete, in the Palaeolithic the veneration, revivification and fear of vengeance of the dead appear to have constituted the general attitude towards the mystery of death. The sacredness of the event rendered it a taboo condition to be approached and treated with the utmost caution and respect. That it was not the final end of life seems to have been taken for granted, though precisely what lay beyond the grave doubtless was as obscure for Early Man as it is for many who foregather at the obsequies of their relatives and friends in a modern community. That it was a life like that to which the deceased had been accustomed in the days of his flesh, where food and raiment, tools and weapons and ornaments would be required, is indicated by the grave-goods. But in addition to this material equipment the body had to be restored to life by magical devices and adorned

The Cult of the Dead

with ornaments, partly as vitalizing agents but also as a mark of respect and of status here and hereafter. The horn of a bison hidden under a block of stone in the funerary trench at the entrance to the cave at La Chapelle-aux-Saints,[22] recalling the horn held by the woman in the bas-relief at Laussel,[23] and the large tusk of a mammoth at Brünn above the skeleton in a bed of ochre with an ivory male figure and shell ornaments,[24] together with the mammoth skull at Paviland in association with the ochreous burial,[25] may have been for the purpose of placing the dead under the protection of these mighty creatures so frequently depicted on the walls of the caves and in bas-reliefs.

With the transition from the precarious life of the chase to the cultivation of the soil and the keeping of flocks and herds under rather more secure Neolithic conditions, the sequence of the seasons and its ritual had its counterpart in the cult of the dead with a common symbolism. The "Venus" figures, which represent the earliest indications of a maternal cult in the Upper Palaeolithic, now began to find a place in the prehistoric graves at Badari, Arpachiyah, and throughout the Fertile Crescent and Western Asia, together with cowrie shells, red ochre and such closely related cult objects as the double axe, the dove, the bucrania and the serpent. Although female figurines have not been found in the earliest Neolithic sites, from the Halaf levels of Hassuna they occur everywhere west of Iran when the Goddess cult became the dominating influence, and eventually, as has been considered, she herself appeared in funerary architecture and its symbolism in her life-giving capacity to the dead.

Ancient Egypt

In Egypt, however, the desiccation of the bodies buried in the hot dry sand of the desert emphasized the continuation of life after death, and led to the elaborate efforts to preserve and reanimate the corpse and to erect the rectangular mastaba tombs of mud brick which developed through the palace façade mastaba into the vast royal pyramids at the beginning of the Dynastic period, when the divine kingship centred the cult of the dead in the throne. But while immortality then became the prerogative of the pharaohs who alone were destined to enter the realms of the gods after death as themselves gods, the royal tombs were, in fact, only a very complex development of the simple prehistoric Amratian and Gerzean trench-graves enlarged to contain an increasing number of food offerings and funerary gifts. At length a shaft was added and the superstructure erected over the series of chambers. Moreover, burial in mastabas was not confined to pharaohs. Therefore, although the nature of the continued existence of commoners in and before the Old Kingdom is not known, the prehistoric cemeteries in the desert graves on the margin of the alluvium disclose a relatively advanced belief in a future life from the fifth millennium B.C. in which all were destined to share. That it was centred in the tomb is shown by the increasing care bestowed upon its construction and furnishing, and the provision made for the comfort and well-being of those who "went down into the pit" lest they should molest the living. In fact, offerings to the dead were made in accordance with a prescribed ritual in the predynastic period long before the Pyramid Texts were drawn up.

From very early times each individual was believed to have an invisible immortal "soul" or ghost which often assumed the form of a bird with a human head, that either survived death or came into existence at the time of the dissolution. To this conception of the *ba* that of the *ka* eventually was added. Originally it was exclusively a royal attribute of divine creative power conceived as a beneficent and protective genius, or spiritual double, who guided the fortunes of the pharaoh primarily in the after-life when he went to his *ka* at death. Since, however, the king was a god, he held communion with his *ka* to some extent during his lifetime. In the Middle and New Kingdoms, when the *ka* became the possessions of commoners as well as of the pharaohs, it acquired a more impersonal character as the vital principle in this life, born with the individual, sustained through his life, and preceding him to

The Cult of the Dead

he next world. It was symbolized by two raised arms with utspread hands, distinct from the bird-shaped *ba* with its hostly attributes and functions in the grave and in relation to he mummy or portrait statue.

To what extent these highly complex interpretations of the constitution and survival of human personality can be regarded as of prehistoric origin and significance is difficult to say. The conception of the *ka* as a vital essence, a guardian spirit and an alter ego would seem to represent very ancient and primitive connotations, as does that of the ghostly *ba* of the dead man. The primitive mind, as we have seen, has always conceived of human survival in terms of some kind of concrete entity, and in Egypt attention was concentrated on the preservation and reanimation of the body and its burial in an "everlasting tomb", together with the portrait statue as its surrogate, after "life" had been imparted to them by the "Opening of the Mouth" ceremony—an extension of the Palaeolithic practice of revivification. While mummification became an elaborate re-enactment of the treatment of the body of Osiris, behind this myth and ritual lay a very long history of the preservation and restoration to life of the dead by magical and mechanical methods.

As Breasted has pointed out, although among no people ancient or modern has the idea of a life beyond the grave held so prominent a place as among the Egyptians, the belief in the immortal and imperishable soul cannot be attributed to them.[26] The purpose of their mortuary ritual was to reconstitute and resuscitate the deceased after the dissolution by magico-mechanical processes and ceremonies external to him, to enable him to continue his existence in the hereafter. And this is precisely what Early Man endeavoured to do in the cult of the dead. To achieve the resurrection of his predecessor the pharaoh erected the *Djed* column, which Frankfort suggests may have represented the Goddess Hathor,[27] thereby effecting his rebirth by an efficacious symbolic act in accordance with established primitive procedure. Or, again, all men could find a place in the everlasting kingdom of Osiris by undergoing the same rites of mummification that were performed on his dismembered and restored body, though eventually in the Middle Kingdom they had to be able to show that like him they were "true in heart and voice" when their hearts were weighed by Thoth against the feather of truth.

Mesopotamia

In Mesopotamia the cult of the dead never assumed the same proportions as in the Nile valley, where vast tombs, elaborate methods of mummification, judgment after death and resurrection dominated Egyptian religion. The Babylonian conception of the hereafter was that of a semi-conscious survival in the House of Darkness, a withering away like the generative force in nature in the devitalizing heat of a Mesopotamian summer. This mood of despair found expression in the lamentations for Tammuz or Marduk imprisoned in the "mountain" which symbolized the nether regions. Even though his liberation was celebrated at the New Year Festival with rejoicings when death appeared to have been vanquished in nature at the return of the rains, it was only life on earth that was renewed. For man, although the grave was not the absolute end of existence, beyond it lay the dreaded abode of Irkalla which none could leave once it was entered, for the gods had made immortality their own prerogative. Thus, Gilgamesh when he went in search of everlasting life failed in his quest, cheated by a serpent of the magic rejuvenating plant he had secured to renew his youth.[28] The gods, and heroes like Utnapishtim, his wife and daughter, alone could be revived and live for ever. This is confirmed in the myth of Adapa, where again mankind is represented as having lost immortality by a trick of the gods.[29] Therefore, the decline and restoration in nature is as near as the Babylonians ever got to the renewal of life emerging from death.

Nevertheless, behind this sinister conception of human destiny it seems that a prehistoric cult of the dead was sufficiently developed to require some equipment for the hereafter. Thus, apart from the elaborate ceremonial practised at the royal tombs at Ur, the normal Sumerian custom was to bury the

The Cult of the Dead

dead in earth and brick graves with an adequate supply of food and drink, which sometimes appears to have been renewed by monthly offerings,[30] together with certain personal belongings.[31] Both extended and flexed burial were practised, the corpse frequently being clothed or wrapped in a mat or winding-sheet and interred, usually in the house under the floor of the court or of a room rather than in a cemetery. The grave-goods, though on the whole meagre, suggest a belief in survival, but individual immortality probably had not acquired a cultic significance except in the case of the royal obsequies with their galaxy of wealth and large-scale immolation of members of the king's household. These rites show that in contradistinction to the later notion of kings and commoners suffering the same fate in the nether regions, at the beginning of the Dynastic period at Ur great importance and significance was attached to status in the after-life. But for the rest of mankind survival readily became a static condition approached with resignation coupled with apprehension, and interpreted as a hopeless quest and divine deprivation arising from the jealousy of the gods who made themselves exclusively the partakers of a blessed immortality in their own realms.

The Indus Valley

Similarly, in India the cult of the dead in prehistoric times is very obscure. In the hill-villages adjacent to the Indus civilization the extensive cemetery at Nal in Southern Baluchistan has revealed, as we have seen,[32] that among the various methods of inhumation employed, "fractional" burial was the dominant practice in the third millennium B.C., suggestive of secondary interment after exposure elsewhere. No attempt was made to protect the bones beyond placing them in small rectangular chambers at Damb Buthi, and in similar brick constructions at Nal. But the pottery vessels, copper axes, beads and red pigment are indicative of a continued existence requiring provision for the well-being of the deceased.

At Mohenjo-daro scant attention appears to have been paid to the disposal of the dead, as the alleged fractional burials and the bones showing signs of incineration are probably relics of attacks by raiders rather than intentional interments. It was only in the cemetery discovered at Harappa in 1937 to the south of the citadel (R37) that definite evidence of ceremonial sepulture has come to light in the Indus valley. There personal ornaments worn by the dead included necklaces, shell bangles, steatite anklets, copper rings and mirrors, and in the thick wooden coffin found in one of the graves traces of a reed shroud reminiscent of similar burials in Sumer in the Early Dynastic period (c. 2800 B.C.),[33] suggesting a possible link with the Mesopotamian cult of the dead.

In the post-Harappan Cemetery H to the south of the citadel, the alleged mythological scenes depicting the journey of the soul to the next life, as described in the Rig-veda, painted as a frieze on a mortuary vat[34] might have a Vedic significance. The fate of the dead, however, in the early texts is very obscure, and in any case the paintings at Harappa are too late to be of much help in the elucidation of the prehistoric beliefs. Both cremation and inhumation were practised by the Indo-European invaders in the second millennium B.C.[35] and as the ashes were buried after incineration, interment probably was the original mode of disposal, though eventually cremation became the dominant rite in India. But at first it was to Mother-earth that the dead were committed and covered by her "as a mother wraps her skirt about her child". There they remained until they embarked on their journey across the rivers to the land of Yama, the king of the dead and the ruler of the abode of bliss, or wherever they might be destined to dwell ultimately. That cremation came to play some part in the process is suggested by the reference in the Rig-veda to the appeal to Agni, the fire-god, in a funeral hymn to bring the deceased to maturity and send him on his way to the Fathers, but not consume him.[36]

The Mediterranean

In its western extension the cult of the dead increasingly came under the influence of that of the Mother-goddess in and after

The Cult of the Dead

the Chalcolithic period, when her emblems are of frequent occurrence in the tombs and in the mortuary ritual. Burial in the contracted position was prevalent, and collective interment in tholoi was widely adopted in the Eastern Mediterranean, while rock-cut and chamber-tombs abounded in the Iberian megalithic region in the west. In Crete the vaulted tombs never reached the height of magnificence attained on the mainland by the great Mycenaean beehives, like the Treasury of Atreus at Mycenae and the Treasury of Munyas at Orchomenos. The Minoan funerary ritual appears to have been relatively simple, consisting in placing the body in the burial chamber unburnt, though fires were lighted in the tholoi for some ceremonial purpose and the offerings deposited in annexes to the circular tombs, unless they were votive deposits rather than offerings made at the time of the funeral. Sometimes libations were poured within a special enclosure, and at Knossos in the Tomb of the Double Axes vessels had been placed before a sacred pillar against the inner wall, evidently as an offering to the Minoan Mother-goddess on behalf of the dead.[37]

The scenes on the Late Minoan sarcophagus from Hagia Triada are very difficult to interpret, but, as has been pointed out,[38] they appear to have some relation to the Goddess cult in its funerary setting, connected probably with the journey of the soul to its final abode, and possibly with its deification. Dr Paribeni compares the figure with open eyes standing before a building, said to be a tomb, with the "Opening of the Mouth" ceremony in Egypt,[39] though there are no indications that actually it was a mummy. The scenes, he thinks, represent a series of episodes derived from the mortuary ritual and the current beliefs respecting the human destiny depicted to gain for the deceased the assistance of the gods in his transition to the next life. Sir Arthur Evans, however, regards the sacrificial scenes as the means whereby the dead hero was summoned back temporarily to the land of the living and the divinity charmed down into its material resting-place by the offerings and with the aid of music and ritual chants and the sacred symbols of the Minoan Goddess.[40] Miss Jane Harrison and Dr Petersen, on the other hand, interpret the picture in terms of the seasonal cycle myth and ritual.⁴¹ But as the scenes decorate a tomb, the natural conclusion is that they had reference to the cult of the dead in the first instance, whatever secondary and subsidiary purposes they may have served. That they are of a composite character is suggested by the symbolism with its double axes, horns of consecration, imagery of bulls, sacred trees and pillars, votive boat, griffins, a hide-dress and the sacrificial scene. A combination of a mortuary ritual with the worship of the Minoan Goddess is indicated, coupled with the cult of the Double Axe as depicted on the walls of the palace at Knossos. Thus, Nilsson has been led to suppose that in Late Minoan times the dead were deified and worshipped in the form of a divine cult, perhaps under Egyptian influence. Therefore, he regards the scenes not as those of funeral ceremonies but of acts of worship consequent upon apotheosis when the deceased hero had been transported by griffins and accompanied by goddesses to the realms of the gods and there deified,⁴² like the Roman emperors who were thought to be carried to the divine world on the back of an eagle.

The griffins, however, on the Ring of Nestor are associated with the Goddess seated in front of her companion and with tokens of her life-giving powers, representing apparently a rite of initiation into the halls of the blest in the underworld over which she presided.⁴³ And in Greece heroes were denizens of the nether regions however mighty and venerated they might be. But a composite cult along the lines indicated by Nilsson need not be incompatible with the conception of the illustrious dead acquiring from the Goddess a derived divine sanctity and exerting a beneficent influence with the deity on behalf of the living, and, therefore, the object of worship and the recipient of offerings in their magnificent tombs. In Malta, for instance, Evans has suggested that the baetylic worship in the megalithic sanctuaries of Hagiar Kim and Gigantea, in which the hero was represented by a pillar, developed out of the cult of the dead.⁴⁴ While the side-chambers in which it is alleged to have occurred may not have been dolmens in which deified heroes were buried, the worship may nevertheless have originated in a cult of the illustrious dead.

Western Europe

The baetylic tradition recurred in Minorca and in the great Spanish megalithic sepulchral structures at Los Millares, while the numerous stylized figurines, plaques and "idols" in Almerian and Portuguese graves show that the Mother-goddess continued to play a prominent part in the mortuary ritual, especially in the south-west of the peninsula and in the Balearic Islands. In France the juxtaposition of the Goddess cult with that of the Axe was of frequent occurrence as it was in the Aegean, Sicily, Malta and the Iberian region. In Western Europe, Brittany, being one of the principal centres of religious activity, attracted apparently many "pilgrims" to worship at the megalithic sanctuaries, and perhaps to bring the remains of their powerful chiefs and venerated heroes to be interred within their sacred precincts. Thus, in addition to the vast array of dolmens and passage-tombs in Morbihan and the surrounding district, the alignments of menhirs at Carnac, covering 2,800 metres and divided into three distinct groups—the Field of Ménec with a cromlech to the north of the village, the Field of Kermario, and the Field of Kerlescan at the west also having a stone circle with rounded corners—and those of S. Pierre, Quiberon, are orientated in relation to the solstices. Therefore, they may have constituted the meeting-places for seasonal gatherings; those at Ménec and Quiberon for the celebration of the midsummer rites, and those at Kermario for the equi-noxial ceremonies in the spring and autumn. But as the align-ments so often end in tumuli (e.g. at Carnac, Mané-er-Hroeck, Locmariaquer, Clud-er-Yer and Kergo) they appear to have had a funerary origin and significance in which the worship of the dead was a conspicuous feature.

The construction, orientation and equipment of the sepul-chral monuments in this area indicate a highly developed cult of the dead. This is clear from great dolmens like the Table des Marchands at Locmariaquer, or corridor-tombs such as that on the island of Gavr'inis, Morbihan, covered by a tumulus nearly 200 feet in diameter, the circular chamber 6 feet high, roofed by a huge block measuring 13 by 10 feet, approached by a corridor 40 feet long, and having no less than twenty-two upright blocks covered with engraved symbolic cult designs. Sometimes, as at Mont S. Michel, the central burial chamber was covered with a huge artificial mound, while at Calvados no less than twelve circular corbelled chambers, each with its own entrance passage, were concealed beneath a mound. As in the case of the Palaeolithic decorated caves, it is only a very profound religious motive that can explain either the sanctuaries or tombs of this character and of these proportions.

This is confirmed by the contents of these megalithic tumuli, which include, besides necklace beads and the usual trinkets, fine stone celts pierced at one end for amuletic uses and giving every appearance of having been votive axes placed beside the burial, perhaps as the emblem of or offering to the tutelary spirit to whom the tomb was consecrated unless they were for the benefit of the deceased in the next life. The bones of horses and oxen in some of the monuments, and what seem to be the bones or ashes of slaves and servants near by, suggest that both animal and human sacrifices on occasions formed part of the obsequies of chiefs and rulers in this region. Ritual urns ornamented with sacred designs often have been ceremonially broken, and show traces of incineration as if used for cooking purposes. But the normal mode of disposal of the dead among the megalithic folk being inhumation, cremation was only adopted sporadically (e.g. in Finistère, Marne and Aisne), doubtless as a result of a secondary intrusion from Central Europe. Whether or not the contracted position, which was freely adopted, had at this stage in cultural development any reference to that of the embryo before birth and the idea of rebirth beyond the grave, we do not know.

In the Early Bronze Age, as we have seen,[45] secondary interment of cremations, sometimes later than the primary inhumations, frequently occurred. When they are of the same period as the original interments they may represent human

The Cult of the Dead

victims sacrificed at the death of a chieftain, but although this is a well-attested practice, especially in Mesopotamia as has been demonstrated, it has to be accepted with caution. When bones, burnt or unburnt, have been intentionally broken, as, for example, in the Cotswold Long Barrows in Britain, a ritual motive is indicated,[46] and when these are found in great tombs in association with a "royal" burial equipment the presumption is that they originally had a sacrificial significance, especially if the sepulchre was sealed at the end of the obsequies. Hemp has argued in favour of large rock-cut tombs having been monuments of individuals closed after the interment, which had included the sacrifice of relatives and servants, and were subsequently used by the deceased's descendants until eventually they became a tribal tomb.[47] In chamber-tombs, however, successive burial has been extensively practised, and the considerable number of skeletons in them (e.g. at Mesara in Crete, and Västergötaland and Troldhöj in Zealand, and Pant y Saer and Tinkinswood in Britain), ranging from a hundred to fifty bodies, is unquestionably the result of their having been used as ossuaries for several generations. The chaotic disorder in most of them is due to the older contents of the tomb having been disturbed by later additions of fresh burials or bones, sometimes after burial or exposure elsewhere.[48]

This doubtless explains some of the fragmentary and fractional burials which recur from the Indus valley to Britain. Thus, at the Pole's Wood South Barrow in Gloucestershire the rifling and destruction were most conspicuous, nine or ten skeletons having been packed away in a chamber measuring 7 by 4 feet. In the entrance, however, one skeleton was in almost perfect condition. This suggests that the fragmentary state of the rest was the result of re-burial, and Crawford thinks that "the perfect skeleton in the entrance passage suggests the immolation of a victim",[49] a practice in his opinion that may have been in vogue also at Belas Knap. But if successive burial was practised it may have been merely the last addition to the ossuary, the bones of the rest having been broken either accidentally in re-interment, or intentionally for ritual purposes.

Against this, as Dr Daniel points out, is the fractional condition of some of the bones.[50]

What is clear, as he says, is that when skeletal and artifactual material is heaped up outside the passage-tomb, as in the Scandinavian examples,[51] there must have been successive burial, and in Britain most of the chambers were collective graves of this kind. It may also be agreed that intentional breaking of the bones requires a ritual explanation, as does fractional burial; even granting, as Keiller, Alexander and Piggott have argued, that it could have been caused in some instances by the seeping of water through part of the filling of the grave.[52] But whatever may have been the precise mode of disposal, the obsequies must have entailed an elaborate ceremonial involving a funeral feast, the equipment of the dead with an adequate supply of grave-goods, sometimes including animal or human victims, to facilitate the journey to the next life and to make every provision and comfort for the well-being of the deceased, and to guard against his return to molest the living. These were the primary purposes and functions of the cult of the dead in prehistoric times.

THE SKY-RELIGION

The Celestial After-life

The widespread adoption of cremation in the Middle Bronze Age was indirectly if not directly associated with an orientation in the conception of the hereafter in a celestial direction. It is true that the practice was only gradually adopted side by side with that of inhumation, often in the form of partial incineration. Nevertheless, once it was established and had become the dominant mode of disposal of the dead, especially in Central and Northern Europe as an intrusion from the Near East, it could hardly fail to influence the conception of the location and nature of the after-life and that of the constitution of man as a duality of body and soul. Moreover, as it coincided with the development of the Sky-religion the way was open for a less materialistic interpretation of the idea of immortality in terms of the return of the soul or ghost to the spirit-world in the

The Sky-religion

smoke of its physical integument.⁵³ Here, however, extreme caution is needed in assuming a correlation between this mode of disposal of the body and an underlying belief about the destiny of the soul.

At death, it seems, the human organism was thought to undergo a process of dissolution in which the body lost its animating principle associated with the breath, blood and its mental and psychical attributes and functions. Ritual reanimation was an attempt to restore these vital elements, coupled sometimes with the preservation of the bones or the mummification of the corpse. What survived, or then came into being, was an independent shadowy entity—the shade or ghost—as a reflection or replica of the living person, which carried on an independent existence either in the grave or in the spirit-world, unless it returned to earth to be reborn in another body.

If in the first instance the Mother-goddess was the producer of life *par excellence*, when the dead were interred in "mother-earth" doubtless it appeared that they were returning whence they came. But in the background stood the obscure figure of the transcendent Supreme Being in the sky who as the Creator became the begetter, breathing into man the breath of life and, in union with the Earth-mother and personification of birth and generation, bestowing upon man and nature their fecundity. As a consequence, since, when the life left the body, it was frequently supposed to go back to the god from whom it came, in the Sky-religion normally it was to the celestial realms that it returned at death. Cremation was calculated to facilitate this transition, though the correlation of the practice with the belief in a heavenly hereafter is too sporadic to indicate that the one was dependent upon the other.

As an ancient funeral custom cremation was sometimes associated with the notion of a continued life in the grave or in the nether regions, as in Greece when after the Minoan-Mycenaean period it was introduced by the Dorians without any very marked change regarding the after-life for ordinary mortals. Nevertheless, it does appear to have been connected with a less concrete conception of the future life and of the grave as an "everlasting tomb" by placing the emphasis on the liberation of the human spirit, and of the immortal element even in the grave-goods, and so to have stressed the idea of a spiritual existence independent of a material matrix. Moreover, its frequent adoption as the mode of disposal of rulers, heroes and the more distinguished dead suggests that it was often related to an abode reserved for the privileged section of the community, and this tended to be located in the divine celestial realms.

The Concept of the Universal Sky-god
The supreme God in the sky being the highest expression and evaluation of Deity, everything that was "above" was naturally associated with him, from celestial phenomena and spirits of the air to kings, chieftains and rulers on earth. But while he was, therefore, liable to become remote and detached from the world and its affairs, he was none the less as all-encompassing —like the sky itself, the air and the wind "blowing where it listeth", with which often he has been associated—as he was all-powerful and all-seeing. Consequently, although the archaeological evidence is very meagre prior to the rise of civilization, the idea of the Sky-god as the universal spirit becomes such a basic assumption that it has every appearance of having been one of the fundamental religious concepts of mankind.

In any case, once the Sky-religion was an established cult, it was the celestial deity who was the Supreme Being responsible for sending rain and giving fertility to the soil (often in conjunction with the Mother-goddess) prior to the advent of the Sun-god with whom he became identified, or by whom he was obscured and even transplanted, as in Egypt. To meet all the requirements of such a celestial deity he was surrounded with a glorious company of gods and spirits with their sacred avocations in relation to the divine ordering of all things in heaven and on earth. Looked at from one angle he could be regarded as "monotheistic" in the sense of being wholly supreme and transcendent in his own domain and in respect of his divine attributes and functions. Conversely, the system could be

The Sky-religion

described as polytheistic and animistic inasmuch as gods many and lords many unquestionably existed and played their allotted roles in the pantheon and in natural phenomena and human society, either for weal or for woe.

Under prehistoric conditions there are no indications that at any time or place, or in any cultural level, one single all-supreme Deity was believed to have existed to the exclusion of all other divine beings. That conception of monotheism is the prerogative of the higher religions (Zoroastrianism, Judaism, Christianity and Islam), but it has not evolved from polytheism or animism in the manner formerly supposed. Each and all of these different expressions of theistic faith and practice have arisen apparently within their own proper contexts and conditions, and at particular levels of thought and evaluation. Having coexisted for their specific purposes and functions they represent degrees of spiritual penetration and experience of the numinous, and different reactions to supernatural effects and relations in the phenomenal world, determined very largely by the religious and cultural environment and the social structure in which they function.

Thus, the Sky-religion cannot be assigned to any one phase or condition of religious development, monotheistic, polytheistic or animistic; or indeed to any type of society or geographical region. It has been a recurrent phenomenon, and, as we have seen,[54] to fulfil the needs of mankind it was brought into relation not only with the solar cult but also with that of the Earth-gods and goddesses. In this way the beneficence of the celestial realms was made accessible on earth providing fruitful seasons, destroying the forces of evil and giving immortal life to the dead. But notwithstanding this syncretism, the Sky-god in his own right normally was regarded as the ultimate source of the plenitude of divine power, omniscience and wisdom, even though the Sun-god was sometimes raised to the dignity of the Supreme Being, as, for example, by Ikhnaton in Egypt, among the Inca in Peru, and some of the Algonquian tribes in North America. Usually, however, he was originally in a subordinate position like Shamash in Mesopotamia, or Marti in the Vedic pantheon, where Dyaus Pitar held pre-eminence as the Sky-father and personification of the heavens, the giver of the fructifying rain to water the earth, until gradually he was displaced, first by the all-encompassing Varuna and then by the Vedic nature gods and goddesses. Later, after Varuna in conjunction with Rta had been resolved into a monistic unity as the universal cosmic and moral order immanent in all phenomena, and the neuter Brahman emerged as the Absolute, the ancient gods of the sky and of the earth were retained as the aspects and attributes of the One Ultimate Reality of universal Being.

In Iran, Zarathushtra having transformed and sublimated the ancient chief god of the vault of heaven into the All-wise Lord Ahura Mazda, and firmly established him as the one and only God of all the earth, he made the earlier polytheistic *daevas* and *ahuras* modalities of divine activity in the perennial struggle between good and evil, light and darkness. In so doing, he raised the prehistoric Sky-god Varuna, brought into relation with the celestial Mitra under the guise of Ahura Mazda, to the level of a genuine ethical monotheistic deity, comparable to Yahweh in post-exilic Judaism. Both of the ancient gods who lie behind the All-wise Lord of the Avesta were heavenly beings representing the all-encompassing sky in its complementary aspects, nocturnal and diurnal. Although Mitra was not the sun, as is clearly maintained in the Avesta,[55] his celestial origins and connexions with the light opened the way for him to acquire solar attributes and functions until in the Mithraic mystery cult the identification became complete. Therefore, Ahura Mazda before his transformation by Zarathushtra had behind him a long history going back to its prehistoric antecedents in the Sky tradition.

The universal Sky-god, in fact, in his divers forms and functions and syncretisms lies at the base of all the higher religions of the Orient and the Mediterranean deeply laid in their prehistoric foundations. Yahweh, the god of the sacred mountain whose voice was heard in the thunder, appears to have been a Western Semitic deity, Ya, or Yami, or Yahu, with celestial affinities before he became the consolidating centre of the Hebrew tribes, and eventually, under prophetic influence, the Creator of the universe and the Lord of history and of nature, controlling all things in accordance with his righteous will and purposes. Zeus, although a composite figure in the Olympian religion, was originally the prehistoric sky- and weather-god like Varuna and Ahura Mazda, long before he became the head of the mountain pantheon in Thessaly and then "the father of gods and men". In Crete, as we have seen,[56] he was brought into relation with the Minoan Goddess as the son of Rhea. In this capacity he was a more primitive figure than the Indo-European Sky-god, being concerned with the renewal of vegetation as a fertility deity. As the giver of fruitfulness and the divine farmer ($\gamma\epsilon\omega\varrho\gamma\acute{o}\varsigma$) he was the vitalizing power in the soil ($\chi\theta\acute{o}\nu\iota o\delta$). In fact, so close was his relationship with the Corn-goddess Demeter that he became virtually a chthonic god in his agricultural aspects.[57] But so comprehensive was his role that all natural phenomena fell within his domain. This universality of Zeus, which finds its roots in his celestial origins and control of the weather, is an indication of his fundamental nature as the Sky-god *par excellence* which could never be obliterated in the religious consciousness of the Greeks, notwithstanding his endless transformations and syncretisms.

The antiquity of this concept of the universal Sky-god going back to prehistoric times can be explained no doubt by a general inclination everywhere to look to the heavens as a seat of supernatural power. Therefore, the various aspects of celestial phenomena—the sky and its constellations, the sun, the moon, the air, the wind and the clouds—have acquired their places and functions in the ever-increasing pantheon of heavenly divine beings, together with their vital and arresting manifestations in the rain, the storm, the thunder and the tempest; beneficent or destructive, awe-inspiring or terrorizing.

Thus, in Egypt the four pairs of gods representing pre-cosmic disorder stood over against the Heliopolitan Ennead of cosmic order—the air and moisture, the sky and the earth, in their male and female forms—grouped round the self-created Sun-god Atum. From the union of Geb and Nut, the Earth and the Sky, Osiris and Isis, and Seth and Nephthys, were born; the posthumous son of Isis, Horus, being destined to engage in mortal combat with his Uncle Seth. Here the conflict in prehistoric times between the northern Horus invaders of the southern valley of the Nile and the indigenous inhabitants who were Seth worshippers may have been interpreted in terms o a more fundamental cosmic struggle in which the forces o "good" and "evil" were opposed, Horus and Seth playing the roles assigned to the Sky-god and the Storm-god in earlier cosmogonies.

Since the Supreme Being in the sky invariably has been regarded as the ultimate source of beneficence, sending the fructifying rain to fertilize the earth and bestowing upon mankind life and sustenance, very seldom has he been held responsible for malign and destructive influences. Nevertheless, while the archaeological evidence suggests that his primary function was the conservation and promotion of life and general well-being, often effected through his sacred marriage with the Earth-goddess, this aspect of the Sky-religion was only one of many manifestations of celestial divine power in connexion with natural phenomena. Thus, meteorites, thunder and lightning, constellations, sacred mountains and certain animals, rainbows, translucent stones, menhirs, and many other similar objects, have been emblems and expressions of the Sky-god in his manifold representations, attributes and functions, iconic and aniconic, in prehistoric religion.

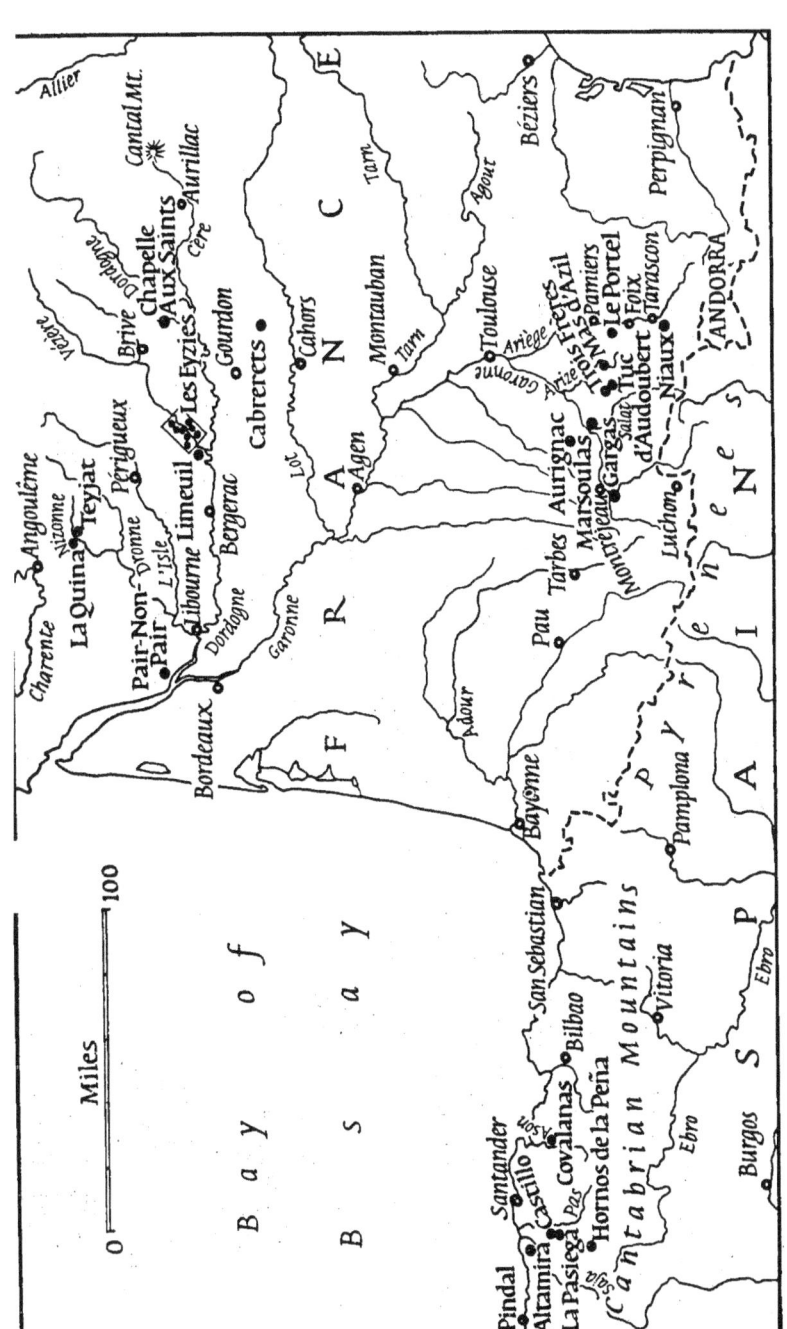

Map showing the principal groups of painted caves and other Palaeolithic sites in France and northern Spain

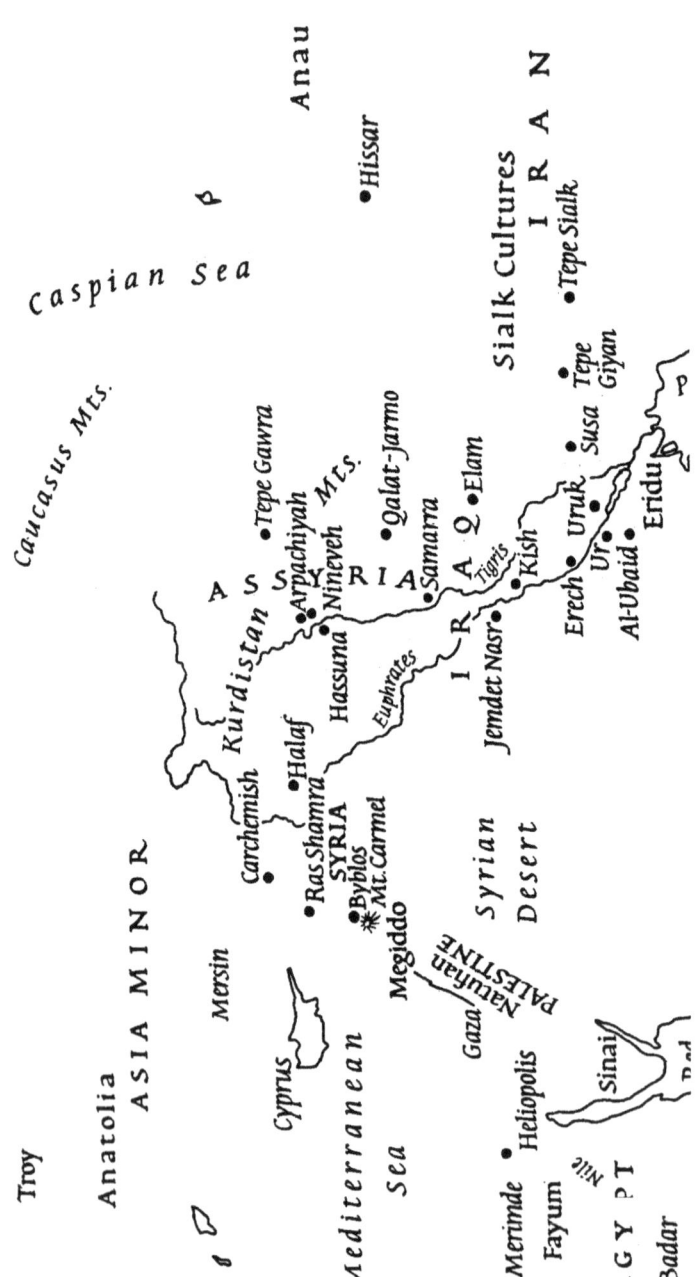

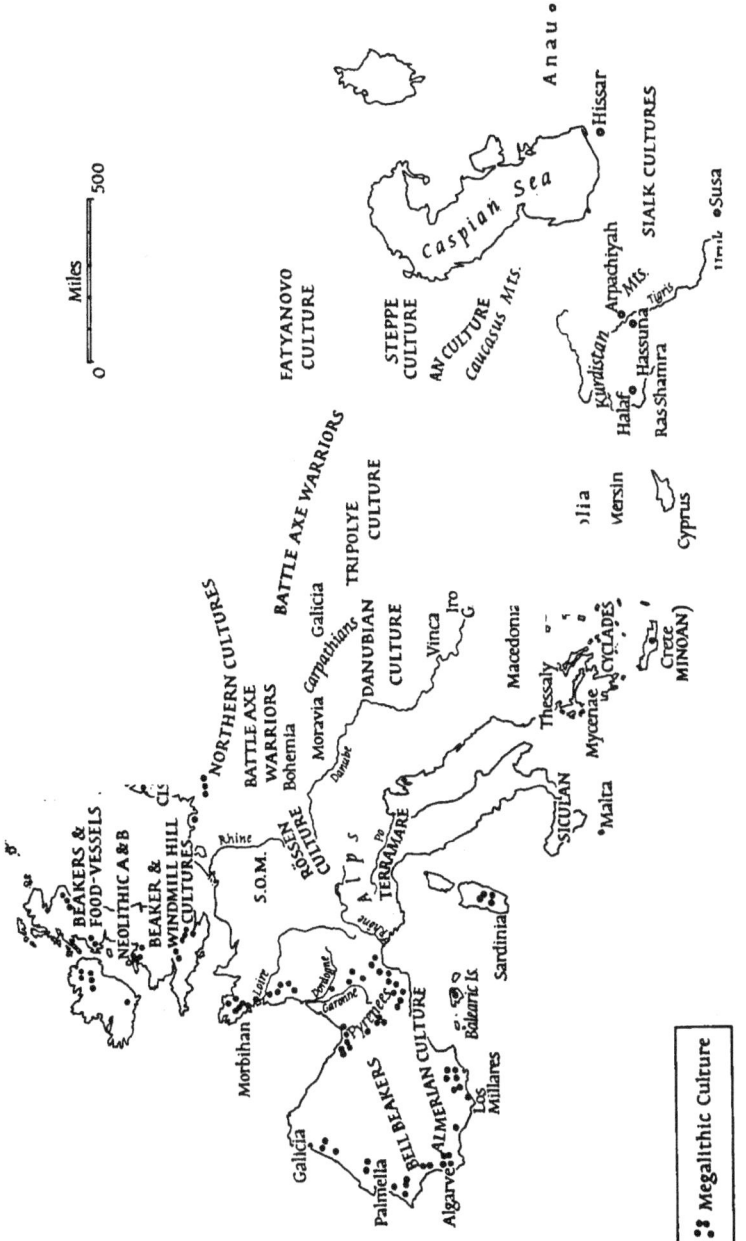

Map showing Neolithic and Bronze Age cultures in Europe and the Near East

NOTES

CHAPTER I

1. Black, Teilhard du Chardin, Young, Pei, *Fossil Man in China*, Peiping, 1933, pp. 5 ff., 60.
2. *Dating the Past*, 3rd ed., 1953, pp. 274 ff.
3. D. Black, *Palaeotologia Sinica*, vol. ii, 1927, pp. 1 ff.; *Fossil Man in China*, pp. 83 ff.; Koenigswald, *Nature*, vol. cxliv, 1939, pp. 926 ff.; Weidernreich, *op. cit.*, vol. cxliii, 1938, p. 715.
4. J. H. Hutton, *J.R.A.I.*, vol. lviii, 1928, pp. 403 ff.; Hose and McDougall, *The Pagan Tribes of Borneo*, vol. i, 1912, pp. 114 f.; vol. ii, pp. 20 ff.; H. I. Marshall, *The Karen People of Borneo*, Ohio, 1922, p. 222.
5. Obermaier, *Fossil Man in Spain*, 1925, pp. 136 f., 339; P. Wernert, *Histoire Générale de Religion*, vol. i, p. 56.
6. Oppenoorth, *Early Man*, ed. MacCurdy, Philadephia, 1937, pp. 349 ff.
7. Breuil and Obermaier, *L'Anthropologie*, vol. xx, 1909, p. 523.
8. K. Gorjanovic-Kramberger, *Mittheilungen der Anthropologischer Gesellschaft in Wien*, vol. xxii, 1902, p. 189; vol. xxiv, 1904, pp. 187 f.
9. R. R. Schmidt, *Die diluviale Vorzeit Deutschlands*, Stuttgart, 1912.
10. Treat and Couturier, *L'Anthrop.*, vol. xxxviii, p. 235; Vernert, *op. cit.*, p. 65.
11. Kinyar, *Antiquity*, vol. xxvii, 1953, pp. 105 f.
12. O. Menghin, *Wienerprähistorische Zeitschrift*, vol. xiii, 1926, pp. 14 ff.; Wernert, *op. cit.*, p. 58.
13. Hauser, *Archiv. für Anthropologie*, vol. vii, 1909, p. 290.
14. Boule, *Annales de paléontologie*, 1911–13; A. and J. Bouyssonie and L. Bardon, *L'Anthrop.*, vol. xix, 1908, p. 513.
15. *L'Anthrop.*, 1913, pp. 616 ff.
16. Breuil, *L'Anthrop.*, vol. xxxi, 1921, pp. 343 ff.
17. Verneau, *Les Grottes de Grimaldi*, vol. ii, Monaco, 1906, pp. 23, 260, 277 ff.
18. Keith, *The Antiquity of Man*, vol. i, 1929, p. 99.
19. C. L. de Villeneuve, *Les Grottes de Grimaldi*, vol. i, p. 64; vol. ii, pl. ii; *L'Anthrop.*, vol. xiii, 1902, p. 561.
20. *Grimaldi*, vol. ii, pp. 298 ff.
21. *Op. cit.*, pp. 33, 298, fig. 4, p. 12.
22. Sollas, *J.R.A.I.*, vol. xliii, 1913, pp. 325 ff.
23. Obermaier, *Der Mensch der Vorzeit*, p. 298; Breuil, *L'Anthrop.*, 1924, pp. 549 ff.
24. L. Testut, *Bulletin de la société d'anthrop. de Lyon*, vol. viii, 1889; *L'Anthrop.*, vol. i, 1890, p. 716; Hardy, *La station quarternaire de Raymonden*, Paris, 1891, pp. 49 ff.; Sollas, *Ancient Hunters*, 1915, pp. 485 ff.
25. A. Arcelin, *L'Anthrop.*, vol. i, 1890, pp. 307 ff.

26. *Textbook of European Archaeology*, Cambridge, 1921, p. 502.
27. J. W. Jackson, *Shells as Evidence of the Migrations of Early Culture*, Manchester, 1917, pp. 138 ff.
28. *Comptes-Rendus de l'Acad. des Sciences*, vol. lxxiv, 1872, pp. 1060 f.
29. M. and St J.-Péquart, *Arch. de l'Inst. de la Pal. Hum. Mémoires*, 19, 1937.
30. Mendes Correa, *Congrès Internat. d'anthrop. et d'archéol. préhistorique*, Paris, 1931, p. 362; Obermaier, *Fossil Man in Spain*, 1925, p. 324.
31. P. R. de Azua, *Bol. de la Soc. Española de hist. Nat.*, December 1918; cf. Burkitt, *Our Early Ancestors*, Cambridge, 1926, p. 22.
32. Dupont, *Mémoires de l'Academie royale des Sciences, des Lettres, et des Beaux-arts Belgiques*, vol. xix, 1867, pp. 1 ff.
33. E. Piette, *L'Anthrop.*, vol. vi, 1895, pp. 276 ff.; Zaborowsky, *Bull. et Mém. Soc. Anthrop. de Paris*, series v, vol. vii, 1906, p. 416.
34. Cf. *Fra Nationalmuseums Arbejdsmark*, 1945, p. 6.
35. Nordman, *Finskt Museum*, 4, 1929; *Acta Arch.*, vol. ii, p. 2651; Curwen, *Antiquity*, vol. xii, 1938, pp. 146 ff.
36. Childe, *Antiquity*, vol. xxiii, 1949, pp. 129 ff.
37. *A.A.*, N.S. vol. xxxiii, 1930, p. 39.

CHAPTER II

1. Brunton, *Mostagedda*, 1937, pp. 5 f., 7 f., 25 ff.
2. Baumgärtel, *The Cultures of Prehistoric Egypt*, Oxford, 1955, p. 20.
3. Brunton and Caton-Thompson, *The Badarian Civilization*, 1928, p. 18.
4. *Op. cit.*, pp. 181 ff.; Brunton, *Mostagedda*, pp. 26 ff.; Baumgärtel, *op. cit.*, pp. 21 ff.
5. *Mostagedda*, pp. 71 ff.
6. Cf. Caton-Thompson and E. W. Gardner, *The Desert Fayum*, 1934, p. 90.
7. J. E. Quibell and F. W. Green, *Hierakonpolis*, vol. ii, 1902, pp. 20 ff.; H. J. Kantor, *J.N.E.S.*, vol. iii, 1944, pp. 110 ff.
8. Breasted, *Religion and Thought in Ancient Egypt*, 1914, pp. 100 f.
9. Cf. Petrie, *The Royal Tombs of the First Dynasty*, 1900, pp. 8 ff.; *Abydos*, vol. i, 1902; vol. ii, 1903.
10. Petrie, *Pyramids and Temples at Gizeh*, 1885; C. M. Firth and J. E. Quibell, *The Step Pyramid*, 1936.
11. Watelin, *Kish*, vol. iv, Paris, 1934, pp. 17 ff.
12. Woolley, *The Sumerians*, Oxford, 1929, p. 36.
13. Seton Lloyd and Fuad Safar, *J.N.E.S.*, vol. iv; October 1945, pp. 267 f., figs. 17, 27, pl. iii, 1, 2, 3; A. L. Perkins, *The Comparative Archaeology of Early Mesopotamia*, Chicago, 1949, p. 5.
14. Perkins, *op. cit.*; E. E. Herzfold, *Archaeologische Mitteilungen aus Iran*, vol. v, 1935, p. 29.
15. Tobler, *The Excavations at Tepe Gawra*, vol. ii, 1950, pp. 105, 124.

16. Cf. E. A. Speiser, *The Excavations at Tepe Gawra*, vol. i, Philadelphia, 1935, p. 177; Tobler, vol. ii, 1950, pp. 51 ff.
17. Perkins, *op. cit.*, pp. 22, 42.
18. Woolley, *The Antiquaries Journal*, vol. x, 1930, pl. xliv (a); Speiser, *Smith. Report*, 1939, p. 444.
19. Mallowan and C. Rose, *Iraq*, vol. ii, 1933, pp. 34 ff.; Perkins, *op. cit.*, pp. 74, 81.
20. *New Light on the Most Ancient East*, 1952, p. 115.
21. Lloyd and Safar, *Sumer*, vol. iv, no. 11, 1948, pp. 117 f.
22. Woolley, *The Antiquaries Journal*, vol. x, October 1930, pp. 327 ff.; cf. *Ur Excavations*, vol. ii, 1934, pp. 35 ff.
23. *Excavations at Ur*, 1954, pp. 16 ff.; *Ur of the Chaldees*, 1950, pp. 29, 68.
24. *Ur Excavations*, vol. ii, 1934, pp. 33 ff.; *Ur of the Chaldees*, pp. 35 ff.; cf. Parrot, *Syria*, vol. xviii, 1937, p. 60.
25. Woolley, *Ur Excavations*, vol. ii, pp. 33 ff.
26. *Op. cit.*, p. 51.
27. Cf. Jacobsen, *The Sumerian King List*, Chicago, 1939, p. 58.
28. *Mémoires de la Mission Archéologique en Iran*, vol. xxx, Paris, 1947, pp. 177 ff.
29. D. E. McCown, *The Comparative Stratigraphy of Early Iran*, Chicago, 1942, pp. 43 ff.
30. *Mémoires*, vol. xxix, 1943, pp. 5 ff.
31. R. de Mecquenem, *Fouilles préhistoriques en Asie occidentale*, 1934, p. 190; *L'Anthrop.*, vol. xlviii, 1938, pp. 67 ff.
32. E. Pottier, *Délégation en Perse, Mémoires*, vol. xiii, 1912, fig. 168, pl. xxx, 7.
33. De Mecquenem, *Mémoires*, vol. xxv, 1934, figs. 60, 3; 12; 61, 1; 62, 1–2.
34. Piggott, *Antiquity*, vol. xvii, 1943, pp. 162 ff.; *Ancient India*, no. i, 1946, pp. 8–26; no. iv, 1948, pp. 162 ff.
35. Piggott, *Prehistoric India*, 1950, pp. 72 ff.; *Ancient India*, no. 1, 1946, pp. 8 ff.; no. 3, 1947, pp. 113 ff.
36. *Annual Survey of India*, 1904–5, p. 105, pl. xxxiii, xxxiv.
37. H. Hargreaves, *Excavations in Baluchistan*, 1925; *Memoirs Arch. Survey of India*, no. 35, Calcutta, 1929, pp. 17 ff.
38. Mockler, *J.R.A.S.*, vol. ix, 1877, pp. 121 ff.
39. E. J. H. Mackay, *Further Excavations at Mohenjo-daro*, vol. i, 1938, pp. 116 ff., 615, 648 ff.
40. *Op. cit.*, p. 117.
41. Marshall, *Mohenjo-daro and the Indus Civilization*, vol. i, 1931, pp. 79 ff.
42. Mackay, *op. cit.*, pp. 94 f.
43. Mackay, *Chanhu-daro Excavations*, New Haven, 1943, pp. 137 ff.
44. Vats, *Excavations at Harappa*, vol. i, 1940, pp. 198 ff.
45. *Op. cit.*, p. 161 f.
46. *The Cambridge History of India*, "The Indus Civilization", Cambridge, 1953, pp. 24 f.
47. Cf. p. 53.

Notes

48. Wheeler, *op. cit.*, pp. 48 f.; *Ancient India*, no. 3, 1947, pp. 85 ff.
49. Vats, *op. cit.*, vol. i, pp. 203 ff.
50. R. E. M. Wheeler, *Ancient India*, no. 3, 1947, pp. 76 ff.; *Cambridge History of India*, 1954, pp. 23, 33.

CHAPTER III

1. Cf. chap. ii, pp. 46 f.
2. Dikaios, *Syria*, 1932, pp. 345 ff.
3. Dikaios, *Iraq*, vol. vii, 1940, pp. 72 ff.
4. *Op. cit.*, pp. 77 ff.
5. Dikaios, *Archaeologia*, vol. lxxxviii, 1938, pp. 4 ff., 95 ff.
6. S. Xanthoudides, *The Vaulted Tombs of Mesara*, 1924, pp. 4 ff.
7. Petrie, *Royal Tombs*, vol. i, p. 18; vol. ii, p. 38.
8. Evans, *The Palace of Minos*, vol. i, 1921, pp. 125 ff.; vol. ii, p. 45.
9. R. B. Seager, *Explorations in Mochlos*, Boston, 1912, pp. 13 ff.; *The Cemetery of Pachyammos, Crete*, Univ. of Penn. Anthrop. Pub. VII, no. 1, Philadelphia, 1916, pp. 9 ff.
10. C. C. Edgar, *B.S.A.*, vol. iii, 1896, pp. 35 ff.
11. Cf. Bent, *J.H.S.*, vol. v, 1884, pp. 48 ff.
12. C. C. Edgar, *Excavations at Phylakopi*, Society Hellenic Studies, no. 4, 1904, pp. 234 ff.
13. T. E. Peet, *The Stone and Bronze Ages in Italy and Sicily*, Oxford, 1909, pp. 223 ff.
14. F. von Duhn, *Italische Grabenkunde*, Heidelberg, 1924, pp. 71 ff.
15. *Op. cit.*, p. 76
16. D. Mackenzie, *British School of Rome*, vol. v, no. 2, 1910, pp. 101 ff.
17. *Op. cit.*, pp. 89 ff.
18. Pallottino, *La Sardegna nuragica*, 1950, pp. 29 ff., 41 f.
19. Hemp, *The Antiquaries Journal*, vol. xii, 1932, pp. 127 ff.
20. Hemp, *Archaeologia*, vol. lxxvi, 1927, pp. 121 ff.
21. *The Antiquaries Journal*, vol. xii, 1932, p. 134.
22. *Malta: Origini della civilta mediterranea*, Rome, 1934.
23. *Prehistoric Malta*, Oxford, 1930, p. 44.
24. Cf. Hawkes, *The Prehistoric Foundations of Europe*, pp. 153 f.
25. J. B. Ward-Perkins, *Antiquity*, vol. xvi, 1942, pp. 30 ff.
26. Zammit, *The Neolithic Temples at Hajar Kin and Mnaidra*, Valetta, 1927, pp. 9, 28.
27. Zammit, *Prehistoric Malta*, "The Tarxien Temples", Oxford, 1930, pp. 7 ff.
28. Zammit, *Antiquity*, 1930, p. 26.
29. *Op. cit.*, p. 17.
30. Chap. vi, pp. 166 f.

31. *The Antiquaries Journal,* vol. viii, 1928, p. 483.
32. L. Siret, *Revue préhistorique,* 1908, nos, 7, 8; *L'Anthrop.,* 1892, no. 4, pp. 391 ff.; Leisner, *Arqueologia e Historia,* vol. i, Lisbon, 1945, pp. 13 ff.; Siret, *Les premiers Ages du métal dans le sud-est de l'Espagne,* 1888.
33. Siret, *Revue des questions scientifiques,* Bruxelles, 1893, pp. 522 ff.
34. Leisner, *Die Megalithgräber der iberischen Halbinsel.* i. *Der Süden,* Berlin, 1943, pp. 59, 63, 73.
35. *Op. cit.,* pp. 174 ff.; C. de Mergelina, *Actas y Memorias Sociedad Española de Antropologia Etnografis y Prehistoria,* Madrid, 1921–2; Hemp, *The Antiquaries Journal,* vol. xiv, 1934, pp. 404 ff.
36. Siret, *Proceedings Congress Prehistoric and Protohistoric Sciences,* 1932, pp. 250 ff.; Obermaier, *El Dolmen de Matarrubilla Sevilla, Comisión de Investigaciones paleontológicas y prehistóricas,* Madrid, 1919, 21, no. 267.
37. Estacio de Veiga, *Antiguidades monumentaes do Algarve,* Lisbon, 1886–91, pp. 248 ff.; no. 3, p. 137.
38. *O Archaeologo Portugués,* vol. xii, Lisbon, 1907, pp. 210, 320; Cartailhac, *Les Ages préhistoriques de l'Espagne et du Portugal,* Paris, 1886, p. 119.
39. Cf. Hawkes, *The Prehistoric Foundations of Europe,* pp. 166 f., 169 ff.
40. Cf. Forde, *A.A.,* vol. xxxii, 1930, p. 39.
41. Cf. pp. 74 f.
42. Cf. Forde, *op. cit.,* pp. 70 ff.; Le Rouzic, *L'Anthrop.,* vol. xliii, 1933, pp. 233 ff.
43. Forde, *P.P.S.,* 1940, pp. 170 ff.; Piggott, *Antiquity,* 1937, pp. 441 ff.; Fleure, *Corridors of Time,* vol. vi, Oxford, 1929, pp. 81 ff.; *Arch. Camb.,* 1924, pp. 249.
44. *P.P.S.,* 1939, pp. 159 ff.; *The Antiquaries Journal,* vol. xix, 1939, pp. 157 ff.
45. Piggott, *op. cit.,* pp. 447 f.
46. Daniel, *P.P.S.,* 1939, pp. 161 ff.
47. Forde, *op. cit.,* pp. 77 f.
48. Le Rouzig, *L'Anthrop.,* vol. xliii, pp. 251 ff.
49. *Mém. Soc. académique d'Archéol. du Dép. de l'Oise,* vol. iv, Beauvais, 1860, p. 465; *Bulletin de la Société préhistorique française,* vol. viii, Paris, 1911, p. 669; Forde, *op. cit.,* pp. 63 ff.
50. E. C. Curwen, *Antiquity,* vol. iv, 1930, pp. 32 ff.; Piggott, *The Neolithic Cultures of the British Isles,* Cambridge, 1954, pp. 17 ff.
51. G. E. Daniel, *The Prehistoric Chamber Tombs of England and Wales,* Cambridge, 1950, pp. 38 ff.
52. Hawkes, *The Prehistoric Foundations of Europe,* pp. 175 ff.; Piggott, *op. cit.,* pp. 50 ff.
53. Hemp, *Trans. Bristol and Gloucester Archaeol. Society,* vol. li, 1929, pp. 261 ff.; Berry, *op. cit.,* vol. lii, 1930, pp. 123, 295; Crawford, *The Long Barrows of the Cotswolds,* Gloucester, 1925, pp. 67 ff.; Daniel, *op. cit.,* pp. 73 ff.
54. Cf. chap. i, pp. 18 ff.

Notes

55. J. Ward, *Archaeologia Cambrensis*, 1915, p. 79.
56. *Proceedings of the Cotteswold Naturalists Field Club*, vol. v, p. 340.
57. Hemp, *Archaeologia*, vol. 80, 1930, pp. 183 ff.; vol. 76, 1926, pp. 126, 128.
58. Hemp, *op cit.*, vol. 85, 1935, p. 253.
59. Daniel, *Prehistoric Chamber Tombs of England and Wales*, p. 57; *Antiquity*, vol. xi, 1936, p. 190.
60. G. Coffey, *New Grange and other Incised Tumuli of Ireland*, 1912; T. G. E. Powell, *P.P.S.*, vol. iv, 1938, pp. 243 ff.
61. Macalister, *The Archaeology of Ireland*, 1928, p. 127.
62. Breuil and Macalister, *Proc. Royal Irish Academy*, vol. xxxvi, p. 1; Coffey, *Trans. R.I.A.*, vol. xxx, 1891, pp. 1 ff.
63. *The Antiquaries Journal*, vol. xiv, 1934, p. 204.
64. Powell, *P.P.S.*, vol. iv, 1938, pp. 239 ff.; Piggott, *Neolithic Cultures of the British Isles*, pp. 193 ff.
65. *Co. Louth Archaeological Journal*, vol. ix, 1939, pp. 1–18.
66. Breuil, *P.P.S.(A.)*, vol. vii, 1934, pp. 293 ff.
67. Childe, *Prehistoric Communities of the British Isles*, 1940, p. 53.
68. Childe, *The Prehistory of Scotland*, 1935, pp. 41 ff.
69. Cf. p. 87.
70. Childe, *The Prehistory of Scotland*, p. 34.
71. Cf. Crawford, *Ordinance Survey Professional Papers*, N.S., no. 8, p. 3; R. F. Jessup, *The Archaeology of Kent*, 1930, pp. 70 ff.; Daniel, *op. cit.*, pp. 80 f.
72. Piggott, *P.P.S.*, N.S., vol. i, 1935, p. 122.
73. Coon, *The Races of Europe*, New York, 1939, p. 111.
74. Daniel and Powell, *P.P.S.*, vol. xv, 1949, p. 178.
75. Chap. i, pp. 33 f.
76. Childe, *Antiquity*, vol. xxiii, 1949, p. 134.
77. The passage-grave at Karleby near Falköping has a chamber 16·65 metres long and a passage 12 metres in length.
78. Cf. C. A. Nordman, *Jaettestuer i Danmark nya fynd, Nordisker Fortisminder*, vol. ii, 1918, p. 118; H. Shetslig and Falk, *Scandinavian Archaeology*, E.T. by E. V. Gordon, Oxford, 1937, pp. 56 f.
79. Nordman, "Megalithic Culture in Northern Europe", *Suomen Muinais- muistohydistyksen Aikakauskirja*, Helsinki, 1935, xxxix, 3, p. 28.
80. Childe, *Dawn of Civilization*, pp. 162 f.

CHAPTER IV

1. Greenwell, *British Barrows*, 1878, pp. 506 f.
2. *Op. cit.*, p. 19.
3. Hogg, *P.P.S.*, vol. iv, 1938, pp. 335 f.
4. S. Rudder, *A New History of Gloucestershire*, 1779, p. 306.

5. J. R. Mortimer, *Forty Years' Researches in British and Saxon Burial Mounds of East Yorkshire*, 1905, pp. 298 ff.; cf. p. 240.
6. *Prehistoric Communities of the British Isles*, 1940, p. 63.
7. Cf. chap. v, p. 123.
8. J. F. S. Stone, *P.P.S.*, vol. xv, 1949, pp. 122 ff.
9. M. E. Cunnington, *Woodhenge*, Devizes, 1929, p. 88; Piggott, *Antiquity*, vol. x, 1936, pp. 221 f.
10. Piggott, *Aspects of Archaeology*, 1951, pp. 274 ff.
11. Piggott, *Antiquity*, vol. iv, 1938, pp. 58 ff.
12. Cf. R. C. C. Clay, *Wilts. Archaeological Magazine*, vol. xliv, 1928, p. 103; R. S. Newall, op. cit., vol. xlv, 1931, pp. 432 ff.; Piggott, *Neolithic Cultures in Britain*, 1954, pp. 355 ff.; L. V. Grinsell, *Ancient Burial-Mounds of England*. 1953, pp. 17 ff.
13. Childe, *The Danube in Prehistory*, Oxford, 1929, p. 295.
14. Cf. Hawkes, *The Prehistoric Foundations of Europe*, pp. 343 f.
15. *Villanovans and Early Etruscans*, Oxford, 1924, pp. 5 ff., 267 f.
16. Pigorini, *Bulletina di Palalnologia Italiana*, vol. xxix, 1903, pp. 76, 169.
17. Childe, *The Bronze Age*, 1930, p. 202.
18. Childe, op. cit., p. 204; Randall-MacIver, op. cit., pp. 35 ff.
19. Gozzadini, *La nécropole de Villanova découverte et décrite*, Bologna, 1870, p. 14.
20. Childe, *Antiquity*, vol. ii, 1928, pp. 37 ff.
21. Childe, *The Danube in Prehistory*, p. 334.
22. Peake, *The Bronze Age and the Celtic World*, 1922, pp. 81 ff.
23. Hawkes, *P.P.S.*, vol. xiv, 1948, p. 199.
24. Woolley, *Annals of Archaeology and Anthropology*, vol. vi, Liverpool, 1914, pp. 95 ff.; *Antiquaries Journal*, vol. xviii, 1938, p. 4.
25. Childe, *P.P.S.*, vol. xiv, 1948, p. 183.
26. Cf. chap. v, pp. 122 f.
27. Cf. chap. v, pp. 123 f.
28. Elliot Smith, *The Migrations of Early Culture*, Manchester, 1915, pp. 32 ff.; Elliot Smith and W. R. Dawson, *Egyptian Mummies*, 1924, pp. 23 f., 73.
29. Quibell, *Report of Brit. Assoc.*, Dundee, 1912, p. 612.
30. Garstang, *Burial Customs of Ancient Egypt*, 1907, p. 30.
31. Petrie, *Medum*, 1892, pp. 17 ff.
32. Petrie, *Deshasheh*, 1898, p. 15.
33. *J.E.A.*, vol. i, 1914, pp. 252 f.
34. Cf. Blackman, op. cit., vol. iii, 1916, pp. 253 f.
35. N. G. Davies and A. H. Gardiner, *The Tomb of Amenembet*, 1915, pp. 57 f.
36. Gardiner, *E.R.E.*, vol. viii, p. 23; Breasted, *Religion and Thought in Ancient Egypt*, p. 54.
37. Cf. chap. ii, pp. 40 f.
38. Sethe, *Urkunden*, vol. i, p. 114; *Palermo Stone*, vol. i, no. 3, p. 4.

Notes 271

39. Budge, *The Book of Opening the Mouth*, 1909, 2 vols.
40. Lepsius, *Denkmäler*, vol. ii, p. 4; *Pyramid Texts*, 1929, E.T. by Mercer, vol. iv, pp. 36 ff.
41. Budge, *op. cit.*, vol. i, p. vii.
42. Blackman, *J.E.A.*, vol. xxi, 1935, pp. 6f.
43. *The Tomb of Amenemhet*, pp. 56 ff.; Moret, *Le Rituel du Culte divin journalier en Egypte*, Paris, 1902, pp. 147 ff.; Wilson, *J.N.E.S.*, Chicago, 1944, vol. iii, pp. 201 ff.; Schiaparelli, *Il libro dei Funerali*, Turin, 1882–90, 3 vols.; Baly, *J.E.A.*, vol. xvi, 1930, pp. 176 ff.; Blackman and Fairman, *op. cit.*, vol. xxxii, 1946, pp. 75 ff. For a parallel rite in connexion with the statue of a god in Babylonia, cf. Blackman, *op. cit.*, vol. v, 1918, pp. 117 ff.; vol. x, 1924, pp. 47 ff.; S. Smith, *J.R.A.S.*, 1925, pp. 37 ff.
44. Cf. W. R. Dawson, *J.E.A.*, vol. xiii, 1927, pp. 40 ff.; *Egyptian Mummies*, 1924, pp. 45 ff.; T. J. Pettigrew, *History of Egyptian Mummies*, 1834, pp. 44 ff.
45. Wilson, *Journal of Near Eastern Studies*, 1944, pp. 201 ff.; Davies, *The Tomb of Rekh-mi-Re at Thebes*, 1943, pp. 70 ff.

CHAPTER V

1. *Het Animisme in der Indischen Archipel*, 1906, p. 372.
2. J. G. F. Riedel, *De Sluik en Kroeshaarige rassen tusschen Selebes en Papua*, 1886, pp. 410 f., 460, 466.
3. Routledge, *The Mystery of Easter Island*, 1919, pp. 231 f.
4. G. Brown, *Melanesians and Polynesians*, 1910, p. 396.
5. Codrington, *The Melanesians*, Oxford, 1891, p. 272.
6. Rivers, *History of Melanesian Society*, vol. ii, Cambridge, 1914, pp. 264 ff., 530 ff.; Seligman, *The Melanesians of British New Guinea*, Cambridge, 1910, pp. 715 ff.; Codrington, *op. cit.*, p. 288, n. 1.
7. Cf. chap. i, pp. 17 ff.
8. Cf. chap. iii, p. 75.
9. Codrington, *op. cit.*, pp. 261 ff.
10. Riedel, *op. cit.*, p. 483.
11. Seligman, *op. cit.*, pp. 728 f.
12. B. Spencer, *Wanderings in Wild Australia*, vol. ii, 1928, pp. 489 ff.
13. H. Basedow, *The Australian Aboriginal*, 1925, p. 214.
14. J. Dawson, *Australian Aborigines*, Melbourne, 1881, p. 67.
15. W. E. Roth, *Bull. of Records of the Australian Museum*, vol. vi, 1907, p. 393; A. P. Elkin, *The Australian Aborigines*, Sydney, 1938, p. 249.
16. Codrington, *op. cit.*, p. 267.
17. *Contrib. to N. Amer. Ethnol.*, vol. iv, 1881, pp. 218, 220 f.
18. Reutter, *De L'embaumement avant et après J. Xt.*, Paris, 1912, p. 142.
19. Gann, *64th Bull. B.A.E.*, Washington, 1918, p. 127.

20. H. C. Mercer, *Public. Univ. Penn.* no. 6, 1897, pp. 93 ff.; Bushnell, *71st Bull. B.A.E.*, 1920, pp. 58 f.
21. *12th Report B.A.E.*, 1894, p. 379; J. W. Foster, *Prehistoric Races*, 1878, pp. 149 ff.; Willcox, *Proc. Acad. Nat. Sci.*, 1874, pp. 165 ff.
22. Le Plongeon, *Queen Mao and the Egyptian Sphinx*, 1896, p. 138.
23. Pepper, *Amer. Mus. Nat. Hist. Anunal Report*, 2, 1902, no. 44; Guernsey and Kidder, *Papers of Peabody Mus.*, 1921, pp. 13 ff.; 19 f.; Z. Nuttall, *The Book of the Life of the American Mexicans*, Berkeley, 1903, pp. 54 ff.; Duc de Loubat, *Codex Magliabecchiano*, 3, Rome, 1904, p. 13.
24. *65th Bull. B.A.E.*, 1919, p. 83.
25. J. W. Fawkes, *Smith. Misc. Collections*, no. 63, 1914, pp. 50 ff.; C. L. Webster, *Archaeol. Bulletin*, no. 3, pp. 70, 73.
26. Chap. iv, p. 104.
27. Lumholtz, *Unknown Mexico*, vol. i, 1903, pp. 71 ff.
28. *Trans. & Coll. Amer. Antiq. Soc.*, vol. i, 1820, pp. 318 ff., 359 f., 362.
29. *Contrib. to N. Amer. Ethnology*, vol. i, 1887, pp. 90 f.
30. *Billings Expedition*, 1802, p. 161.
31. Dall, *Smithsonian Contributions*, 1878, pp. 31, 84 ff.
32. R. Beverley, *History of Virginia*, 1772, p. 185.
33. Turner, *Samoa*, 1884, pp. 148 f.; *Nineteen Years in Samoa*, 1861, p. 232.
34. Hare Hongi, *Journal of the Polynesian Society*, vol. xxv, 1916, pp. 169 ff.
35. *Op. cit.*, p. 172.
36. W. Ellis, *Polynesian Researches*, vol. i, 1829, pp. 520 ff.
37. G. de Mendieta, *Historia eclesiastica Indiana*, Mexico, 1870, p. 358.
38. Brasseur de Bourbourg, *Histoire des nations civilisées du Mexique et de l'Amérique*, vol. iv, Paris, 1859, 3, pp. 239 ff., 407 ff.
39. *A.A.*, N.S. vol. 16, 1914, pp. 62 ff.
40. *18th Report B.A.E.*, 1899, pp. 317 ff.
41. *Contrib. Mus. Amer. Ind.; Heye Foundation*, vol. v, 1919, pp. 9 ff.; *A.A.*, N.S. vol. 7, 1905, pp. 625 f.
42. Sophocles, *Trachiniae*, pp. 1191 f.; Hyginus, *Fab.*, p. 36.
43. Iamblicus, *De Mysteriis*, p. 12.
44. Monier-Williams, *Brahmanism and Hinduism*, 1887, pp. 283 f.
45. Turner, *Samoa*, p. 335; *Contrib. to N. Amer. Ethnol.*, vol. iii, 1877, pp. 181 f.
46. *History of Melanesian Society*, vol. ii, pp. 546, 549 ff.
47. Hill-Tout, *British North America*, 1907, pp. 178 ff.
48. Evans-Pritchard, *African Affairs*, vol. xlviii, no. 190, January 1949, pp. 56 ff.
49. *Op. cit.*, p. 59.
50. Bushnell, *83rd Bull. B.A.E.*, 1927, p. 25.
51. Kruijt, *Het Animisme in der Indischen Archipel*, 1906, pp. 369 ff., 380.
52. *Op. cit.*, pp. 371, 381.
53. Skeat and Blagden, *Pagan Races of the Malay Peninsula*, vol. ii, 1906, pp. 103, 110, 114.
54. *Op. cit.*, pp. 208 ff.

Notes 273

1. H. N. Evans, *Ethnology and Archaeology of the Malay Peninsula*, Cambridge, 1927, pp. 18 ff.
2. P. Schebesta, *Among the Forest Dwarfs of Malaya*, 1929, p. 255.
3. Cf. Perry, *J.R.A.I.*, vol. xliv, 1914, pp. 281 ff.; *Folk-Lore*, vol. xxvi, 1915, pp. 138 ff.; Riedel, *De sluik en Kroeshaarige rassen tussehen Selebes en Papua*, 1886, pp. 334 ff., 360.
4. Kruijt, *op. cit.*, p. 373.
5. Seligman, *The Melanesians of British New Guinea*, Cambridge, 1910, p. 616.
6. Kruijt, *op. cit.*, pp. 345 f.
7. *Op. cit.*, vol. ii, pp. 262 f.
8. Codrington, *The Melanesians*, p. 258.
9. Rivers, *op. cit.*, p. 267.
10. Wheeler, *Archiv. für Religionwissenschaft*, vol. xvii, 1914, p. 64.
11. R. W. Williamson, *The Mafulu Mountain People in British New Guinea*, 1912, pp. 258 ff., pls. 87, 88, 89.
12. B. Thomson, *The Fijians*, 1908, pp. 120 ff.
13. *Op. cit.*, p. 132; Fison, *Tales of Old Fiji*, 1904, p. 168; J. J. Williams, *Fiji and the Fijians*, vol. i, 1870, pp. 200 ff.; Frazer, *Belief in Immortality*, vol. i, 1913, pp. 424 f.
14. Frazer, *op. cit.*, p. 399.
15. Keysser, Neuhauss, *Deutsch New Guinea*, vol. iii, Berlin, 1911, pp. 82 f., 143.
16. Brinton, *Myths of the New World*, Philadelphia, 1896, p. 280.
17. *J.A.I.*, vol. xxi, 1891, pp. 18 f.; Bancroft, *Native States of North America*, vol. iii, New York, 1883, p. 520.
18. J. Franklin, *Second Expedition*, 1828, pp. 291 ff.
19. A. Henry, *Travels and Adventures in Canada*, Toronto, 1901, p. 144; *71st Report B.A.E.*, 1920, p. 30.
20. Copeway, *Ojibway Nation*, 1847, p. 32; Schoolcraft, *Indian Tribes*, Philadelphia, 1853, vol. i, p. 321.
21. Pinkerton, *Voyages and Travels*, vol. xiii, 1812, p. 41.
22. Sahagun, *Hist. Gen. de las cosas de Nueva España*, vol. i, Mexico, 1829, lib. ii, p. 164; Brasseur de Bourbourg, *Histoire Nat. Civ.*, vol. iii, p. 497.
23. Sahagun, *op. cit.*, vols. II, vii, pp. 253 ff.
24. H. Ling Roth, *Natives of Sarawak and British North Borneo*, vol. i, 1896, pp. 204 ff.
25. Hose and McDougall, *The Pagan Tribes of Borneo*, vol. ii, 1912, pp. 32 ff.
26. O. Rutter, *The Pagans of North Borneo*, 1929, p. 216.
27. Skeat and Blagden, *Pagan Races of the Malay Peninsula*, vol. ii, 1906, pp. 99 ff., 106 ff.
28. *Melanesians*, p. 255.
29. *Op. cit.*, p. 285.
30. Malinowski, *Argonauts of the Western Pacific*, p. 513.
31. Hocart, *J.R.A.I.*, vol. lii, 1922, p. 84.

CHAPTER VI
1. *Golden Bough*, vol. iv, part 1 (Adonis), p. 5.
2. *L'Anthrop.*, vol. xx, 1911, pp. 257ff.; vol. xxiii, 1912, pp. 129, 143; *Revue préhistorique*, vol. v, 1910, p. 33; Capitan, *Rev. de l'Ecole d'anthrop.*, vol. xxii, 1912, pp. 316ff.
3. L. Passemard, *Les statuettes féminines dites Vénus stéatopyges*, Nimes, 1938, pp. 121f; Luquet, *The Art and Religion of Fossil Man*, Oxford, 1930, pp. 85, 110.
4. Capitan, *Peintures et gravures murales des cavernes paléolithiques. Les Combarelles aux Eyzies*, 1924, pl. vi.
5. *The Gate of Horn*, 1948, p. 57.
6. G. Clark, *Savagery to Civilization*, 1946, p. 56.
7. E. A. Golomshtok, *L'Anthrop.*, vol. xliii, 1933, pp. 334ff.; S. N. Zamiatnine, *Paleolit. S.S.S.R.*, Moscow, 1935, pp. 26ff.
8. Burkitt, *Eurosia Septentrionalis Antiqua*, ix. Helsinki, 1934, p. 113.
9. J. W. Jackson, *Shells as Evidence of the Migration of Early Culture*, Manchester, 1917, pp. 135ff.
10. Cf. Didon, "L'Abri Blanchard, Périgueux, 1911", extract from *Bull. de la Soc. Hist. et Archéol. du Périgord*, pl. vi, no. 28; Mortillet, *Musée Préhistorique*, 2nd ed., no. 189.
11. Boule, *Les Hommes Fossiles*, Paris, 1923, p. 266.
12. *L'Anthrop.*, vol. xxiii, 1912, p. 657; *C.R. Acad. Inscrip. et Belles-Lettres*, 1912, pp. 532ff.
13. Breuil and Calve Aguilo, *L'Anthrop.*, vol. xx, 1909, p. 1.
14. Cf. chap. vii, pp. 172f.
15. Only four Magdalenian figurines have been discovered, all of them in France.
16. Breuil, *L'Anthrop.*, vol. xxiii, 1912, p. 529.
17. Cf. Obermaier, *Fossil Man in Spain*, 1925, pp. 257ff.; *L'Anthrop.*, vol. xxxvi, 1926, pp. 5–6.
18. Cf. E. S. Hartland, *Primitive Paternity*, 1909–10; Malinowski, *The Father in Primitive Psychology*, 1927, pp. 28ff., 43ff.; *Sexual Life of Savages in North-Western Melanesia*, 1929, pp. 146ff.
19. Petrie, *Prehistoric Egypt*, 1920, pp. 8f.; Brunton and Caton-Thompson, *The Bedarian Civilization*, 1928, p. 29.
20. M. E. I. Mallowan and J. Cruikshank Rose, *Iraq*, vol. ii, 1935, pp. 79ff.
21. *The Archaeology of Palestine and the Bible*, New York, 1932, p. 109.
22. *Excavations at Tepe Gawra*, Philadelphia, 1950, p. 163.
23. *Op. cit.*, p. 165.
24. Seton Lloyd and Fuad Safar, *J.N.E.S.*, vol. iv, 1945, p. 270.
25. Mallowan, *Iraq*, vol. iii, 1936, pp. 19f.
26. Woolley, *The Development of Sumerian Art*, 1935, pp. 37f., pls. 6a–e, f, h; *Antiq. Journal*, vol. x, no 4, 1930, p. 338, pl. xcviii.
27. *J.E.A.*, vol. ix, 1923, pp. 191f.

Notes

28. *Deutsche Forschungsgemeinschaft in Uruk-Warka*, vol. vii, Berlin, 1936, pl. 47; cf. vol. viii, p. 50.
29. *Op. cit.*, vol. viii, p. 52, pl. 49 e.
30. R. de Mecquenem, *L'Anthrop.*, vol. xlv, 1935, pp. 93 ff., pls. 1–2.
31. *Op. cit.*, pls. 7 i.
32. Contenau, *Syria*, vol. viii, 1927, p. 198, figs. 2, 3; *La Déesse nue babylonienne*, Paris, 1914, p. 59, fig. 58; cf. p. 62, fig. 59; *Délégation en Perse, Mémoires*, vol. i, p. 125, fig. 276; cf. p. 130, pls. vii, 14, viii, 19.
33. Pézard et Pottier, *Les Antiquités de la Susiane*, Paris, 1913, p. 129.
34. *Op. cit.*, p. 149.
35. *De Morgan Collection*, no. 276.
36. Cf. *Délégation en Perse*, vol. i, p. 130, pls. vii, 10; Pézard, *op. cit.*, p. 129; Contenau, fig. 60.
37. *Explorations in Turkestan*, 1904; Pumpelly, vol. i, 1908, p. 171, pl. 46, figs. 13, 14.
38. *Op. cit.*, pl. 46, fig. 11.
39. *Op. cit.*, figs. 10a, 10b.
40. *Op. cit.*, pls. 4, 55.
41. Piggott, *Prehistoric India*, 1950, p. 127; Stein, *Memoirs Arch. Survey of India*, no. 37, 1925, pp. 38, 42, 60, 75, pls. ix, P.W. 9, P. 262; xii, K. 14; xvi, D.N. d. 9, S.J. 68; Piggott, *Ancient India*, 1950, pp. 107 f., 126 ff.
42. Stein, *op. cit.*, p. 60.
43. *Op. cit.*, pl. ix, P.C. 17.
44. Cf. Brunton and Cater-Thompson, *Badarian Civilization*, p. 29; Woolley, *Antiq. Journal*, vol. xi, p. 368; Zammit, *Archaeologia*, vol. lxx, p. 197.
45. Mackay, *Further Excavations at Mohenjo-daro*, vol. ii, 1937, pls. xci, 12; xcii, i, a; vol. i, pp. 257 ff.; Marshall, *Mohenjo-daro and the Indus Valley Civilization*, vol. i, 1931, pp. 338 ff.; Vats, *Excavations at Harappa*, vol. i, 1940, pp. 292 ff.; Piggott, *Ancient India*, no. 3, 1946, pp. 126 ff.
46. Marshall, *op. cit.*, vol. i, p. 339.
47. Mackay, *op. cit.*, p. 259; *The Indus Civilization*, 1948, pp. 53 f.
48. Marshall, *op. cit.*, pl. xciv, 11; Mackay, *op. cit.*, vol. ii, pl. lxxii, 7; pl. lxxvi, 5; Vats, *op. cit.*, pls. lxxvi, lxxvii.
49. Marshall, *op. cit.*, pl. xciv, no. 11.
50. *Op. cit.*, pl. xii, no. 17.
51. Marshall, *op. cit.*, vol. i, pp. 53 ff.
52. Mackay, *Further Excavations at Mohenjo-daro*, vol. i, pp. 335 ff.
53. Marshall, *op. cit.*, pls. xiii, 1, 7; xiv, 2, 4.
54. *Op. cit.*, pls. xiii, 1, 2, 8.
55. *Op. cit.*, pls. cxxx, 21, 23.
56. Mackay, *op. cit.*, pp. 407 f.
57. Vats, *Excavations at Harappa*, 1940, pp. 51, 53, 55 ff.
58. *Op. cit.*, p. 370.   59. Cf. p. 140.   60. p. 371.

61. Pumpelly, *Exploration in Turkestan*, vol. i, 1908, p. 47.
62. Cf. chap. ix, pp. 237f.
63. Oikaios, *Iraq*, vol. vii, 1940, p. 78.
64. *Cambridge Ancient History*, vol. i, 1923, p. 91.
65. C. W. Blegen, *American Journal of Archaeology*, vol. xli, 1937, p. 569, pl. xx.
66. J. T. Bent, *J.H.S.*, vol. v, 1884, pp. 49ff.
67. Cf. Evans, *The Palace of Minos*, vol. i, 1921, p. 49, figs. 12, 13.
68. *Op. cit.*, p. 52.
69. Cf. Homer, *Odyssey*, pp. 125–7; Hesiod, *Theogony*, p. 969; *Diodorus*, vol. v, pp. 25ff.; J. E. Harrison, *Themis*, Cambridge, 1912, pp. 54 n. 7, 164; *Prolegomena to Study of Greek Religion*, 1903, p. 456.
70. Harrison, *Prolegomena*, fig. 86.
71. Solinus, vol. xi, p. 8; Nilsson, *The Minoan-Mycenaean Religion*, 1927, p. 439.
72. Evans, *op. cit.*, pp. 500ff., figs. 359, 362, 377; Nilsson, *op. cit.*, pp. 268ff.; B. E. Williams, *Gournia*, Philadelphia, 1908, pp. 47ff., pl. xi.
73. Evans, *op. cit.*, vol. iv, p. 559, figs. 522a, b; *B.S.A.*, vol. vii, 1900, p. 29, fig. 9.
74. *B.S.A.*, *op. cit.*, p. 101; vol. ix, fig. 38.
75. *J.H.S.*, vol. xxii, p. 77, fig. 2.
76. Diodorus, *I*, iv, c. 79, 3.
77. Evans, *op. cit.*, vol. iv, pp. 959ff.
78. Evans, *op. cit.*, vol. i, pp. 438f.; Nilsson, *op. cit.*, pp. 368ff.; Paribeni, *Mon. ant.*, vol. xix, pp. 1ff.
79. Evans, *B.S.A.* vol. viii, pp. 101ff.; *op. cit.*, vol. i, p. 447.
80. Zammit and Singer, *J.R.A.I.*, vol. liv, 1924, pp. 79ff.; pls. v, 6, 7, 9; vol. xix, pl. 10.
81. Zammit, *Prehistoric Malta*, Oxford, 1930, p. 80, pl. xxii.
82. *J.R.A.I.*, *op. cit.*, pl. xv, 49.
83. *Op. cit.*, pl. xviii, 53.
84. *Op. cit.*, pl. xviii, 54.
85. *Op cit.*, pl. xi, 29.
86. *Op. cit.*, pl. xx, 30.
87. M. A. Murray, *Excavations in Malta*, 1929, pp. 11, 29.
88. Zammit, *The Hal-Saflieni Prehistoric Hypogeum*, Malta, 1910, p. 40 *J.R.A.I.*, *op. cit.*, pl. ix, 22.
89. *J.R.A.I.*, pl. x, 23.
90. Cf. chap. iii, pp. 70f.
91. Zammit, *Prehistoric Malta*, pp. 13, 15, 84, 96.
92. Siret, *Revue préhistorique*, 1908, pp. 10, 21.
93. Correia, *Comisión de investigaciones paleontológicas y prehistóricas*, Madrid, 1921 pp. 27, 63ff., figs. 50, 56, 58.
94. Cf. chap. iii, pp. 76f.   95. Correia, *op. cit.*, p. 75.
96. *Junta superior para excavaciones archeologicas*, Madrid, 1930, *Mems.*, p. 112.

97. Z. le Rouzic, *Carnac, Menhir-Statues avec signes figuratifs et Amulettes ou Idoles des Dolmens du Morbihan*, Nantes, 1931, pp. 13 ff.
 98. Kendrick, *The Archaeology of the Channel Islands*, vol. i, 1928, p. 32.
 99. *Op. cit.*, pp. 21 ff.; *Antiq. Journal*, vol. v, 1925, pp. 429 f.
100. Et Michon, *Rés. des mém. Soc. de Antiq. de France*, Centenaire, 1904, p. 299.
101. E. MacCulloch, *Proc. Soc. Antiq.*, vol. viii, 1881, p. 32.
102. A. de Mortillet, *Bull. Soc. d'Anthrop.*, Paris, 1893, p. 664.
103. *Association Française pour l'avancement des Sciences*, Paris, 1890, p. 629.
104. *Bull. Soc. préhistorique française*, vol. viii, Paris, 1911, p. 669.
105. V. C. C. Collum, *The Tressé Iron-Age Megalithic Monument*, Oxford, 1935.
106. Piggott, *The Neolithic Cultures of the British Isles*, 1954, p. 42; Childe, *Prehistoric Communities of the British Isles*, 1949, 3rd ed., p. 40.
107. Piggott, *op. cit.*, p. 88, figs. 14, 1–4, 10.
108. Piggott, *P.P.S.*, N.S. vol. ii, 1936, p. 87.
109. C. Fox, *The Early Cultures of North-west Europe*, Cambridge, 1950, pp. 59 f.
110. Philippe, "Cinq Années de Fouilles au Fort-Harrouard, 1921–5", *Société normande d'études préhistoriques*, vol. xxv, *bis* Rouen, 1927.
111. *Manuel d'archéologie préhistorique*, Paris, 1908, p. 603.

CHAPTER VII

 1. Spencer and Gillen, *Native Tribes of Central Australia*, 1938, pp. 167 ff.
 2. Cf. chap. iv, p. 148.
 3. Breuil, *Quatre cents siècles d'art pariétal*, Montignac, 1954, pp. 166, 176 f.
 4. *Antiquity*, vol. iii, no. 9, 1929, p. 17.
 5. *Science, Religion and Reality*, 1926, p. 44.
 6. Bégouen, *C. r. Ac. Inscrip.*, 1923, p. 14; Breuil, *op. cit.*, pp. 236 ff.
 7. A. Lemozi, *La Grotte-Temple du Pech-Merle*, Paris, 1929; Breuil, *op. cit.*, pp. 266 ff.
 8. F. Windels, *The Lascaux Cave Paintings*, 1949, pp. 27 ff.; A. H. Brodrick, *Lascaux: A Commentary*, 1948, pp. 81 ff.
 9. Breuil, *op. cit.*, pp. 131, 134 f.
10. Windels, *op. cit.*, p. 63; Levy, *The Gate of Horn*, 1948, p. 21.
11. Spencer and Gillen, *op. cit.*, pp. 171 ff.
12. *Op. cit.*, pp. 614 ff.
13. Spencer and Gillen, *Northern Tribes of Central Australia*, pp. 436 ff.
14. *La Caverne d'Altamira*, Monaco, 1909, p. 139.
15. Cf. chap. ix, pp. 23 f.
16. Cf. Marett, *The Threshold of Religion*, 1914, pp. 40 ff.; J. E. Harrison, *Ancient Art Ritual*, 1913, p. 26.

17. Driston, *L'Egypte*, Paris, 1938, p. 597.
18. Cf. chap. viii, pp. 210f.
19. Frazer, *Golden Bough*, part IV (Adonis II), p. 219.
20. Pyr. Texts, 466b, Sethe, *Urgeschichte und älteste Religion der Aegypter*, Leipzig, 1930, p. 99.
21. Frankfort, *Kingship and the Gods*, Chicago, 1947, pp. 150ff.; *The Birth of Civilization in the Near East*, 1951, p. 54.
22. *Religion and Thought in Ancient Egypt*, 1914, pp. 8f.
23. Cf. Frankfort, *Kingship and the Gods*, pp. 123ff.
24. Blackman, *Studia Aegyptiaca*, "Analecta Orientalia", vol. xvii, 1938, p. 2.
25. Wainwright, *The Sky-Religion in Egypt*, Cambridge, 1938, pp. 11f.
26. Blackman, *Luxor and its Temples*, 1923, pp. 179ff.
27. A. Erman and A. M. Blackman, *The Literature of the Ancient Egyptians*, 1927, p. 137.
28. *J.E.A.*, vol. ii, 1915, p. 125.
29. Brugsch, *Zeitschrift für aegypt. Sprache und Altertumskunde*, vol. xix, 1881, pp. 71–111; Loret, *Recueil de travaux relatifs à la Philologie et à l'archéol. Egyptiennes et Assyriennes*, vol. iii, 1882, pp. 43ff.; vol. iv, 1883, pp. 21ff.; vol. v, 1884, pp. 85ff.
30. Brugsch, *Religion und Mythologie der alten Aegypter*, Leipzig, 1885–8, p. 621.
31. Gardiner, op. cit., p. 123; Brugsch, *Zeitschrift*, pp. 84, 94; *Rel. und Myth.*, p. 618.
32. S. N. Kramer, *Sumerian Mythology*, Philadelphia, 1944, pp. 83ff.
33. Langdon, *The Babylonian Epic of Creation*, Oxford, 1923, p. 37, line 14.
34. *Folk-lore*, 1939, p. 140.
35. Cf. T. Jacobsen, *The Intellectual Adventure of Ancient Man*, Chicago, 1946, pp. 126ff.; Frankfort, *Ancient Egyptian Religion*, Chicago, 1948, pp. 54ff.
36. Ezek. viii. 14.
37. Pallis, *The Babylonian Akitu Festival*, Copenhagen, 1926, pp. 193ff., 252ff.; Langdon, *The Babylonian Epic of Creation*, Oxford, 1923, pp. 34ff.
38. S. Smith, *J.R.A.S.*, 1928, pp. 849ff.; Pallis, op. cit., p. 109; Tallquist, *Sumerisch-akkadische Namen der Totenwelt*, Helsingfors, 1934, p. 26, n. 4.
39. A. J. Wensinck, *Acta Orientalia*, vol. i, pp. 169ff.
40. Jacobsen, *The Sumerian King List*, Chicago, 1939; Assyr. Studies, no. 11, p. 58.
41. Admon., 12, 1; Cairo, 34501.
42. E. Chiera, *Sumerian Ritual Texts*, vol. xxxi, Upland Pa., 1924, 24, i, 22–5.
43. Frazer, *Golden Bough*, part IV, pp. 9ff.; B. Z. and C. G. Seligman, *The Pagan Tribes of the Nilotic Sudan*, 1932, pp. 90ff.; *Egypt and Negro Africa*, 1934, pp. 28ff.; Meek, *The Northern Tribes of Nigeria*, vol. i, 1925, pp. 255ff.; vol. ii, pp. 58ff.; Evans-Pritchard, *The Divine Kingship of the Shilluk of the Nilotic Sudan*, Cambridge, 1948, pp. 18f., 21, 36f.
44. Moret, *Du caractère religieux de la royauté Pharaonique*, Paris, 1902, pp. 256ff.;

Notes

Breasted, *Religion and Thought in Ancient Egypt*, p. 39; Murray, *Ancient Egypt*, vol. ii, 1926, pp. 33 ff.; Seligman, *Egypt and Negro Africa*, p. 2; Frankfort, *Kingship and the Gods*, 1948, pp. 79 ff.

45. *J.E.A.*, vol. ii, 1915, p. 134.
46. *J.E.A.*, vol. xxviii, 1942, p. 71; *Kingship and the Gods*, p. 79.
47. Sethe, *Untersuchungen zur Geschichte und Altertumskunde aegyptens*, vol. iii, 1905, pp. 134 ff.
48. T. H. Gaster, *Thespis*, New York, 1950, pp. 57 ff.; R. de Langhe, *Les textes de Ras Shamra-Ugarit*, Paris, 1945.
49. Cf. C. H. Gordon, *Ugaritic Literature*, Rome, 1949, pp. 3 ff.
50. *Baal-'Anat Cycle*, p. 67; vol. ii, pp. 5–6.
51. *Palace of Minos*, vol. ii, p. 842; vol. iii, p. 142; cf. Nilsson, *Minoan-Mycenaean Religion*, pp. 296 f.
52. A. W. Persson, *The Religion of Greece in Prehistoric Times*, California, 1942, p. 34.
53. Evans, *op. cit.*, vol. i, pp. 161 f.
54. *Op. cit.*, vol. ii, pp. 838 ff.
55. Nilsson, *op. cit.*, p. 230, pl. i, 4.
56. Cf. Evans, *Archaeologia*, vol. xv, 1914, pp. 10 f., fig. 16; Persson, *op. cit.*, p. 49.
57. Evans, *op. cit.*, vol. i, p. 432, fig. 310 a; vol. iii, pp. 220, 225, figs. 154, 158.
58. Cf. Persson, *op. cit.*, pp. 91 ff.; Malten, *Archäologisches Jahrbuch*, 1928, pp. 90 ff.
59. Cf. Deedes, *The Labyrinth*, 1935, pp. 27 ff.
60. Chap. viii, pp. 221 ff.
61. *The Golden Bough*, part II, p. 140.
62. Nilsson, *Greek Popular Religion*, New York, 1940, pp. 51 ff.
63. *Refutatio omnium haeresium*, vol. v, p. 8; cf. Farnell, *Cult of the Greek States*, vol. iii, pp. 177, 183.
64. Artemidorus, vol. i, p. 8.
65. Proclus ad Plato, *Timaeus*, p. 293 (Lobeck).
66. Farnell, *op. cit.*, vol. iii, p. 184.
67. Euripides, *Bacchae*, pp. 20 ff.; Farnell, *op. cit.*, vol. v, pp. 86 ff.; Rhode, *Psyche*, 1925, pp. 250 ff.
68. These examples are quoted from notes made by the author during a visit to the museum at Eleusis.
69. Farnell, *op. cit.*, vol. iii, pl. xxi b, p. 256.
70. *Minoan-Mycenaean Religion*, p. 490.
71. *Op. cit.*, pp. 153 f., figs. 28, 29.
72. *Op. cit.*, p. 155.
73. Tacitus, *Germania*, 40.
74. Lucretius, vol. ii, pp. 600–43.
75. Cf. Crawford, *Antiquity*, 1954, pp. 25 ff.; R. J. C. Atkinson, *P.P.S.*, vol. xviii, part II, 1952, p. 236; *Stonehenge*, 1956, pp. 33 f., 84 f., 163 f.

76. *Stonehenge*, p. 165.
77. Hawkes, *P.P.S.*, 1948, pp. 196 ff.; Navarro, *The Early Cultures of North-west Europe*, Cambridge, 1950, pp. 77 ff.; Atkinson, *op. cit.*, pp. 162 ff.
78. Cf. Childe, *Prehistoric Communities of the British Isles*, p. 122, n. 14.
79. Piggott, *P.P.S.*, 1938, pp. 58 ff.

CHAPTER VIII

1. *Primitive Culture*, 4th ed., vol. i, 1903, pp. 426 ff.
2. *Op. cit.*, vol. ii, pp. 113 f., 247 ff., 311 f.
3. *Principles of Sociology*, vol. i, 1885, p. 411.
4. Frazer, *The Worship of Nature*, 1926, pp. 9 f.
5. *The Making of Religion*, 1898, pp. 160 ff.; cf. Howitt, *Native Tribes of South-east Australia*, 1904, pp. 488 ff.
6. Cf. Schmidt, *Der Ursprung der Gottesidee*, Munster, 1912–54.
7. Spencer and Gillen, *Native Tribes of Central Australia*, 1938, p. 246, n. 1.
8. *Nuer Religion*, Oxford, 1956, pp. 2 ff., 118, 124, 200 ff.
9. *Op. cit.*, p. 316.
10. *Bulletin Société préhistorique française*, vol. iv, 1907, p. 215.
11. A. B. Cook, *L'Anthrop.*, vol. xiv, 1903, pp. 34 ff.
12. Cf. A. C. Haddon, *The Study of Man*, 1898, pp. 277 ff.; Marett, *The Threshold of Religion*, 1914, pp. 17 f., 145 f.; Howitt, *op. cit.*, pp. 578 f.; Spencer and Gillen, *Native Tribes of Central Australia*, pp. 246 n., 634.
13. Cf. Wainwright, *The Sky-Religion in Egypt*, Cambridge, 1938.
14. *Religion and Thought in Ancient Egypt*, 1914, p. 9.
15. Pyr. Texts, p. 1105.
16. Budge, *Tutankhamon, Amenism, Atonism and Egyptian Monotheism*, 1923, p. 79.
17. Frankfort, *Kingship and the Gods*, 1948, p. 38.
18. Cf. Davies, *J.E.A.*, vol. ix, 1923, pp. 133 ff.; *Journal of the Society of Oriental Research*, vol. x, Chicago, 1926, pp. 25 ff.
19. Langdon, *Babyloniaca*, vol. xii, Paris, 1931, p. 11, lines 11–12.
20. Gadd, *The Idea of Divine Rule in the Ancient East*, Oxford, 1948, p. 34.
21. Cf. F. Nötscher, *Ellil in Sumer und Akkad*, pp. 56, 66.
22. Cf. Frankfort, *op. cit.*, p. 228; F. Thureau-Dangin, *Sumerische und Akkadische Königschriften*, Leipzig, 1907, pp. 156 f.
23. Heidel, *The Babylonian Genesis*, Chicago, 1950, pp. 20 ff.; vol. ii, pp. 60 ff.
24. *Op. cit.*, p. 47; vol. ii, pp. 31 ff.
25. Heidel, *The Gilgamesh Epic*, Chicago, 1951, p. 229.
26. Cf. Cook, *Zeus*, vol. i, pp. 577 ff., 635; Garstang, *The Hittite Empire*, 1929, pp. 204 f.
27. S. Mercer, *The Tell El Amarna Tablets*, vol. ii, Toronto, 1939, pp. 483 (13 f.).

28. Konow, *The Aryan Gods of the Mitanni People*, Kristiana, 1921, pp. 1 f.
29. *Rig-veda*, vi, 27, 8; x, 33, 2; *Atharvaveda*, v, 22, 5, 7, 9.
30. The Sanskrit form of the Avestan *Ahura* adopted by Zarathushtra as the designation of the All-wise Lord, Ahura Mazda, the Supreme Being of Zoroastrian monotheism, whose power was limited only by the spirit of evil, Angra Mainyu or the Druj. The Avesta, *Yasna*, xxx.
31. Cf. Keith, *Indian Culture*, vol. iii, p. 421.
32. *Satapatha Brahmana*, v, 1, 1, 2; iii, 2, 2, 4.
33. *Chandogya-Upanishad*, vi, 8, 7 f.; *Brihadaranyaki*, i, 4, 10; *Isa Upanishad*, 1 ff.
34. *Yasna*, 34, 44, 45, 48.
35. *Yasna*, 30.
36. *Five Stages of Greek Religion*, Oxford, 1925, p. 65.
37. Nilsson, *History of Greek Religion*, Oxford, 1925, p. 31.
38. Cf. Rose, *Handbook of Greek Mythology*, 1933, pp. 49 f.
39. Cf. Aeschylus, *Danaids*, *Tragg. Graec.*, Fr. ed., Nauck, p. 44; Euripides, Fr. 898, pp. 7 ff.; Cook, *Zeus*, vol. iii, pp. 456 ff.; Farnell, *Cult of the Greek States*, vol. i, pp. 244 ff.
40. Chap. vii, p. 197.
41. Rose, *op. cit.*, pp. 102 ff.
42. Frazer, *The Golden Bough*, part II, p. 140.
43. *The Aryans*, 1926, p. 81.
44. Shetelig and Falk, *Scandinavian Archaeology*, Oxford, 1937, pp. 156 f.
45. *The Golden Bough*, part x, pp. 160 ff.
46. Chap. vii, p. 203.
47. Cf. Atkinson, *Stonehenge*, 1956, p. 172.

CHAPTER IX

1. *Elementary Forms of the Religious Life*, 1913, p. 206.
2. A. R. Radcliffe-Brown, *A.A.*, 1935, pp. 394 ff.; *J.R.A.I.*, vol. lxxv, 1945, p. 33.
3. *Op. cit.*, pp. 47, 206.   4. Cf. chaps. v, vi.
5. *Les fonctions dans les Sociétés Inférieures*, Paris, 1915; *La Mentalité primitive*, Paris, 1921; *L'Expérience mystique et les symboles chez les primitifs*, Paris, 1938.
6. Evans-Pritchard, *Nuer Religion*, Oxford, 1956, pp. 77, 82, 132 f., 140 f.
7. Chap. vii, p. 180.
8. Newberry, *Annals of Archaeology and Anthropology*, vol. v, Liverpool, 1913, p. 136.
9. Baumgärtel, *The Cultures of Prehistoric Egypt*, Oxford, 1955, p. 31.
10. Hornblower, *J.E.A.*, vol. xv, 1929, p. 39.
11. Levy, *The Gate of Horn*, 1948, p. 116.
12. *Op. cit.*, pp. 38, 43.
13. Winckler, *Rock-Drawings of Southern Upper Egypt*, 1938, p. 22.

14. Gadd, in Hall and Woolley, *Ur Excavations*, vol. i; *Al 'Ubaid*, Oxford, 1927, pp. 142f.
15. *Op. cit.*, p. 143.
16. Cf. chap. vi, p. 159.
17. Chap. vi, p. 158.
18. Capitan, *Les Combarelles aux Eyzies*, 1924, pl. vi; Picard, *Revue de Philologie*, 1933, pp. 344ff.
19. Cf. Malton, *Archäologisches Jahrbuch*, 1928, pp. 90ff.
20. Capitan and Peyrony, *Revue anthropologique*, vol. xxxi, 1921, pp. 92ff.
21. Chap. vii, p. 178.
22. *L'Anthrop.*, vol. xxiv, 1913, pp. 627ff.
23. Cf. chap. vi, p. 146.
24. A. Makowski, *Mittheilungen der Anthropologischen Gesellschaft in Wien*, 1892, p. 73; Obermaier, *Der Mensch der Vorzeit*, p. 298; Breuil, *L'Anthrop.*, 1924, pp. 549ff.
25. Buckland, *Reliquiae Diluvianae*, 1823, pp. 82ff.
26. *Religion and Thought in Ancient Egypt*, p. 61.
27. Frankfort, *Kingship and the Gods*, p. 178.
28. Tablet XI.
29. Cf. Heidel, *The Gilgamesh Epic and the Old Testament Parallels*, Chicago, 1949, pp. 207ff.
30. F. Thureau-Dangin, *Hilprecht Anniversary Volume*, Leipzig, 1909, p. 161.
31. Chap. ii, p. 43.
32. Chap. ii, p. 53.
33. Chap. ii, pp. 48f. Also, Woolley, *Ur Excavations, The Royal Cemeteries*, vol. ii, 1934, pp. 135ff.; Mackay, *Report on the Excavations of the "A" Cemetery at Kish*, vol. i, Chicago, 1925, pp. 13f.
34. Vats, *Excavations at Harappa*, vol. i, 1940, pp. 207ff.
35. *Rig-veda*, x, 18.
36. *Rig-veda*, x, 1, 4, 16.
37. Evans, *Palace of Minos*, vol. ii, p. 279.
38. Chap. vi, p. 164.
39. *Monumenti Antichi*, vol. xix, pp. 5–86, pls. i–iii.
40. *Palace of Minos*, vol. i, pp. 439, 447.
41. Harrison, *Themis*, 1912, p. 178; Petersen, *Arch. Jahrbuch*, vol. xxiv, 1909, p. 162.
42. *Minoan-Mycenaean Religion*, pp. 378ff.
43. Evans, *J.H.S.*, vol. xlv, 1925, pp. 68ff.
44. *Mycenaean Tree and Pillar Cult*, 1901, pp. 98ff.
45. Chap. iv, p. 108.
46. Cf. Crawford, *The Long Barrows of the Cotswolds*, 1925, p. 14.
47. *P.P.S.*, N.S. 1, vol. ii, 1935, p. 108.
48. C. A. Nordman, *The Megalithic Culture in Northern Europe*, Helsinki, 1935, p. 28; Crawford, *op. cit.*, p. 13.

49. *Op. cit.*, p. 127.
50. *Prehistoric Chamber Tombs of England and Wales*, 1950, p. 110.
51. Nordman, *op. cit.*, p. 29.
52. *P.P.S.*, N.S. IV, 1938, p. 128.
53. Chap. v, p. 133.
54. Chap. viii, p. 224.
55. *Yasht.*, x, 13.
56. Chap. viii, p. 222.
57. Cf. Nilsson, *History of Greek Religion*, pp. 121f.

ABBREVIATIONS

A.A.	American Anthropologist.
L'ANTHROP.	L'Anthropologie.
B.A.E.	Bureau of American Ethnology.
B.S.A.	British School of Athens, Annual of.
E.R.E.	Encyclopaedia of Religion and Ethics.
J.E.A.	Journal of Egyptian Archaeology.
J.H.S.	Journal of Hellenic Studies.
J.N.E.S.	Journal of Near Eastern Studies.
J.R.A.I.	Journal of the Royal Anthropological Institute.
J.R.A.S.	Journal of the Royal Asiatic Society.
P.P.S.	Proceedings of the Prehistoric Society.

BIBLIOGRAPHY

CHAPTER I

Black, D., *Fossil Man in China*, Peiping, 1933.
Boule, H., *Les Hommes Fossiles*, 3rd ed., Paris, 1946.
Broderick, A. H., *Early Man*, 1946.
Burkitt, M. C., *Prehistory*, 2nd ed., Cambridge, 1927; *Our Early Ancestors*, Cambridge, 1926; *The Old Stone Age*, 3rd ed., 1955.
Clark, J. G. D., *The Mesolithic Settlements of Northern Europe*, Cambridge, 1936.
Hose, C., and McDougall, W., *The Pagan Tribes of Borneo*, 1912.
Jackson, J. W., *Shells as Evidence of the Migrations of Early Culture*, 1917.
Keith, A., *The Antiquity of Man*, 2 vols., 2nd ed., 1929.
Luquet, G. H., *The Art and Religion of Fossil Man*, 1930.
Macalister, R. A. S., *Textbook of European Archaeology*, Cambridge, 1921.
Marshall, H. I., *The Karen People of Borneo*, Ohio, 1922.
Obermaier, H., *Fossil Man in Spain*, New Haven, Yale Press, 1925.
Oppenoorth, W. F. F., *Early Man*, edited by MacCurdy, Philadelphia, 1937.
Osborn, H., *Men of the Old Stone Age*, 1918.
Sollas, W. J., *Ancient Hunters*, 3rd ed., 1924.
Teilhard de Chardin, *Early Man in China*, Peiping, 1941.
Verneau, R., *Les Grottes de Grimaldi*, Monaco, 1906.
Zeuner, F. E., *Dating the Past*, 1952; *The Pleistocene Period*, 1945.

CHAPTER II

Baumgärtel, E. J., *The Cultures of Prehistoric Egypt*, Oxford, 1955.
Breasted, J. H., *Religion and Thought in Ancient Egypt*, 1914.
Brunton, G., *Mostagedda*, 1937.
Brunton, G., and Caton-Thompson, G., *The Badarian Civilization*, 1928.
Caton-Thompson, G., and Gardner, E. W., *The Desert Fayum*, 1934.
Childe, V. G., *New Light on the Most Ancient East*, new edition, 1952.
Hargreaves, H., *Excavations in Baluchistan*, 1925.
Jacobsen, T., *The Sumerian King Lists*, Chicago, 1939.
Lloyd, Seton, *Mesopotamia*, 1936.
Mackay, E. J. H., *Further Excavations at Mohenjo-daro*, 1938; *The Indus Civilization*, 1935; *Chanhu-daro Excavations*, New Haven, 1943.

Marshall, Sir J., *Mohenjo-daro and the Indus Civilization*, 2 vols., 1931.
McCown, D. E., *The Comparative Stratigraphy of Early Iran*, Chicago, 1942.
Perkins, A. L., *The Comparative Archaeology of Early Mesopotamia*, Chicago, 1949.
Petrie, Sir Flinders W. M., *Prehistoric Egypt*, 1920; *The Royal Tombs of the First Dynasty*, 1900; *Abydos*, vol. i, 1902; vol. ii, 1903; *Pyramids and Temples at Gizeh*, 1885.
Piggott, S., *Prehistoric India*, 1950; *Some Ancient Cities of India*, 1945.
Pumpelly, R., *Explorations in Turkestan*, Carnegie Institute, 1906–8.
Quibell, J. E., and Green, F. W., *Hierakonpolis*, vol. ii, 1902.
Speiser, E. A., *The Excavations at Tepe Gawra*, vol. i, Philadelphia, 1935.
Tobler, A. J., *The Excavations at Tepe Gawra*, vol. ii, Philadelphia, 1950.
Vats, M. S., *Excavations at Harappa*, New Delhi, 1940.
Watelin, L. C., *Kish*, vol. iv, Paris, 1934.
Wheeler, Sir Mortimer R. E., *The Cambridge History of India; The Indus Civilization*, Cambridge, 1953.
Woolley, Sir Leonard, *The Sumerians*, Oxford, 1929; *Ur of the Chaldees*, 1950.
Woolley, L., and Hall, H. R., *Ur Excavations*, vol. i, Al 'Ubaid, 1927; *The Royal Cemetery*, 1934.

CHAPTER III

Crawford, O. G. S., *The Long Barrows of the Cotswolds*, Gloucester, 1925.
Childe, V. G., *The Dawn of European Civilization*, 3rd ed., 1950; *Prehistoric Communities of the British Isles*, 1940; *The Prehistory of Scotland*, 1935; *Skara Brae*, 1931.
Curwen, E. C., *The Archaeology of Sussex*, 2nd ed., 1954.
Daniel, G. E., *The Prehistoric Chamber Tombs of England and Wales*, Cambridge, 1950; "The Dual Nature of the Megalithic Colonisation of Prehistoric Europe", *Proceedings of the Prehistoric Society*, vol. vii, 1941.
Evans, Sir Arthur, *The Palace of Minos*, vols. i–iv, 1922–35.
Forde, C. D., "Early Culture of Atlantic Europe", *American Anthropologist*, 32, pp. 19–100, 1930.
Hawkes, C. F. C., *The Prehistoric Foundations of Europe*, 1940.
Jessup, R. F., *The Archaeology of Kent*, 1930.
Macalister, R. A. S., *The Archaeology of Ireland*, 1928.
Nordman, C. A., *The Megalithic Culture in Northern Europe*, 1935.

Bibliography

Peet, T. E., *The Stone and Bronze Ages in Italy and Sicily*, Oxford, 1909.
Petrie, Sir Flinders, *Royal Tombs of the First Dynasty*, 1900–1.
Piggott, S., *The Neolithic Cultures of the British Isles*, Cambridge, 1954.
Seager, R. B., *Explorations in Mochlos*, Boston, 1912.
Siret, L., *Les premiers Ages du metal dans le sud-est de l'Espagne*, Paris, 1888.
Xanthoudides, S., *The Vaulted Tombs of Mesara*, 1924.
Zammit, T., *Prehistoric Malta;* "The Tarxien Temples", Oxford, 1930; *The Neolithic Temples at Hajar Kin and Mnaidra*, Valetta, 1927.

CHAPTER IV

Breasted, J. H., *Religion and Thought in Ancient Egypt*, 1914.
Budge, Sir Ernest A. W., *The Book of the Opening of the Mouth*, 2 vols., 1909.
Childe, V. G., *Prehistoric Communities of the British Isles*, 1940; *The Danube in Prehistory*, Oxford, 1929.
Davies, N. G., and Gardiner, A. H., *The Tomb of Amenembet*, 1915.
Elliot Smith, Sir Grafton, and Dawson, W. R., *Egyptian Mummies*, 1924.
Garstang, J., *Burial Customs of Ancient Egypt*, 1907.
Greenwell, W., *British Barrows*, 1877.
Grinsell, L. V., *Ancient Burial-Mounds of England*, 1953.
Hawkes, C. F. C., *The Prehistoric Foundations of Europe*, 1940.
Mercer, S., *The Pyramid Texts*, 1929.
Moret, A., *Le Rituel du Culte divin journalier en Egypte*, Paris, 1902.
Peake, H. J. E., *The Bronze Age and the Celtic World*, 1922.
Petrie, Sir Flinders, *Medum*, 1892; *Deshasheh*, 1898.
Piggott, S., *Aspects of Archaeology*, 1951.
Randall-MacIver, *Villanovans and Early Etruscans*, Oxford, 1924.

CHAPTER V

Basedown, H., *The Australian Aboriginal*, 1925.
Brasseur de Bourbourg, *Histoire des nations civilisée du Mexique et de l'Amérique*, vol. iv, Paris, 1859.
Brown, A. R., *The Andaman Islanders*, Cambridge, 1922.
Brown, G., *Melanesians and Polynesians*, 1910.
Codrington, R. H., *The Melanesians, their Anthropology and Folklore*, Oxford, 1891.
Dawson, J., *Australian Aborigines*, Melbourne, 1881.

Ellis, W., *Polynesian Researches*, 1829.
Elkin, A. P., *The Australian Aborigines*, Sydney, 1938.
Evans-Pritchard, E. E., *Nuer Religion*, Oxford, 1956.
Evans, I. H. N., *Ethnology and Archaeology of the Malay Peninsula*, Cambridge, 1927.
Frazer, Sir J. G., *Belief in Immortality*, vol. i, 1913.
Hose, C., and McDougall, W., *The Pagan Tribes of Borneo*, 2 vols., 1912.
Lumholtz, C., *Unknown Mexico*, 1903.
Malinowski, B., *Argonauts of the Western Pacific*, 1922.
Rivers, W. H. R., *History of Melanesian Society*, vol. i, Cambridge, 1914.
Routledge, W. S., *The Mystery of Easter Island*, 1919.
Rutter, O., *The Pagans of North Borneo*, 1929.
Schebesta, P., *Among the Forest Dwarfs of Malaya*, 1929.
Seligman, C. G., *The Melanesians of British New Guinea*, Cambridge, 1910.
Skeat, W. W., and Blagden, C. O., *Pagan Races of the Malay Peninsula*, 2 vols., 1906.
Spencer, B., *Wanderings in Wild Australia*, 2 vols., 1928.
Turner, G., *Samoa*, 1884; *Nineteen Years in Samoa*, 1861.
Williamson, R. W., *The Mafulu Mountain People in British New Guinea*, 1912.

CHAPTER VI

Brunton, G., and Caton-Thompson, G., *The Bedarian Civilization*, 1928.
Childe, V. G., *Prehistoric Communities of the British Isles*, 1949.
Evans, Sir A. J., *The Palace of Minos*, vols. i and iv, 1922–35.
Harrison, J. E., *Prolegomena to the Study of Greek Religion*, Cambridge, 1903; *Themis*, Cambridge, 1912.
Kendrick, T. D., *The Archaeology of the Channel Islands*, 1928.
Levy, G. R., *The Gate of Horn*, 1948.
Luquet, G. H., *The Art and Religion of Fossil Man*, Oxford, 1930.
Mackay, E. J. H., *Further Excavations at Mohenjo-daro*, 1937.
Malinowski B., *The Father in Primitive Psychology*, 1927; *Sexual Life of Savages in North-western Melanesia*, 1929.
Marshall, Sir John, *Mohenjo-daro and the Indus Valley Civilization*, 1931.
Obermaier, H., *Fossil Man in Spain*, Yale Press, 1925.
Petrie, Sir Flinders, *Prehistoric Egypt*, 1920.
Piggott, S., *Prehistoric India*, 1950; *The Neolithic Cultures of the British Isles*, 1954.
Pumpelly, R., *Explorations in Turkestan*, Carnegie Institute, 1906–8.

Stein, Sir A., *Memoirs Arch. Survey of India*, No. 37, 1925.
Tobler, A. J., *Excavations at Tepe Gawra*, Philadelphia, 1950.
Vats, M. S., *Excavations at Harappa*, 1940.
Woolley, Sir L., *The Development of Sumerian Art*, 1935.
Zammit, T., *Prehistoric Malta*, Oxford, 1930; *The Hal-Saflieni Prehistoric Hypogeum*, Malta, 1910.

CHAPTER VII

Atkinson, R. J. C., *Stonehenge*, 1956.
Blackman, A. M., *Luxor and its Temples*, 1923.
Breasted, J. H., *Religion and Thought in Ancient Egypt*, 1914.
Breuil, H., *Quatre cents siècles d'art pariétal*, Montignac, 1954; *La Caverne d'Altamira*, Monaco, 1909.
Brodrick, A. H., *Lascaux: A Commentary*, 1948.
Erman, A., and Blackman, A. M., *The Literature of the Ancient Egyptians*, 1927.
Evans, Sir A. J., *The Palace of Minos*, vols. ii and iii, 1928–30.
Farnell, L. R., *Cult of the Greek States*, vol. iii, Oxford, 1907.
Frankfort, H., *Kingship and the Gods*, Chicago, 1947; *Ancient Egyptian Religion*, Chicago, 1948; *The Intellectual Adventure of Ancient Man*, Chicago, 1946.
Frazer, Sir J. G., *The Golden Bough*, part iv, 1914.
Gaster, T., *Thespis*, New York, 1950.
Harrison, J. E., *Ancient Art and Ritual*, 1913.
Kramer, S. N., *Sumerian Mythology*, Philadelphia, 1944.
Langdon, S., *The Babylonian Epic of Creation*, Oxford, 1923.
Lemozi, A., *La Grotte-Temple du Pech-Merle*, Paris, 1929.
Levy, G. R., *The Gate of Horn*, 1948.
Marett, R. R., *The Threshold of Religion*, 1914.
Moret, A., *Du caractère religieux de la royauté Pharaonique*, Paris, 1909.
Nilsson, M. P., *Minoan-Mycenaean Religion*, Oxford, 1927; *Greek Popular Religion*, New York, 1940.
Pallis, S. A., *The Babylonian Akitu Festival*, Kobenhavn, 1926.
Persson, A. W., *The Religion of Greece in Prehistoric Times*, California, 1942.
Spencer, W. B., and Gillen, F. J., *The Native Tribes of Central Australia*, 1938; *Northern Tribes of Central Australia*, 1904.
Wainwright, G. A., *The Sky-Religion in Egypt*, Cambridge, 1938.
Windels, F., *The Lascaux Cave Paintings*, 1949.

CHAPTER VIII

Breasted, J. H., *Religion and Thought in Ancient Egypt*, 1914.
Budge, Sir E. A. W., *Tutankhamon, Amenism, Atonism and Egyptian Monotheism*, 1923.
Childe, V. G., *The Aryans*, 1926.
Cook, A. B., *Zeus*, 3 vols., Cambridge, 1914-38.
Evans-Pritchard, E. E., *Nuer Religion*, Oxford, 1956.
Farnell, L. R., *The Cult of the Greek States*, vol. i, Oxford, 1896.
Frankfort, H., *Kingship and the Gods*, Chicago, 1948.
Frazer, Sir J. G., *The Worship of Nature*, 1926; *The Golden Bough*, parts ii and x, 1914.
Gadd, C. J., *The Idea of Divine Rule in the Ancient East*, Oxford, 1948.
Haddon, A. C., *The Study of Man*, 1898.
Heidel, A., *The Babylonian Genesis*, Chicago, 1950; *The Gilgamesh Epic*, Chicago, 1951.
Howitt, A. W., *Native Tribes of South-east Australia*, 1904.
Lang, A., *The Making of Religion*, 1898.
Murray, G., *Five Stages of Greek Religion*, Oxford, 1925.
Nilsson, M. P., *History of Greek Religion*, Oxford, 1925.
Rose, H. J., *Handbook of Greek Mythology*, 1933.
Schmidt, P. W., *Der Ursprung, der Gottesidee*, Munster, 1912-54.
Shetelig, H., and Falk, H., *Scandinavian Archaeology*, Oxford, 1937.
Spencer, W. B., and Gillen, F. J., *Native Tribes of Central Australia*, 1938.
Tylor, Sir E. B., *Primitive Culture*, 4th ed., 2 vols., 1903.
Wainwright, G. A., *The Sky-Religion in Egypt*, Cambridge, 1938.

DIVISIONS OF PLEISTOCENE	GLACIATIONS AND INTERGLACIALS	FLINT INDUSTRIES	HUMAN TYPES	CULT PRACTICES
Lower c. 1000000–500000 years	Pre-glacial and Günz glaciation Günz-Mindel Interglacial	Pre-Crag Abbevillian Clactonian Cromerian		
Middle 250000 years c. 200000	Mindel glaciation Mindel-Riss Interglacial Riss glaciation	Clactonian Abbevillian Lower Acheulian Late Clactonian Lower Tayacian Levalloisian I, II, and III Upper Acheulian	Pithecanthropus Sinanthropus Heidelberg Swanscombe Mount Carmel	Cult of skulls
Upper c. 150000	Riss-Würm Interglacial Würm I glaciation (maximum)	Levalloisian III, IV Latest Acheulian Mousterian Levalloisian V-VII Châtelperron	Neanderthal Man	Ceremonial interments
c. 72000 c. 25000–10000	The Upper Palaeolithic Interstadial Würm II Würm III	Aurignacian Gravettian Solutrean Magdalenian and Grimaldian	Homo sapiens Crô-Magnons Combe Capelle Grimaldi	Venuses, Ochre-burials, Hunting ritual, Increase rites, sacred dance

The provisional time-scale is based on Prof. E. F. Zeuner's estimates.
cf. *Dating the Past*, 3rd edition, 1952, pp. 286, 299.

The Mesolithic Period

| 10000 B.C.
c. 7000 B.C.
c. 2500 B.C. | Late Glacial and Pre-Boreal
Boreal
Sub-Boreal | Capsian, Azilian-Tardenoisian
Maglemosean
Ertebølle (Denmark)
Asturian (Spain)
Natufian (Palestine) | Upper Palaeolithic survivors and precursors of the modern races of Europe | Cult of skulls (Ofnet ritual burial)
Sacred dance
Ossuaries (Téviec)
Danish *Dyssers* |

Sequence of Cultures in Western Europe

Neolithic (Stentinello)	Mesolithic	Mesolithic	Mesolithic	Mesolithic Ertebølle	Danubian I
Siculan I (Chalcolithic)	Almerian (El Garcel)	Neolithic I	Neolithic A Windmill Hill	Neolithic II	Rössen Lengyel
Siculan I	Los Millares Portuguese megaliths	Chalcolithic Cists, Passage-graves	Barrows Clyde-Carlingford		Early Saxo-Thuringian
Siculan I	Beakers, Palmella Alcala	Chassy S.O.M. Channelard	Galleries Neolithic B Peterborough	Passage-graves	Jordansmühl Beakers
Siculan I	Early Bronze Age	Chalcolithic II Beakers	Neolithic Beakers B Round barrows Avebury	Single graves Stone cists culture	Corded-ware warrior-cultures Globular ware
Siculan I	Viejo	Megalithic culture Breton Early Bronze Age	Stonehenge		Altheim Early Bronze Age
Siculan I	El Argar	Barrow cult	Wessex Early Bronze Age		Aunjetitz West Alpine Lake dwellings
Siculan I Siculan II (Middle Bronze Age)		Corded ware Bronze Age III	Food-vessels Wessex warrior culture	Early Bronze Age Stone cists	Apennine I Middle Bronze Age Terremare
			Middle Bronze Age Urnfields	Bronze Age II	Apennine II Tumulus culture Lausitz

B.C.	CRETE	THESSALY		TROAD	DANUBE
3000	Neolithic				Danubian I
c. 2600	Early Minoan I	Dimini-Vardar	Early Helladic I	Troy I	Vinča
					Butmir
2400	Early Minoan II	Early Macedonian	Early Helladic II	Troy II	Danubian II
2200	Early Minoan III		Early Helladic III	Troy III and IV	Tripolye, Tordos
2000	Middle Minoan I	Middle Macedonian	Middle Helladic I	Troy V	Danubian III
1800	Middle Minoan II		Middle Helladic II	Troy VI	Bronze Age
			Minyan		
1600	Late Minoan I	Late Macedonian	Late Helladic I		Baden
1400	Late Minoan II	Mycenaean	Late Helladic II		Perjamos
1300	Fall of Knossos	Mycenaean	Late Helladic III	Troy VIIa, VIIb	

| \multicolumn{5}{c}{*Sequence of Cultures in the Near East*} |
B.C.	EGYPT	MESOPO-TAMIA	SUSA AND IRAN	SIND AND PUNJAB
From c. 4000	Tasian Fayum Badarian Merimdian Amratian Naqada I Gerzean Naqada II	Qalat Jarmo Hassuna Samarra, Halaf Gawra Arpachiyah Nineveh I Ubaid Uruk Gawra XII Nineveh II Hassuna V Uruk Jemdet Nasr.	Sialk I Sialk II Hissar I Sialk III Susa I. Anau I Susa B Sialk IV Anau II Susa C	Harappa I
c. 3000	1st Dynasty	Ur I–*III*	Hissar III Susa D	Mohenjo-daro Harappa II (R.37)
c. 2800	Old Kingdom	Sargon (c. 2300)	Hissar III Anau III	Chanhu-daro I
c. 2000	Middle Kingdom	Hammurabi		Harappa III (H) Chanhu-daro II

INDEX

Abri-Mège, 146, 149
Abri-Murat, 146
Absolon, C., 147
Abydos, tombs at, 40, 115 f.
Adad, 215 f.
Adonis, 195
Addington, 92
Aegean, 61, 162, 195, 221
After-life, the, 131 ff., 136, 138, 143 f., 248, 254 f.
Ahura Mazda, 217 f., 219, 258
Akitu, the, 191
Almerian megaliths, 73 f.
figurines, 154, 235 f.
goddess cult, 167 f.
Alpera, 150 f.
Alpine urnfields, 105
Altamira, 146, 149, 177, 179
Al 'Ubaid, burials, 46
Amon-Re, 211, 212
Amratian, burials, 35
figurines, 153
Animism, 204 ff.
Anau, 51, 156 f.
Anu, 213 f., 229
Annual Festival, the, 187 ff., 191 f.
Apsu, 214
Asura, 217
Athena, 163
Atkinson, R. J. C., 280, 289
Aton, 211 f.
Attis, 196, 199
Atum-Re, 186, 210 f.
Aurignacian cultures, 26, 30, 150
Australian funerary rites, 120 f.
Intichiuma, 172, 179 f.
Avebury, 84, 85, 100, 202, 227
Axe cult, the, 162 f., 226, 249

Ba, the, 114, 244 f.
Baal, (Aleyan), 194
Badarian burials, 25 f., 73
figurines, 153
Baluchistan, 51 f., 157
Balearic Isles, tombs, 66 ff., 97, 100, 202, 227

Barrows, long, 84 f., 98 f.
round, 99 ff.
Battle-axe warriors, 95 f., 97, 202, 227
Beaker folk, 82, 96, 97, 100, 202, 227
Bégouen, Count, 148 f., 173, 175
Beehive tombs, 45, 61
Belas Knap, 86, 92, 253
Birth, mystery of, 145 ff., 148, 152, 172, 230, 235 f., 239, 255
Black, Davidson, 17, 264
Blackpatch, 84, 171
Body and soul, 130 f., 244, 255 (see also Ba, Ka, Mummy)
Boule, H., 264, 285
Boyne passage-graves, 88 ff.
Brahman, 218
Brain extraction, 18 f., 28, 125
Brassempouy, 146 f.
Breasted, J. H., 185, 210, 245, 265, 270, 278
Breuil, Abbé, 152, 168, 178, 180
Brünn (Brno), 23, 26 f.
Brodrick, A. H., 285, 289
Bronze Age, the, 69, 97 f., 242, 252
Brunton, G., 35 f., 265 f., 270, 285
Bryn Celli Ddu, 87, 91 f., 99
Bull cult, 197, 237 f., 240
Bull-roarers, 208 f.
Burial ritual, 17 ff. (see Dead, cult of; Skulls, cult of)
Burkitt, M. C., 148, 265, 274, 285

Cairns, horned, 88, 90
long, 92 f.,
Cannibal feasts, 17 ff.
Capsian culture, 151, 241
Carnac, 79 ff., 251
Carn Brae, 84
Castillo, 179
Causewayed camps, 85
Cave-burial, 21 ff., 34, 63, 118 ff.
Chancelade burial, 26, 27, 30
Chanhu-daro, 54 f., 260
Childe, V. G., 49, 91, 92, 99, 225, 265 f., 285 ff.
Choukoutien, 17 f.

Index

Cissbury, 84
Cists, 73, 78, 96, 101, 169, 170
Clactonian implements, 18
Clark, J. G. D., 264, 285
Clyde-Carlingford graves, 89, 90 ff., 93
Coldrum, 92
Combarelles, 146, 240
Corbelled vaults, 73, 79, 82
Corridor-tombs, 73, 79, 82
Cogul, 149
Combe Capelle, 23 f., 27
Collorgues, Gard, 170
Cotswold-Severn barrows, 86 f., 90, 92, 253
Cow symbolism, 235 ff.
Cowrie shells, 21, 25, 29, 148, 157
Crawford, O. G. S., 92, 253, 282 f., 286
Cremation, 54, 56, 98 ff., 122 f., 131 f., 248, 252, 254 f.
  partial, 98 f.
Crete, tombs, 61 f.
  goddess cult, 162 f., 222, 239 f.
Crô-Magnon Man, 23, 24, 26, 29
Curwen, E. C., 268, 286
Cycladic tombs, 63 f.
Cyprus, tholoi, 58 f.
  goddess cult, 59, 161

Damb buthi cemetery, 53 f., 247
Daniel, G. E., 80, 88, 254, 283, 286
Dances, fertility, 149 f., 232, 254
Dead, the cult of in
  British Isles, 83 ff., 253
  Brittany and S.O.M., 79, 97 ff., 251
  Central Europe and Italy, 102 ff.
  Crete and the Aegean, 61 ff., 249
  Egypt, 34 ff., 109 ff., 244
  Elam and Baluchistan, 50 ff.
  Iberian Peninsula, 72 ff.
  Indus valley, 54 ff., 247 ff.
  Mesolithic, 30 ff.
  Mesopotamia, 43, 246
  Palaeolithic, 21 ff., 241
  Scandinavia, 94 ff., 254
  Western Mediterranean, 65 ff.
Dead, land of, 38, 43 f., 50

Death, mystery of, 17 ff., 143 f., 242
Decapitation, 171
Déchelette, J., 171
Desiccation of the corpse, 109, 114, 119 f., 123, 126, 130
Deverel, 106
Djed-column, the, 187, 245
Dolmens, 33
Dove, symbol of, 163 f., 195
Dowth, 89
Drachenhöhle, cave, 21
Drachenloch, 21
Dumézil, J., 220
Dumu-zi, 189, 193, 214
Durkheim, E., 230
Dyaus Pitar, 210, 217, 258
Dyssers, 33, 76

Ea (Enki), 214 f.
Eleusinian mysteries, 198
El Garcel, 73 f., 167 f.
Elliot Smith, Sir G., 109
Embalmment, 109 f., 114, 116, 125 f.
Enlil, 213 f.
Ennead, the Heliopolitan, 184, 186, 259
Enuma elish, the, 191
Ertebølle culture, 32
Evans, Sir A., 162, 196, 249, 250
Evans-Pritchard, E. E., 134, 207, 233, 288, 290
Evisceration of the corpse, 114, 121, 123 f.

Farnell, L. R., 200, 289
Feasts, funerary, 18, 21, 49, 119, 120, 135, 254
Fertile Crescent, the, 34, 58, 182, 198
Fertility cults, 148 ff., 152, 172 ff., 182
  dances, 149, 172 f., 180
Figurines, 65, 73, 76, 82, 145 ff., 153 ff., 161 ff., 167 ff., 171, 238, 241, 243
Fires in graves, 62, 98 ff., 119, 123
Flexing of the body, 29, 30, 45 f., 49, 121, 126
Font-de-Gaume, 173, 177
Food-vessel folk, the, 101
  offerings (*see* Grave-goods)

Index

Forde, C. Daryll, 33, 268, 286
Fractional burial, 46, 53, 55, 56, 247
Frankfort, H., 194, 245, 289
Frazer, Sir J. G., 145, 190, 198, 205

GADD, C. T., 282
Gallery-graves, 63 ff., 73 ff., 78, 80 ff., 90 ff.
Gardiner, A. H., 187, 194
Gaster, T. H., 279, 289
Gawra, Tepe, burials, 45
  figurines, 154
Gavr'inis, 82, 168, 252
Gerzean cemetery, 37
Gigantea, 68, 70, 250
Giganti (Giants' tombs), 65 f., 80, 90
Gilgamesh, 246
Giyan, 51 f.
Goddess cult, the:
  Baluchistan, 157
  British Isles and Northern France, 171 ff., 201 f., 203
  Brittany and Channel Islands, 168 f., 241, 251
  Crete, 162 ff., 222
  Eastern Mediterranean and Aegean, 161 ff., 195 ff., 222 ff.
  Egypt, 236
  Indus valley, 157 ff., 238
  Malta, 165 ff., 241
  Palaeolithic, 147 ff., 255
  Spain, 167 ff., 241, 251
  Western Asia, 153 ff., 188, 193, 237, 241
Grave-goods, 20, 24 ff., 35 f., 48, 56, 60, 75 ff., 82, 96, 105, 124, 139 f., 241, 254
Gravettian culture, 27, 145, 147, 153, 208
Greenwell, W., 98, 287
Grimaldi burials, 23 ff., 146, 148
Grimes' Graves, 84, 171
Grinsell, L. V., 100, 287
Griffiths, F. Ll., 194

HAGIA KIM, 68, 165 f., 250
Hagia Triada, tombs, 61, 62
  goddess cult, 164, 249

Hal Tarxien, 68 ff., 72, 165 f., 167
  Saflieni, 70, 166
Halaf, Tell, burials, 45
  figurines, 153, 165, 167
Hallstatt cemetery, 107 f.
  culture, 107
Harappa civilization, 54 ff.
  cemetery R 37, 55 f., 248
  figurines, 157 f., 160
Hargreaves, H., 52
Harrison, J. E., 249, 288
Harvest festivals, 186, 193 (*see* Annual Festival)
Hathor, 236, 245
Hawkes, C. F. C., 85, 268 ff., 286, 287
Head, preservation of the, 18
Heliopolis, 184 f., 210 f., 236
Hierakonpolis, tomb, the, 37
Hindu origins, 54 ff., 160, 217 ff., 237
Homo neanderthalensis, 17
  sapiens, 17
Hooke, S. H., 189
Hornblower, G. D., 236, 281
Horus cult, the, 37, 114, 184, 212
  eye of, 115
  sky-god, 183, 210, 212, 216, 236
Huns'-beds, 96
Hunting ritual, 172 ff., 180
Hypogeum (*see* Hal Saflieni)

IKHNATON, 211 f., 257
Immortality, 143 (*see* After-life)
Inanna, 188, 193
Indo-Europeans, 217, 221, 223, 225
Indus valley culture, 54 ff., 157 (*see* Harappa)
Ishtar, 188, 193
Isis, 183, 260 (*see* Osiris and Horus)

JACOBSEN, T., 266, 285
Java man (*see Pithecanthropus*)
Jemdet Nasr period, 47, 51

KA, the, 244 f.
Keith, A., 24, 264, 285
Kercado, passage-grave, 79 f., 81
Khoiakh festival, 187 f.

Index

Kingship, sacral:
  Egypt, 184 ff., 194, 241
  Indus valley, 57
  Mesopotamia, 188 ff., 192, 213 f., 241
Kish, cemetery, 51
Kit's Coty House, 92
Knap Hill, 84
Knossos, goddess cult at, 164, 196, 250
Koenigswald, R., 264
Kore, 198 f., 201
Krapina, 19
Kulli culture, 52, 157 f.

LA CHAPELLE-AUX-SAINTS, 21 f., 243
La Ferrasie, 22, 242
Lalanne, G., 146
La Madeleine, 146
Lang, A., 206
Laugerie-Basse, 26, 29, 148, 208
Lausitz, culture, 102, 107
  urnfields, 104 f.
Laussel, 146, 243
Le Moustier, 21
Larnake, 43
Lascaux, 177 ff., 181, 242
Lemozi, Abbé, 176
Les Eyzies, 23, 26, 146, 173, 208
Lespugne, 148
Les Trois Frères, 149, 173 f., 179, 180
Lévy Bruhl, L., 232
Levy, G. B., 274, 289
Lloyd, Seton, 266, 285
Locmariaquer, 251 f.
Los Millares, 73 f., 80, 94, 167, 241, (*see* Almerian)
Lourdes, 146, 149, 232
Luquet, G. H., 264, 285
Lyle's Hill, 93

MACALISTER, R. A. S., 158, 266, 285
Mackay, E. J. H., 28, 285, 288
Magdalenian culture, 26, 148, 150, 178, 208 f.
Maglemosean culture, 31

Maiden Castle, 84, 86, 171
Malta, "temples" in, 68 f.
Malta (Siberia), 147
Malinowski, B., 174, 288
Mané-er-Hroeck, 81, 251
Mané-Lud, 82
Marduk, 188, 191, 213 f.
Marriage, the sacred, 188, 224
Marshall, Sir J., 52, 54, 158, 286, 288
Marsoulas, 146, 149, 177
Mastaba tomb, the, 40 f., 110 f.
Maz d'Azil, 31
Megalithic culture in:
  British Isles and Channel Islands, 83 f.
  Brittany, 79 ff.
  Crete and the Aegean, 61 ff.
  Denmark and Scandinavia, 33, 94
  Eastern Mediterranean, 58 ff.
  Pyrenees, 78 f.
  S.O.M., 83
  Spain, 73 ff.
  Western Mediterranean, 65 ff. (*see also* Malta)
Merimdian burials, 37 f., 73
Mersin, 161
Mesara, tholoi, 62, 74, 253
Min, 186 f., 216
Minateda, 152
Minoan Goddess, the, 162 ff., 195 f., 239, 249 f.
Minotaur, the, 240
Mnaidra, 68 f., 166
Mochlos, 62
Mohenjo-daro, 54 ff., 160, 167
Monotheism, 208 ff., 256 f.
Monte Circeo, 19
Montelius, O., 33, 66
Mont St Michel, 82, 252
Montespan, 174 f.
Mousterian culture, 18 f., 21, 22, 208
Mourning ceremonies, 121 f., 141
Mummification in Egypt, 109 ff., 116, 129 f., 131 f.
  Mexico and Kentucky, 123 ff.
  The Pacific, 126 ff.
Mummy, making of, 114

bundles, 120f., 122, 124, 130
burial rites, 115
"opening of the mouth", 112f., 245, 249
Murray, G., 222
Murray, M. A., 166, 276, 279
Myres, J. L., 161
Mystery cults, 186, 198

NAL cemetery, 53, 56, 247
Naqada cemetery, 34
Navetas, 66f., 80
Neanderthal Man, 17f., 19, 29
Neolithic, A culture, 84f., 92
  B culture, 93
New Grange, 88f.
Nordman, C. A., 269, 286
Niaux, 172, 174, 177, 181
Nilsson, M. P., 198, 250, 289
Nin-Khursag, 236f.
Nuraghi, 66, 69
Nympsfield, 86, 99

OBERMAIER, H., 264, 285
Ochre burials, 20, 24ff., 28, 30, 243
  on figurines, 146, 148
Ofnet, 20, 30, 243
Olympian gods, 221ff., 214
Orientation of the dead, 38, 133f.
Osiris, cult of, 43, 113f., 132, 183ff., 187, 189
  genealogy, 184 (*see* Ennead)
  "gardens", 186f.
Ossuaries, 70, 73, 104, 106, 166
Othin, 225

PASSAGE-GRAVES, 78, 80, 88ff., 93
Paviland, 25f.
Pech-Merle, 176f., 179
Pelos, 63
Perkins, A. L., 45, 286
Persson, A. W., 279, 288
Petrie, Sir Flinders, 34, 265, 286ff.
Phallic symbols, 84, 150, 159f., 171
Piggott, S., 85, 254, 266, 283, 286, 287f.
Pithecanthropus, 18ff.
Pithoi, 43
Placard, 28
Plas Newydd, 88

Pleistocene period, 17f.
Pliocene period, 18
Port-holes, 75f., 82f.
Portrait statues, 111f., 127ff., 130
Prajapati, 218
Předmost, 23f., 147
Pumpelly, R., 51, 286
Pyramids, the, 40ff.
  Age, 40, 110

QALAT JARMO, 182
Quetta, 52

RADCLIFFE-BROWN, A. R., 230, 281
Ras Shamra, 108, 194ff.
Re, 182, 210, 212 (*see* Atum-Re, Amon-Re, Heliopolis)
Rhea, 222, 259
Rimbury, 106
Rites de passage, 143, 192
Ritual experts, 181, 233
  control of natural processes, 229ff.
Rivers, W. H. R., 132
Rock-cut tombs, 60, 63, 65, 66ff., 80f., 82
Rta, 218

SACRIFICE, Human in funeral ritual, 48, 142, 254
Samara burials, 44
  figurines, 161
Sardinian gallery-graves, 65f.
Schmidt, Pater W., 206, 208
Seasonal ritual, 182, 197, 203
Secondary burial, 119ff., 136
Sed-festival, 194
Seine-Oise-Marne, (S.O.M.), megaliths, 83
  goddess cult, 169ff.
Shamash, 215
Shells in graves, 20f., 24ff., 28 (*see* Cowries)
Shiva cult, 160, 238f.
Sialk, 52, 182
Siculan tombs, 65
Sin, 215
Sinanthropus pekinensis, 17f.
Single-graves, 95, 97

Skulls, cult of, 17 ff., 28, 119, 122
Sky-god, the, 208 ff., 216 ff., 221 ff., 256 (*see* Supreme Beings, Zeus, Re, Dyaus Pitar, Yahweh)
   religion, the, 204 ff., 224 f., 255 f., 257
   in Egypt, 210 ff.
   Greece, 221 ff.
   India, and Iran, 217 ff.
   Mesopotamia, 213 ff.
   Scandinavia, 225 f.
   Wessex, 227 f.
Sky-world, the, 132, 254 f. (*see* After-life)
Snake symbolism, 59 ff.
Soan culture, 18
Social structure and religion, 230 f.
Solar cult, 184 ff., 210 ff., 213 (*see* Heliopolis, Re, Atum-Re)
Solutrean culture, 27, 147
"Sorcerer", the (Trois Frères), 173, 175, 232
Soul, conception of (*see* body, Ka, Ba)
Statue-menhirs, 168 ff., 241
Stein, Sir Aurel, 157
Stonehenge, Aegean influences, 202, 227
   barrows, 100
   cremations, 100
   temple, 227 f.
"Substitute heads", 110 (*see* Portrait statues)
Suffering god, the, 189 f.
Supreme Beings, 206 ff., 212, 256
Susa, cemetery, 50 f.
   figurines, 156, 161
Symbolism, 230 ff.

Tammuz, 188 f., 191, 193, 196, 214, 246
Tardenoisian culture, 31
Tasian culture, 35
Terramara cemeteries, 102
Téviec, burial, 31
Teyjat, 172 (*see* Les Eyzies)
Thickthorn barrow, 171
Tholoi, 45, 58, 65, 74, 80, 82, 88, 249
Thor, 225 f.
Tiamat, 192, 213
Tobler, A. J., 154
Toilet ceremonies of the pharaoh, 112
Tombs:
   beehive, 45, 61 (*see* Tholoi)
   rock-cut, 60 (*see* entry)
   vaulted, 61
Tószeg, 102, 108
Totemism, 180, 183, 232, 234 f.
Tree cult, 196 ff.
Trou-Violet, 20
Troy, goddess cult at, 161
Tuc d'Audoubert, 148, 172, 176
Tumulus culture, 105 f., 107
Tylor, Sir E. B., 204 f., 206

Underworld, the, 132 f., 136
Unter Wisternitz, 147
Ur, royal tombs at, 47 ff., 137, 246 f.
Urn burial, 101 f.
Urnfields, 104 ff.
Uruk, 47, 155
Utnapishtim, 215, 246

Varuna, 217 f., 237, 258
Vats, M. S., 56, 286
Vegetation cult, the, 181 ff., 240 f.
"Venuses", 145 ff. (*see* Figurines)
Villanovan cemeteries, 103
Vistonice, 147

Warka (*see* Uruk)
Wessex chieftains, 100 f., 203, 228
West Kennet barrow, 85
Wheeler, Sir R. E. M., 55, 266 f., 286
Whitehawk Camp, 84, 171
Willendorf, 145
Windels, F., 178
Windmill Hill culture, 84 f., 92, 171
Woolley, Sir Leonard, 47

Yahweh, 211, 220, 223, 288
Young god, the, 196 f., 198, 224

Zammit, T., 68, 71 f., 166
Zarathushtra, 220, 258, 281
Zeuner, F. E., 18, 264, 285
Zeus, 198 f., 200, 210, 221 ff., 224, 240, 259
Zhob valley, 52, 157 f.

www.ingramcontent.com/pod-product-compliance
Lightning Source LLC
Chambersburg PA
CBHW061244230426
43662CB00020B/2417